Praise for *The Healing Party*

'A compelling portrait of religious zealotry but also of true goodness. The portrait of the family is wonderfully realised, especially the mother, whom Lee has imbued with warmth and grace, and her own inner mystery.' —Amanda Lohrey

'Micheline Lee excels at drawing the ambiguities and frictions of familial connections: conflict, dislike and difference balanced by enduring love, which, in this family, is felt, but never expressed ... Lee creates a memorable, almost tragi-comic portrait of an Asian-Australian family.' —*Books+Publishing*

'The tenderness and exasperation with which the characters are drawn will ensure comparisons with Amy Tan ... *The Healing Party* succeeds in the aim all novels share: it suggests new ways of seeing.' —*The Monthly*

'The combination of a family on high alert while dealing with terminal illness, cultural difference, blind faith, and grieving provides all the momentum and drama a reader could wish for.' —Booktopia

'A wild family drama, shot through with a furious, pure and grieving love' —Helen Garner

'*The Healing Party* is part reality television and part an anthropological study of a strange foreign culture ... [a] deceptively simple, disciplined work' —*The Saturday Paper*

'Lee is an exceptionally talented writer ... An impressive, unique Australian debut' —*Readings Monthly*

'A striking fictional debut and contemporary parable of religious salvation at all costs' —*The Sydney Morning Herald*

'A gripping family drama concerning love, grief and the complexities of faith' —*Canberra Weekly*

'Incredibly gripping, highly recommended' —Leigh Sales

'I couldn't stop till I finished. Horrifying and wonderful' —David Marr

'Compelling from start to finish, *The Healing Party* is a mature and illuminating account of the complex ties of family.' —*Australian Book Review*

The Healing Party

The Healing Party

Micheline Lee

Published by Black Inc.,
an imprint of Schwartz Books Pty Ltd
Wurundjeri Country
22–24 Northumberland Street
Collingwood VIC 3066, Australia
enquiries@blackincbooks.com
www.blackincbooks.com

This edition published in 2023

9781760644857 (paperback)
9781925435085 (ebook)

A catalogue record for this book is available from the National Library of Australia

Cover design by Lauren Briggs, based on an original design by Peter Long
Text design and typesetting by Tristan Main
Cover photograph by Karen Ilagan, Getty Images
Author photograph by Susan Gordon-Brown

Printed in Australia by McPherson's Printing Group.

For Stephen and Mark

WHO KNOWS HOW MANY MORE YEARS I WOULD have stayed away had I not received the phone call from Anita.

As soon as I picked up and said hello, she said, 'Natasha? Mum has terminal cancer.'

No lead-up, no explanations. It was typical of the way Anita and I talked. Although we could be sweet-tongued with others, we were terse to one another. I leant over the back verandah with the phone to my ear, looking out into the darkness of the garden. The night was cool by Darwin standards. It was early June, the start of the dry, and the usual whirr of fans was absent. I stared into the shadows until the twisted branches of the old frangipani took shape. I listened to the high-pitched scratching of the cicadas until the noise seemed unbearable.

'Are you there?' she said.

'How long has she got?'

'The doctor said five months. But you never know.'

'I want to come home,' I said, like a little girl.

'No one's stopping you. No one has ever told you that you couldn't come home. No one can tell you anything!' She hung up.

*

Four weeks later, after a long day of travel down from Darwin, I stepped off the bus a block from where my parents lived. I had not been back in eight years. In my final year of school, not even waiting to complete my exams, I'd taken off to Darwin, which had seemed to me as far away as you could get from Melbourne without leaving the country. Since then I had met with my family several times, staying with friends or my sisters, but never setting foot in my parents' home.

The rumble of the bus faded. Mid-afternoon and no sign of life in the slow, straight rows of houses. You could wait for a long time for something to happen here.

This was the bus-stop that I had waited at every morning before school. It must have been. That's where it fitted. Opposite, a few doors down, was the Murphy house, and closer to the corner the Jacobs family, who had the child with Down syndrome. I walked past the sites feeling strangely indifferent, until I turned a corner and started to lurch downhill into Aquarius Court. The slope of the footpath seemed innocuous now, but I remembered screeching down with my belly on a skateboard; the treachery of the concrete, my face flying just centimetres above it.

It continued to be called Aquarius Court after Dad failed to persuade the neighbours to support a name change. My sisters and I were sent to door-knock locally with a petition written in his stylish cursive script. The petition stated, 'We, the residents of Aquarius Court, hereby denounce the glorification of astrology and claim the right to a street name that will uphold Australia's Christian values.'

Only the Bolands signed. Mr Boland hooted with laughter when he read the petition. 'Yeah, why not,' he said. 'Let's see where this gets us. This street would be called bloody 'Alleluia' if your father had his way, wouldn't it?'

The square houses were set back comfortably from the street, fronted by generous driveways and neat lawns. The three at the end of the court had been display homes. They were cut from the same pattern but had feature entries. Roman columns lined the driveway of the first, and the second was fronted by Japanese black and white screen doors. The house at the end – the one neighbours called the Spanish house – featured a faux-stone portico with archways and a terracotta roof. People always presumed we lived in the Japanese one, but my parents had chosen the Spanish.

It was the first house my parents had ever owned. In Hong Kong, like most people, we rented. When we moved into Aquarius Court, the suburb was new and many of the houses vacant. After the crowded lanes of Hong Kong, our new street seemed silent, huge and unused. The end of the court opened onto a grass oval that stretched out like the vast open plains we had seen in American movies.

Our furniture and belongings arrived from Hong Kong in large wooden crates. Dad surrounded the house with the emptied crates so that anyone wanting to enter would have first to find their way through a maze. For years the crates sat on the clay soil in the front yard, until, one by one, they fell apart, the rotten planks opening like petals of a strange giant flower.

As I approached the house, the neighbours' green, manicured front gardens gave way to my parents' unkempt one. Despite Mum's constant entreaties to Dad to do some work, the garden had never looked any good, and now it looked even worse. An overblown cactus towered up to the roof, and the few trees that had managed to survive were by now scraggly and rugged, and placed in odd spots around the yard. Weeds grew in clumps; otherwise, there were large patches of bare earth.

I stopped at the driveway to check my clothes. This morning in Darwin before my flight, I had pulled on jeans and a black singlet. Over the top of the singlet, I wore a long-sleeved checked shirt left open except where it was tied at my waist. On arriving in Melbourne's cold, I had pulled on my fleece-lined denim jacket. Putting my backpack down now, I untied my shirt and smoothed it down over my hips so that it covered my bum. Then I did up the buttons, leaving only one undone at the neck.

Mum had visited me in Darwin last year. When I picked her up from the airport, she cast an appraising eye over my clothes and told me I looked like a slut. I was never offended when Mum called me this because she pronounced it 'srut' and had a habit of using such words without knowing their full meaning. I answered back, 'If I look like a slut, then you do too!' I was trying to say that she liked to look sexy too, but was just more devious about it. Her tops may not have been low-cut, or her skirts short, but they were nipped, tucked and tailored to show off her shape. Fluttering over her cleavage would be some maddening lace or semi-transparent voile. Her fabrics were soft and feminine and doused in perfume. Long silk skirts with side splits flowed over her legs. They opened when she sat down, causing her to tug modestly at the fabric and draw even more attention to her thighs.

With slow steps, I walked through the Spanish arches and down the path to the front door with its 'Jesus lives here' sign. I knocked and waited, listening for footsteps. When Dad opened the door, he looked small and ordinary. Gone, I thought, was the scourge, the performer and the visionary. He stood, stooped and sad, making me long to comfort him. At the same time, rising up in me involuntarily as we performed a stiff hug was a faint but familiar repulsion at his touch, and at the sight of his bulging wet eyes and thick lugubrious lips. When I asked how he was, his voice broke and his mouth twisted. 'Well, you know how it is. It's very hard. We can only trust in God. It's good you came. Your mother needs you, Natasha.'

Stepping inside, I recognised the faint odour of soya sauce and brushed carpet. The colours in the house, Dad's colours, seemed more gaudy than I remembered. In the entrance a red Chinese lantern hung low from the ceiling, forcing tall Western visitors to duck. An arrangement of ultramarine blue pots sat in a corner on the bright orange carpet. Some of the furniture had been moved around, probably for the wheelchair. I leant my backpack against the carved mustard-coloured treasure chest that had travelled with us from Hong Kong. Dominating the wall behind the chest was Dad's photomontage of the Rapture. Visitors always commented on this work. He had collaged together portraits of nearly a hundred people, including our family, in a swirling mass of humanity flying heavenwards. But it was the ones who were left behind on the earthly battleground to whom the eye was drawn. Partaking of every earthly vice, their faces were contorted in gluttony, rage and loathing.

I followed Dad into the lounge room. There was Mum, beaming her beautiful lopsided smile at me. Her lips rose up on one side and pulled downwards on the other so that it looked as though she was half laughing, half crying. She raised her shoulders beseechingly. Afraid to cry, I focused on her surroundings – the fact that she was in the lounge room where we would never sit unless there were visitors, the maroon vinyl couches that still looked new, and the showiness of the Chinese cabinet stuffed with modernist sculptures created by Dad in the seventies.

Mum had told me she was using a wheelchair now, but I hadn't realised her appearance would be so changed by it. The wheelchair seemed to encase her in steel, its metal sides almost as high as her shoulders, and its spoked wheels bulky and unstylish. It did not matter how beautifully dressed she was, the wheelchair hospitalised and diminished her. Her head jerked forward as though she wanted to rise to greet me, but she remained where she was, sunk in and bound to the chair.

I could barely speak. She looked at me and said flatly, 'That's how it is, my dear.' And then, in a cheery tone, 'We have to bear our crosses. I put my trust in God. He will heal me.'

'Amen,' Dad said. 'Yes, Lord, we claim the miracle.' I rushed across to my mother so that she would not see the tears in my eyes.

Once when I was in primary school, she had lifted me up onto a high step and I saw the muscles flex in her neck and was aware for the first time that she was young, strong and physical. Now I put my arms on her shoulders and bent low so that she could pat my cheek in the way she sometimes did since becoming born again. As a family, we had seldom hugged or touched before we became Charismatic. Mum's face was still attractive, I noted with relief. Her hair did seem thinner and it occurred to me that this was an effect of the chemotherapy she had started a fortnight ago.

I wondered what Dad was doing, hovering next to me. Then I realised he was offering me an armchair as if to a guest. He waited until I sat down before pulling up a seat for himself.

'How long are you staying?' Mum asked.

'For as long as it suits everyone. I quit my job,' I said.

'What?' Mum said. 'You quit your job? What for quit your job? No need, la. We are okay – your sisters come every day, and we have a carer, Rosa, in the morning.'

'Irene, just accept,' Dad interjected. 'Accept that your daughter wants to help. She's doing the right thing.'

'You had a nice office. Why leave? You think you can just find another job?'

'Of course she will find another job, an even better one!' said Dad.

'It will be a different job when I get back, but I'm sure it will be fine,' I said. A few details were enough to satisfy them, and I was glad not to have to explain why I had few regrets about leaving work. 'What did you have for lunch today?'

'I have taught Rosa how to make Chinese food. Today she made chicken herbal soup. It was quite nice. A little bit salty, though,' Mum said.

'Nothing like your mum's cooking,' Dad said. 'We eat very bland food now.'

'You should learn to eat it, not go out to buy laksa and those oily noodles all the time,' Mum reproached Dad.

I described the baked fish and potatoes they served on the plane, then we talked about the wheelchair and how it got around the house. Dad, looking restless, walked up the stairs to his studio.

I went to make a pot of tea. The kitchen was much cleaner and neater than my mother had ever kept it. Perhaps it was the carer who had cleared the benches and stacked things up in orderly piles. A new poster showed sunlight breaking through clouds. In the bottom right-hand corner were words written in gold letters: *Miracles happen only to those who believe.*

As I returned with the tray of tea, Dad called down to me from the landing that overlooked the lounge room. 'You want to see the works I completed today, Natasha?' he said.

'You are tired, aren't you, Natasha, after the long flight. You should go and rest,' Mum said.

'When you see my pictures, Natasha, you will be filled with new energy.' Chuckling to himself, Dad karate-chopped the air with his hands.

It was good to see Dad still had spirit. 'Of course. Let's have a look at them,' I said.

While Mum and I were drinking our tea, Dad came down the stairs and spread six large prints on the floor. The energy of the line and the boldness of the colour were striking. Black lines slashed across coloured photomontages of tigers crouching, stalking and leaping. In one print, in the midst of the chaos, a lone man wearing a cross sat on a white tiger. In another print, bare-breasted women tumbled with the tigers.

'What do you think? These are my best yet. I feel they are truly inspired. Which do you like best?' He held each of them out in turn. I was immediately nervous about what to say. 'Primal' was how the reviews had described his work, but there had been a perceptible mellowing in his style since becoming Charismatic.

Before I had the chance to respond, he picked up the first one again. 'They are all extraordinary, aren't they?' he exclaimed. 'But if I had to decide, this is the best. Look at the beautiful strong lines and how the colour sings.'

Gazing at the picture he held out to me, I admired the poetry with which he had combined the images of the tigers, and then assaulted this symmetry with his raw, brutal brushstroke.

'You know, Natasha, my movements are instinctive, this is pure energy,' he said in a hushed voice, slowly shaking his head.

'It's good, Dad. I really like the tangle of black lines.' I heard the timidity in my voice.

He nodded and said, 'Yes, a tangle of lines. I said to Jesus, we are your servants, Lord, why have you allowed Irene to be sick with cancer? Do you not want good health and prosperity for us, your followers, so we can manifest your perfection? Then the Lord put it on my heart that He is not a gangster – He does not say, follow me and you have bought yourself special protection! No, it is not like that. He is above petty human calculations. He loves us so much He allows us to tangle ourselves in our webs – like you said, the tangle of lines, see? The cancer may come from my mother's dealings in black magic, or it could be —'

'No, la, Paul, don't talk like that. Such nonsense, what black magic?' Mum implored.

'Irene, let me speak the truth!' Dad cried. 'Black magic exists no matter what you want to believe. I tell you, the cancer was either a manifestation of black magic or it could be somehow connected to the existence of gratuitous evil. We do not know what goes on in the spiritual realm – there is constant warfare between the good and the evil spirits. An evil spirit can infiltrate at any time that we have left ourselves open to it.

'So what is my point, Natasha?' The sudden thickness in his voice alerted me. Dad stared at me with fierce eyes. His nostrils flared and his mouth twisted in an ugly smile. No one had said anything about my leaving, but it had not been forgotten. We had resumed the conversation we were having when I left eight years ago.

I looked away. I knew that face, possessed with anger, almost savage.

'The point is,' he said in a loud voice, 'that only He is perfection and we, until we join Him in heaven, are human. But the miracle is there. He loves us so much that He cannot bear for us to suffer – that is why He died on the cross for us. The miracle is there, we only need to believe. Find it in your heart to believe, Natasha. Will you? Put aside the "smartness"' – he spat that word out – 'and the fashion of ideology and . . . just believe!'

I had anticipated this, but still my whole body prickled with humiliation and anger. I longed to say something that would show how I despised what he had to say. In my teens I had never known how to reply, but at least I would do something surly – roll my eyes, smirk, make a scoffing sound, or pretend I hadn't heard.

Dad looked at me expectantly. Mum said, 'Praise the Lord,' and smiled in silent appeal to me. When I didn't react, Dad started rolling up his prints.

'Now I must make some important phone calls,' he said, and walked up the stairs to his studio. I gathered the cups and took them into the kitchen, washing up slowly to steady my breathing and still my shaking.

As so often happened when I saw my father angry, I thought of that other face – so different and yet so closely aligned with his. Though I tried to suppress the image, it appeared as I had seen it as a ten-year-old in my grandmother's tall, thin terrace house on Rowling Road in Hong Kong, where my father and his twelve brothers and sisters had grown up.

We were not allowed up on the third floor, but once on a visit I had sneaked up the staircase that grew narrower and steeper the higher you got. The door at the top of the landing was not locked. I turned the knob and peered inside. A barely clad man sat on a mattress in a cage almost the size of the small room. When he saw me he lurched over, put two fingers in a V to his mouth, which was covered in sores, and asked me for a cigarette.

The next time I saw him, some cousins and I were playing on the concrete in front of the house. A cousin, laughing, pointed her finger at the top floor. He had escaped from his cage and squatted naked on the window railing. Perched up there like a great ugly eagle, he took in his surrounds. Stretching his thin arms to the sky, he leapt. The sound as he landed was no louder than a coconut falling to earth. His face, which looked so strangely like my father's, lay smashed and seeping into the pavement.

*

When I returned to Mum she was tired, so I supported her while she shifted to the couch. She smelt of powder and soap and something slightly bitter. I helped her rest her head on the armrest and spread a blanket over her. Between bouts of silence, we talked about members of their Christian community or my sisters, until she dozed off and her mouth grew slack.

Dad walked into the lounge room wearing his coat and beret. Seeing Mum asleep, he told me in a quiet voice that he was going out for two or three hours to see Father Lachlan and Geoff Atkins from his ministry team. He explained that they would be doing God's work by witnessing to a woman who wanted an abortion. I asked him which bedroom I should sleep in and he told me to take my pick.

I entered the corridor leading to the three bedrooms and glanced behind me to make sure the door did not swing shut. When the door to the corridor and all the bedroom doors were closed, the corridor became a pitch-black vault.

The first room had belonged to Anita and Maria before Anita moved out, the second room had been shared by Patsy and me, and the bedroom with the ensuite bathroom at the end was my parents'. Thinking I would take the first room, since it was further from Mum and Dad's room than my old bedroom, I opened the door but saw that it was crammed with old furniture and Dad's photos and equipment. I went to the bedroom that Patsy and I had shared. Mostly unchanged, it had two single beds with their own bedside tables, separated by a chipboard wardrobe that we had painted pink to match the walls.

Our room had looked like the bedrooms of our schoolfriends, or so we'd hoped, with its pastel colours and posters of cute animals. No pictures of pop stars had been allowed by Dad, though, and suddenly remembering, I swung the door shut. A poster of Bono that my friend Bonnie had secretly stuck to the back of the door was still there. Bonnie had shared this room with me when she came to us for refuge. She had taken Patsy's bed, while Patsy moved into Maria's room. I ripped the poster off the door and was about to crush it but stopped myself. Since Bonnie's death, I had not been able to throw away anything of hers. Folding the poster, I placed it in my backpack to take to Darwin and add to the cardboard box where I kept her photos, letters and books.

The room had a sour smell of old bedding. I imagined also a hint of vanilla, the scent of the discount moisturiser Bonnie had worn. Opening the window, I gathered the curtains and let them hang on the outside of the window. I stripped the blankets and sheets from the beds and, although the weather was cold and grey, carried them out the back to hang on the Hills Hoist. The large backyard was an intimidating tangle of long grass, teeming weeds and towering cacti. Dad had been meaning to clean it up since we'd moved in thirteen years ago. Only the side edge of the yard where a path led to the Hills Hoist was clear.

Returning to the room, I emptied my backpack and stuffed my clothes into the wardrobe. Then I flopped down on the bare mattress, still wearing my shoes and jacket, meaning to rest for one minute but sinking straightaway into a deep sleep.

I woke up, startled. The phone was ringing in my parents' bedroom and I rushed to pick up. It was Dad, gushing and breathless. 'Where's Mum, Natasha? Wonderful news. Praise the Lord!'

'What is it, Dad?' I was shivering from cold.

'Geoff and I prayed with Father Lachlan, a true man of God. We were singing in the most mellifluous of tongues when suddenly Geoff burst out in prophecy. "Your hands have been blessed so that Irene may live!" Do you understand, Natasha? Jesus will heal your mother through the hands of Father Lachlan. Isn't that wonderful?'

'Do you mean healed of cancer?'

'Of course, Natasha.'

'And when is this to happen?'

'This year – by the end of this year. Alleluia! There is plenty more, but now I must tell Irene. Give the phone to Mum.'

'She's sleeping, Dad.'

'Wake her up.'

'Can't this wait until you come home?'

'She will want to be woken up for this wonderful news. Your mother is healed. Tell her to sing and dance and eat anything she wants – no more hospital, no more chemo, we are going to throw that wheelchair away. A miracle, Natasha. Give the phone to Irene – now!'

Her face was sensitive, sweet and sad while she slept, her brow relaxed, mouth gentle and eyelids lightly flickering. It seemed so cruel to wake her.

'Mum, wake up,' I said, rubbing her shoulder. And louder, 'Mum, Dad's on the phone.' Her eyes opened, shocked and unseeing. The panic on her face subsided as she took in my presence and her surroundings.

'Huh, what?' she said in a hoarse voice.

'It's all right, Mum. It's just Dad on the phone. He says he has some good news for you.' I handed her the phone.

'*Meeyeaah?*' she asked. Dad's excited talking, rising and falling over the line, was loud enough for me to hear. Then the tinny sounds stopped, and she said, 'Praise the Lord. Okay … Alleluia … Yes, I believe … Yes, I am healed …' Her voice sounded tired and dull, but when she put the phone down and I saw her eyes, they were glowing.

PATSY, THE YOUNGEST, RANG WITH A MESSAGE from Anita, the eldest. The family was coming over for dinner at 7 p.m., and Anita said I had to cook. Patsy's voice often trembled from shyness. Now it took on a self-important tone. Everything had to be organic and free-range. No frying, no soya sauce, no chemicals or preservatives, no chillis or pepper. Avoid wheat, oil, butter and sugar. As she reeled off the foods that Mum could not eat, it sounded like a more extreme form of the diet Patsy had been following for the past year.

The bag of chicken livers was sitting in the fridge, as Patsy had said. Liver, rich in iron, was supposed to be good for Mum. She had cooked it for us when we were children. I had seen her pick the livers up with both hands, squish the extra fluid out, massage them with five spice and soya sauce and throw them in a wok of sizzling oil. I couldn't bear to touch the things. I tipped the bag into a mixing bowl and the livers slithered out like large blood clots.

Dad arrived home with a shining face. He went straight to Mum in the family room to talk more about the miracle. Although I could see them from the kitchen, I could not hear what they were saying over the racket I was making. Mum and Dad looked hopeful and happy as they talked. I lit the stove and banged down the pressure cooker.

Dad went up to his studio. I helped Mum lie down and hurried back to the kitchen. I opened and shut cupboard doors searching for implements and ingredients, rinsed, chopped vegetables, scraped out jars, and filled and stirred the pots. At the same time, I ran back and forth to the family room when Mum called for water, or to move her pillows or take her to the toilet. Every few minutes I turned my head to look at the clock.

Five minutes before the family was due to arrive, I had cooked two dishes: a colourless chicken and lentil soup, and steamed liver with vegetables. The liver had lost its plumpness and rich brown sheen, and sat in shrivelled, grey lumps in the steamer.

At least I could make the table look good. My parents still dined as though they were in a cheap Hong Kong eatery. I pulled away the plastic sheet covering the table and replaced it with a pale yellow bedsheet I found in the linen cupboard.

With a clattering of high heels Anita strode in, well groomed, suited and swinging a glossy briefcase. She had recently been promoted to marketing manager of the property development firm she worked for. Her perfume and the corporate air she wore momentarily overpowered the smell of cooked liver. Everything seemed to lift a notch in pace.

'You're looking well,' she said and lifted her eyebrows, code for *You've put on weight.*

'And you are looking exceedingly well,' I responded, puffing out my cheeks and crossing my eyes. We both laughed.

'How was the trip?' she asked. Before I could answer, she walked into the family room to greet Mum and started organising her pillows. When she returned to the kitchen, she lifted the lid of the steamer. 'These are overcooked. Do you know how much organic liver and vegetables cost?' She tasted the soup. Without asking me, she took out a jar of tomato paste from the fridge and scraped half of it into the pot.

She started to make a shopping list. Pushing me aside, she fossicked through the fridge and cupboards, calling out what we had and what we needed to get. She then opened a drawer full of bottles of pills. Pulling out one bottle after another, she said, 'You give two of these blue pills at dinner time, one pink pill, two capsules and a tablespoon of this tonic. Same at breakfast time, except you also give two capsules from this blue bottle and one tablet from this foil pack. Got that, or do I need to repeat?'

Irritation rose in me. 'Do you mind writing that down?'

She raised her voice. 'Look! There are a million and one things to do. Read the labels and ring me tomorrow if you are not clear.'

I was about to say, *What's the matter with you?* but stopped short when I saw the resentment on her face.

Before we could argue, Anita's husband, Charles, came through the door with William on his hip. Anita rushed to them, gushing, 'How's my little boy!' Charles, warm face smiling, put his arm around my shoulder and said, 'Welcome back, Bindi Windi Booroomool! Say something in Aboriginal!' I gave a weak laugh. He came closer and said in a lowered voice, 'It's good you're back. Your mother is really very ill.'

He went into the next room to greet Mum. Charles, a property developer from Shanghai, had converted to Catholicism so he could marry Anita. He was well liked by Mum and Dad, who said he was very 'open'. Anita brought Will over to me. 'Say hello to your Aunty Natasha,' Anita said.

I picked up Will, a solid little bundle in his overalls. He looked me straight in the face, gave me a half smile and squirmed away, saying, 'I want Mummy.'

Patsy was right next to me in the kitchen before I noticed her. 'Hi, nice to have you home,' she said. She wore a cream-coloured pinafore that puffed around her small frame. 'How did you go with the cooking?'

'Don't ask. Anita thinks everything is overcooked,' I said.

'What? The vegetables and liver are organic, you know,' Patsy said, frowning. The furrows made her thin, pale face look even more pinched, and I wanted to reach over and smooth them away. She was supposed to have been cured of her anorexia, but to me she still seemed far too skinny.

'Maria late as usual?' I asked.

'She's on executive time, of course,' Anita said sarcastically.

Just then Maria arrived, carrying three large handbags with their zips undone and contents spilling out. Her evangelical pamphlets, first-aid kit, things she'd picked up at the Salvos; she always carried too much with her in case she needed it. My sister, the bag lady, dressed in a shapeless blue tracksuit, had been unemployed for too long.

'Hi, Nat. Great to have you here,' she said and hugged me. Maria was the most tactile of us, giving big Christian hugs, though she did so with her hands balled up. 'Is that a new jumper? Looks nice on you,' she said. Her face was still pretty despite the dowdy clothes. She was the best-looking among us sisters.

I tugged on the polyester sleeve of her tracksuit top. 'Thanks, Maria – you shouldn't have dressed up for me!'

She laughed. 'Oh, I just came from ministry group. I was in a rush!'

My sisters and I moved to the family room. Mum sat on the sofa watching William propel matchbox cars off the sofa arm. Charles, who was in the armchair opposite Mum, told us to sit down.

'Listen, your mother has news,' he said.

'Natasha, you tell them,' Mum said.

'You can, Mum. I don't really know what it's all about. You talked about it with Dad more than me.' I wanted them to hear it from her, though we all knew how difficult it was for Mum to recount even simple stories.

We waited while Mum picked at the seam in her skirt and fumbled for words. 'Well, you see, your dad and Geoff Atkins, Father Lachlan also ... they were going to pray with this woman ... she wanted to, you know, abortion ... but then, um ... she didn't turn up, la. They thought, let's pray for her anyway but then ... it ended up they were praying for me ... then your dad and Geoff said Irene is healed ... a miracle ...'

Maria and Patsy seemed to pep up as soon as they heard Mum say the word 'miracle', but Anita and Charles started to question her. 'Wait till Dad comes out of his studio – he will explain,' Mum said. She picked up Will's cars from the cushion next to her and busied herself handing them to him.

Dad came down the stairs, rubbing his hands together.

'Wonderful news, everyone. Wonderful news! Is dinner ready? You must all be sitting down when I tell you.' He saw the food had not been laid out and turned back towards his studio. 'Call me when everyone is seated at the table.'

We rushed around, setting the table and putting the food out in serving bowls. I spooned out the liver and vegetables into an oval ceramic dish, garnished it with finely chopped fresh coriander and spring onion and arranged thinly sliced cucumber around the edges of the dish. Anita served the rice while Patsy ladled the soup into each bowl and Maria placed a slice of orange on top.

I went into the family room looking for candles. Next to the TV was the family altar, which was basically a coffee table covered in a pink scarf on which sat a crucifix, a statue of Mary and six candles. A portrait of the face of Jesus derived from the Turin Shroud hung on the wall behind the altar. I grabbed the two long white candles and brought them back with me to the kitchen, where I placed them at the centre of the table. I had picked some jasmine on my walk from the bus and wove the stems around the candles. With the candles lit, the table looked festive and aglow. Patsy fetched Mum. '*Umboy!*' she said, admiring the grandness of the table. Then Maria went to the studio to fetch Dad.

*

'We thank you, Lord, for the great miracle you have bestowed on your faithful servant Irene. We acknowledge you, O Lord, as almighty and powerful saviour. And we thank you for bringing Natasha home. Let us sing.' Dad broke into 'Thank you, thank you, Jesus'. It was a simple, rousing tune. We sang it with gusto, and I enjoyed hearing our voices fill the house.

'So, what's this about a miracle?' Anita asked.

'Let's taste this food first and then I will tell you the whole wonderful story,' Dad answered, scooping the liver onto his plate of rice. He clicked his spoon and fork together enthusiastically and took a large mouthful. Within a few seconds, his face lost all expression and his chewing slowed. He reached for the soup, sipped at it and then moved his mouth around uncomfortably.

Pushing his bowl away, he stood up. 'Thank you to the cooks, but we will agree that this is a time of celebration. Irene, you are healed and can eat anything you want, not this ... this ... bland horse food.' He smiled as though he thought his choice of words was cute. 'I will order noodles from Ting Chu – they are very quick. Charles, leave now to pick it up.'

Dad grabbed the phone and dialled. 'Good evening, it is Paul Chan. I want to order takeaway for a very special occasion. Two large char kway teow, two large hokkien noodles, one roast duck and one large barbeque pork. Are you listening? We must have the dishes cooked now as a matter of great priority – cooked deliciously, but cooked now. You can do that? Can be ready in ten minutes? Very good.' He put the phone down and walked to his studio, calling back to us, 'Fetch me when the food has arrived.'

I continued to spoon soup into my mouth. My throat, hot and constricted, threatened to gag.

'Never mind, Natasha, I like it,' said Maria, always the kind-hearted one.

'It's not too bad,' Mum said, also drinking her soup. 'You know your dad – he wants to celebrate.'

'Let's just say, use a recipe next time,' Anita said, and Patsy was already clearing the table.

Within forty minutes, my carefully presented dishes had been packed away in the fridge. Plastic takeaway boxes, stray noodles and duck bones littered the table, and oil, soya sauce, red barbeque sauce and brown gravy spattered the tablecloth. Dad had eaten and was ready to talk.

'I was summoned this afternoon to do God's work. A young Filipino woman wanted to abort her child. It had been arranged that she would meet Father Lachlan and me for counselling. Geoff Atkins also came to lend his prayers. We sat together in a room in his seminary, waiting to talk with her. We waited and waited but she did not turn up. So we prayed for her and her unborn baby in her absence. This happened for a reason. A reason preordained by the Lord.

'We held hands and I led the prayer. I said, "Dear Lord, we intercede for this woman who holds the decision of life and death in her hands. May she see that it is only you who giveth life and who taketh life. May she see the light, may she manifest your divine will and choose life." As soon as I said this, the Lord put it on our hearts that we were not just praying for this young mother – we were praying for Irene to choose life. Suddenly, a warmth filled my spine and abdomen just where Mum's cancer is. As though it was God speaking through me – I believe it was God's voice – I said, "We denounce the demons of despair and failure and call forth your miracle. Yes, Lord, we claim your miracle. Irene chooses life!" At that moment a fragrance of oranges was in the air and the sky outside seemed suffused with purple light. I burst out into tongues and Geoff and Father Lachlan followed and then we were all singing in the most mellifluous of tongues. It was beautiful. It really was magnificent. When the singing faded away, Geoff uttered forth a prophecy from God that Father Lachlan will be blessed with healing powers so that Irene shall live.

'Isn't that wonderful, everyone? We started praying for a Filipino woman who wanted an abortion and the Lord showed us that just as that woman must choose life for her baby, so must Irene choose life for herself!' He turned to Mum. 'Do you accept God's miracle, Irene?'

Mum closed her eyes. 'Amen,' she said quietly.

Dad turned his attention to the rest of us. 'All must believe! It is only through our belief that it will happen. Jesus cannot force miracles on us. We must accept in faith and not let our doubts prevent the healing which the Lord wants to bestow on Irene. Jesus knocks on our door, but he will not let himself in. Only you can let him in.'

'Alleluia,' Maria responded. Patsy spoke quietly in tongues.

Charles, with Will asleep on his lap, whispered, 'Thank you, God.'

'That's positive news,' Anita said, but her face was troubled. Seeing Dad's eyes on me, I nodded. I was amazed how easy it was to fall back into line.

For a while Dad was silent, holding his hand to his head and occasionally nodding as though listening to something. Suddenly he smacked his knee hard and shouted, 'Yes! Yes, Lord!' Raising both hands, he looked heavenwards. 'Yes, Lord, we will do your will.'

He stood up, now directing his talk to us. 'God has put it on my heart that we must hold a healing party. At this healing party, Father Lachlan will lay his hands on Mum and she will be healed. This party will be the manifestation of our faith. All and sundry will be invited so that they may witness the miracle. We are to start planning for the party immediately!'

*

It was time for night prayers. We moved to the family room. Maria handed me a guitar. 'Do you still play?' she said. I tuned the guitar while she lit two long white candles and four small scented ones on the family altar and turned out the lights. We sang, 'Come back to me with all your heart/ Don't let fear keep us apart.' By the time we reached the chorus, 'Long have I waited for your coming/ Home to me and living/ Deeply our new life,' I was in tears, grateful to be hidden by the darkness and drowned out by the singing. We sang more hymns, each more appealing than the last, and then Dad led us in tongues. Together the incoherent sounds and minor key made the most beautiful discordant song.

For the next part of the prayers, we went around the circle, each taking turns to say a prayer out loud. In the past I would say 'Pass' when it was my turn, but this time, like my sisters before me, I prayed aloud for Mum to be healed. In the flickering light of the candles, I saw Mum looking peaceful and elated. Song and love flowed through my family. God was with us and everything would be all right. Dad called out, 'The fragrance of oranges. Do you all smell it – the fruit of healing?' And we did.

*

That first night, I shoved my feet into sheets and mattress so cold they felt damp. I kicked my legs to warm up and when I stopped, I could no longer move. Too overwhelmed to go over scenes and review the day in my head, I gave in and sank into deep sleep.

The sound of voices woke me. They were coming through the wall. For a moment I thought I was a child again, lying in the dark listening to my parents in the next room. When their voices were raised and angry, I would feel a terrible anxiety. In the middle of the night, when you are woken, anything can seem a catastrophe.

Sometimes I heard them after they had returned from a party or a dinner. The floor would creak, lights would be turned on and off, and as they walked past my bedroom I could smell Mum's perfume, and sometimes cigarette smoke or odours from the restaurant they had been to. When they entered their bedroom and closed the door, Mum's voice would start, low and complaining. She would continue for some time until Dad interjected angrily. Occasionally I could make out the words, 'Always so jealous! Do you want to destroy me?' Once I heard him stomping around, shouting out crazily, 'I will shoot you!'

When the voices were calm, I would feel comforted and fall back asleep to their mumblings, as if to a lullaby. It was lovely when they shared a joke or recounted a funny incident. Mum would say, '*Ho suwey!* How absurd!' as they both laughed. Occasionally, after they had become born-again Christians, they would sing a favourite hymn together and the tune would vibrate through the wall, warming my whole being.

This time, however, even before I was sufficiently awake to make out what the voices were saying, an uneasiness gnawed at my stomach. Mum's voice was unintelligible but insistent. Then I heard Dad's voice, urgent, cajoling. I pulled the blankets away from around my ears and quietened my breathing. Mum's words were now audible. 'How can I sleep with this pain! I can't stand it!' She let out a slow, wounded moan. The suffering in her voice made me sit upright.

Then Dad started to pray, drowning her out. 'You are healed, Irene . . . By the blood of Jesus!' I heard more praying, and he said loudly, 'We reject you, Satan!'

I rose from the bed. The floorboards creaked, sending a crack resonating up the walls and through to the roof. Moving down the corridor, I tiptoed onto the tiles in the bathroom and ran the cold tap. The noise of the pipes cranking up and the water flowing seemed amplified. I rinsed and filled a glass with water. For a few minutes I stood outside their bedroom door with the glass of water, unsure whether to knock. Not a sound could be heard from their room now. I rested the weight of my head against their door and closed my eyes. Eventually, I poured the water down the bathroom sink and returned to bed.

The voices started again, this time calmer. Then Mum and Dad were singing in tongues. When the singing ceased, there was silence for a time, before I heard first his and then her snoring, almost indistinguishable in their low rumbling.

I turned on my side and pulled up the blankets ready to go back to sleep, but an image of Bonnie sleeping in bed face down, bush of hair over the pillow, legs squeezed together and body straight as a pin, came to me. A cold sweat broke over my body. The breath was strangled out of me. The fear had come back;

perhaps it had always been with me. Or waiting here in this room. There was no reason for it. I tried to speak in tongues – '*Unay unay astinor, umbala meshala asti usha* ...' It didn't work. Something terrible was about to happen.

I threw back the blankets and jumped out of bed with my hand outstretched for the light switch. The light hurt, but I kept my eyes open. I stood with my back against the wall, getting my breath back, and scanned the beds, the wardrobe, the clothes that I'd left lying on the floor, making sure that things were as they should be.

When Patsy and I shared this room, I would shake her awake and squeeze into her bed. She would roll on her side towards the wall but put her hand behind her for me to hold. I listened to her breathing. If it became heavy, I would call out, poke and even pinch her, to make her stay awake with me until the terror passed. She would murmur, half-asleep, 'Yep, okay,' and never became angry, even though I was the big sister and should have been looking after her.

After half an hour, I was calm but still wide awake. I pulled out from a deep pocket of my backpack the book Jason had given me before I left Darwin. The title dominated the cover. In black capital letters on a plain grey background were the words *On Death and Dying*. I told myself I would have to cover it in brown paper and hide it.

The interviews with terminally ill patients were detailed and real. Too real. After a few pages, my mind wandered off to thoughts of Jason. On our last night together we rode our bicycles the long way to the Thai restaurant, curving around the foreshore, following the fiery red horizon line. We stopped by the bottle shop on the way and Jason bought a bottle of white wine for me and a six-pack of VB and a bottle of Scotch for himself. He drank every night, but Friday night, with the working week over, was the big one.

He said he wanted to take me to the airport the next morning, but I told him I hated awkward, drawn-out goodbyes at airports. We knew it was our last night and although we ordered our favourite dishes, we had no appetite for them. I drank one glass of wine, he drank the rest of the bottle and then the VBs while we smoked and looked around us and at each other.

We went to my house after dinner. I started to climb the stairs ahead of Jason, but he caught me around the waist and held onto me from behind. Nuzzling his face into the back of my neck, he caressed my breasts. Then he reached down with one hand and slid his fingers inside the front of my pants. I swung around and he kissed me, grasping me to him. His mouth and tongue were urgent and stinking of alcohol.

I wrenched away. 'Fuck off.'

He looked as if he had been struck.

'Sorry,' I said, 'it's just that it doesn't feel right tonight.'

He ran down the stairs, grabbed his bicycle and, instead of using the path, dragged it over the bushy undergrowth of the garden. I followed him, holding my bare arms against my sides to avoid the sharp spines on the twisted straps of the pandanus trees.

'Shit!' Jason shouted as he pulled his arm back from a pandanus. His ugly tone irritated me. The skin of his upper arm was bluish in the moonlight and it oozed a thin line of dark blood.

When he reached the road, he straightened his bicycle and I thought he was going to ride away without saying goodbye. But he turned around. 'I'm sorry,' he said.

For a long time we held each other tight. My last sight of him was his long back loping from side to side as he forced down the pedals.

I put the *Death and Dying* book down, lay back on my bed and closed my eyes. I imagined I had taken his hand and led him back up the stairs. I was slippery and swollen now and beautiful to touch. As my spine began to arch and my toes began to curl, as I drew in deep and stopped breathing, I saw Jason's sweet face, his guarded eyes and crooked nose, and the hurt that suddenly softened his eyes.

On weekday mornings from 7 a.m. till 9 a.m., a carer from Red Cross was scheduled to come to help Mum. Anita, who had made the arrangements, told me how difficult it had been to find a good carer – the first one failed to show up after two days, and the second one couldn't follow even simple instructions. However, Mum was happy with Rosa, who now had the job. Dad would open the door for Rosa when she arrived in the morning and stay in his studio until she left. I stayed out of the way too, hiding in my room.

A few days after my arrival, Mum called me into the bathroom, wanting me to learn the correct way to lift her. Rosa stood next to her in the cramped space between the toilet and the shower. The room was still damp from Dad's shower. Rosa was curly-haired and middle-aged, her box-shaped body wrapped in a Red Cross uniform.

'Hello, my darling. So you're the daughter from Darwin.' She grabbed my shoulders and scanned my face. Looking over to Mum, she said, 'Your daughter has bigger nostrils and lips and her face is wider, but still she has some of her mother's good looks.'

'You mean her mother's used-to-be good looks,' Mum said.

'Too long ago now.' She waved a graceful hand at the distant past. It usually annoyed me when people commented that Mum was prettier than her daughters, but this time I was pleased. Poking out from under the frilled hem of her pink cotton nightgown, Mum's thin legs looked cold.

Rosa picked up the wet bathmat from the floor and hung it over the towel rail. There was barely enough room in the bathroom for Mum's wheelchair to sit next to the toilet and Rosa to stand next to her, so I watched from the doorway.

Rosa manoeuvred the wheelchair so that it was almost touching the toilet. 'I will teach you my way to lift,' she said. 'Don't ask me if it's the doctor's way – it's my way. Many people say do it like this or do it like that. But look, I do it my way and it's been working for over twenty years. You are lucky your mum is light and never complains.' She planted a sneakered foot on each side of the wheelchair so that she was facing Mum.

'Sorry, my darling, do you mind if I use you?' she said to Mum. Mum shuffled her body forward to the edge of the chair and Rosa placed her arms under Mum's shoulders. 'You join your arms around her back so you have a good hold. It's like you are hugging each other. Then you bend your knees. Make sure you use the muscles in your legs and your stomach and lift —'

Mum suddenly pulled away, thumping against the wheelchair's backrest. 'Wait!' Mum cried. 'Close the door, Natasha. Close it! Close it!' Squeezing into the bathroom, I grabbed the door and pulled it shut.

'Always your mum says, close the door, close the door!' Rosa said. 'It's okay, Irene. He's your husband. You should see how my husband sees me – curlers in my hair, fat, no teeth. So what? He still loves me. If not, that's his problem! Bye-bye to him.' She laughed.

Mum's face was closed and her eyes hard. Rosa stopped laughing. 'Never mind, darling. Just remember, you are always gorgeous.'

On a count of three, Rosa hoisted Mum to her feet. Mum clung to Rosa, helpless legs scrabbling. Together they shuffled towards the toilet, locked in a bent and desperate dance. The blue floor tiles, covered in mist, glistened treacherously. One slip and there would be no mercy from the shower ledge or the sharp corner of the vanity bench. With the side of her head pressed against Rosa's bust, Mum watched me watching her. I forced myself not to look away.

Grunting, Rosa lowered Mum's weight onto the toilet seat. Only when Mum had found her balance did Rosa release her. Mum pulled back her shoulders, fixed her hair, smoothed down her nightgown and turned to me.

'So, have you got it, Natasha? You know how it works?' she said, her head held at a stiff angle. I nodded. 'Okay,' she said. 'Go and have your breakfast.'

I left, closing the door behind me as Rosa struggled to pull the nightgown out from under Mum without letting its hem fall into the toilet bowl.

*

Rosa's shift finished. Having showered, dressed, eaten breakfast and taken her medicine, Mum was exhausted. Dad helped her onto the sofa in the lounge room and sat beside her. With their heads bowed, they prayed the rosary. When Mum called me to join them, I said I would pray with them while I finished washing up. I pushed open the bi-fold doors so I could see them from the kitchen. Dad, fingering the baby-blue plastic beads, led the incantation. Mum responded softly. *The first joyous mystery . . . hail Mary . . . blessed are the fruit . . . at the hour of our death . . .* They were phrases that I knew well enough to chant without pause or thought. Disjointed, floating from a distance, the words had an added beauty. Dad's dark skin was pale in the cool grey light and his restless eyes were shut. Mum's body in its stillness, in respite, was graceful. I was reminded of photos of them from when they were young. They had been introduced in church; Dad was a recent convert from Buddhism, in the days before he went wild – or, as Mum put it, before he became modern.

When the rosary was over, Dad laid his right hand first on each of Mum's legs, then on her abdomen. Dipping his finger into a small jar of blessed oil, he drew the sign of the cross on her forehead. He kept his hand on her head and quietly prayed in tongues.

I attended to the dishes in the sink and when I turned back to look at Mum and Dad, they were talking in serious tones. They remained on the sofa, but their heads were turned away from each other, Mum rubbing her sore abdomen. As I drew closer, I heard them talking about the healing party.

Mum was insisting that the guests be limited to thirty. Dad disagreed. 'Open up the doors to everyone,' he was saying. 'It must be a party like no other we have ever had.'

'Don't be absurd! How can everyone fit?' Mum said.

'If they are spilling out into the street, all the more glory to God. Alleluia!'

She touched her throat. 'Then we give them only tea and biscuits.'

'No, Irene, we must be generous. We are doing this for the Lord. There must be plenty of good food. Make everyone happy.'

'We can't do this.'

'We must show God's love, Irene.'

'Okay – the Australian way. Everybody has to bring a plate of food to share.'

'How can you calculate when the Lord has promised a miracle at this party?'

Mum looked away, frowning. In the past, she would have jumped to her feet. 'Aiya, don't show off, how absurd, everyone brings a plate, it's understood,' she would have argued, until, as usual, Dad won. I anxiously anticipated the quarrel to come.

Dad loved to hold parties. It seemed we held a hundred of them in the house on the top of the hill in Hong Kong, where we lived for two years from when I was seven. One side of the hill was dominated by houses and roads, the other side was darkened by deep, dense jungle. Our house was flanked by a grand expanse of lawn that was regularly clipped by a gardener to stop the jungle's encroachment.

The double-storey colonial house was a mansion compared with the narrow shophouses in crowded streets that we usually rented. Although the rent was cheap, it had been vacant for a long time. Dad found out why soon after we moved in: the lawn that had so impressed us had been a burial site for Japanese soldiers during the Second World War. We lived there with a constant feeling of unease – my sisters and I feared walking on the lawn or even entering a bathroom alone. But we stayed on at the house on the hill for the parties. By folding back the French doors that stretched across two sides of the house, we opened up the ground-floor living area to the lawn and the hum, screech and chatter of the jungle. On party nights that lawn, strewn with lanterns casting flickering shadows, could have been a shimmering sea.

Patsy and I would position ourselves between the living room and kitchen. Double doors like those in a Western saloon separated the two rooms and swung back and forth with a *whoomph* as the women pushed through, carrying trays stacked with smoking beef satay, glistening noodles, yellow chicken curry and fragrant roast duck. After the food, Dad would gather everyone on the lawn and Mum would be dragged out of the kitchen. The two of them would stand in front of the guests, the reigning monarchs, the most glamorous of couples. Dad, in a multi-coloured silk shirt, sweat shining on his forehead, teeth showing, would start with a speech in which he simultaneously entertained and inspired, congratulated and challenged his guests. While the guests were still shaking their heads at his brilliance, he would sing a cheeky song or perform a mime specially selected for the night. Next up, he would introduce the party games. This was the part where we saw adults acting like children. Afterwards there would be more food, and then dancing that went on and on until Patsy and I could take no more. We lay on the couch that had been pushed against the wall to make room for the dancing, and before we knew it we would find ourselves being carried up to bed by Agnes.

Agnes was only sixteen, a year younger than Anita, when she came to us from the orphanage as a live-in servant. Patsy and I loved her – she wasn't like the other servants who averted their eyes and helped silently when called and then disappeared. Her skinny arms would wrap around me and I'd hear a whispered *Why you so fat, Nat?* in my ear. *Alamak!* she would cry, hoisting me up. Then *boom, boom* – I would feel each step she took up the stairs, jiggling and rocking to the music with me in her arms.

After we moved to Melbourne when I was eleven, Dad continued to hold parties. Inspecting the house in Aquarius Court for the first time, Dad stood in the large lounge room and saw how it opened up into the kitchen and the family room; he imagined the space thronging with guests, and his mind was made up.

But parties in Australia were not what he expected. I remembered the night he and Mum attended their first Australian party, held by a photographer colleague of Dad's. They left dressed to the nines, excited and carrying a plate of cakes. They returned early that night, hungry and appalled. My sisters and I gathered around Dad to hear about the party. 'No food except a few pathetic bowls of cold chips and crackers ... No games ... No dancing ... Just loud music and people drinking their beer!' Dad could not bring himself to tell the whole of it. Later we learnt about the shameful incident. Dad and Mum had waited to be offered at least a drink, but there was nothing being served. The guests were helping themselves to drinks from a big bin filled with ice. So Dad reached for a bottle but a man called out loudly in front of the other guests, 'Mate, that's mine. Didn't you bring your own? You know, BYO? Aussie for bring *your own*!'

Dad vowed to show the Australians how to hold a party. He invited all his workmates, clients and photographic models. Mum cooked for weeks in advance, and we bought a large freezer just to store the prepared dishes. My sisters and I were the kitchen hands. On the night of the party, the guests, eyes greedy, filled up their plates from two tables laden with hot Chinese dishes, and came back once, twice and even three times for more. After the meal, Dad made a speech, sang a Hakka folksong and invited guests to come up and perform. When no one came forward, he introduced a new game he had made up to mark our first party in Australia. He called it 'Hula-Hula Aussies'. We moved all the furniture aside and the fifty guests sat on the carpeted floor in a large circle. Spinning around in the middle of the circle, Dad explained the game. A grass skirt he had been given as a visiting artist in Hawaii would be passed around while the music played. As soon as the music stopped, the person left holding the skirt had to stand in the middle of the circle, pull on the skirt and do a hula dance. Dad gave a demonstration, wiggling and hamming it up to laughter and wolf-whistles. He called Mum up to demonstrate the swaying hips and rotating pelvis for the women, but, always modest, she refused. Before the party, Dad had instructed me on how to operate the CD player. I would sit next to him, and when he secretly pushed his foot against mine, I was to stop the music. I wondered if anyone else noticed how the music kept stopping every time the skirt reached the hands of a pretty woman.

After we became born-again Christians, we continued with the parties. Instead of games, however, we had dances, songs and acts put on in praise of the Lord. Everybody loved our parties, but they never saw what we, especially Mum, had to go through to hold them. Mum and Dad always had their worst quarrels beforehand. Mum suffered a week of nerves and non-stop cooking. Dad would chide her, 'Be generous, show people a good time.' Mum would snort, 'You just want to show off.'

This time, however, Mum did not seem able to put up a fight. She rubbed her rosary beads on the woollen skirt stretching over her distended abdomen and closed her eyes. Dad continued in a gentle but insistent voice. 'The healing party is our chance to witness to the people. The Lord has promised to heal you. Let this party bring the unbelievers to Him!' Sitting forward on the couch, Dad turned to her, one knee almost touching the ground. 'Say yes, Irene.'

Mum's head tilted to one side. For a moment I imagined how they must have looked when he proposed to her. 'Yes, Boon Chin, we must witness for the Lord,' she said.

'Praise the Lord,' Dad said. They talked some more until Dad climbed the stairs to his studio.

I went into the lounge room once he left. 'You don't have to have a big party if you don't want to,' I said to Mum. 'A small party will be just right. Do whatever *you* feel comfortable with. Don't let anyone bully you into anything.'

'What are you talking about? Your dad is not a bully.'

'I didn't say he was.'

Her hand fluttered around her throat. 'It is not nice to talk like that. We will have a good party. Don't worry.'

*

Later that day, when Mum had woken from her afternoon nap and Dad had gone out to meet with Geoff Atkins, I looked for an opportunity to talk to Mum.

She sat in the family room, listening to an American preacher shout his message from the CD player. 'Amen,' Mum muttered, nodding her head. As he moved into the final part of his sermon, I went to the kitchen to prepare a pot of tea, determined to talk to her when the CD had ended.

Dad had said that when he married Mum, he thought her profound because of her beautiful, enigmatic smile. He would talk about anything on his mind, philosophise, even read her his poetry or sing to her. She would keep quiet and listen, and always that smile played upon her lips. I knew what he meant. I had seen her with some men, particularly those with an eye for women. One of the leaders of the Charismatics was a dashing Maltese man. He knew how to wear a suit and he always smelt good. Everyone wanted a piece of him, but he would always seek Mum out. He would talk and gaze into her smiling face. She would say nothing, and afterwards he would tell Dad, 'You're a lucky man, Paul. What a woman – she just radiates wisdom.' Dad would agree, even though disillusionment had set in soon after their marriage.

'Your mother is a good woman,' he would confide to me in my early teenage years, 'but I am continually offended by the way she speaks. "Boon Chin, what for doing nothing?" she says when I am preparing my next artwork; "Boon Chin, stop showing off!" she says when I am telling interesting stories to try to make people happy. Or else she serves me a wonderful-looking bowl of noodles and spoils it with, "Here, eat it!" or "Why you never do the gardening?"

It seemed to me that Mum was most at ease when she was talking to my sisters, or to her female friends from Hong Kong.

With her I'd always felt left out. I listened jealously to her talk about nothing with my sisters – what they ate for lunch, who the new priest was, the latest news on the neighbours, where to buy cheap meat, who was wearing what and whether it suited them.

When Mum became Charismatic, she found a new voice. She learnt to pray out loud, direct to Jesus. 'Alleluia, praise you, Jesus. You are the way, the truth and the light! I worship you. I love you!' My stomach would squirm, listening to her easy words of love to Jesus.

There were only a few times in my childhood that I could recall being alone with Mum. Once was when we were visiting my grandparents' shophouse on Rowling Road in Kowloon for the New Year holidays. Later, my feelings about that place on Rowling Road, or *Loling Load,* as we pronounced it, were of an infected household. There was my uncle with the gold tooth, who was always making sucking sounds and looking at us girls in a way that disturbed me. There were my aunts, who were not allowed to eat with the rest of us, but instead served us or waited in the kitchen until we had finished, and then were left to finish the scraps. There was the oldest uncle whom I saw torment a servant, making her carry a basin of water over her head and threatening to beat her if she spilt so much as one drop. A few times, screaming and banging broke out and my sisters and I would be forced out of the house. The sickness of my caged uncle seeped through the bars and under the door, wafted down the spiral staircase, found my grandparents, Agnin and Ayer, in their bed, and suffused every corner of the house. Even the unsuspecting guests in the front room below breathed him in. But at this time, when I was about seven, I still did not know of this uncle's existence and Loling Load to me was a thrilling, chaotic place filled with strange and debauched characters.

It was the hot, drowsy part of the day after lunch had been eaten. About twenty of us were staying in the narrow two-bedroom house. My grandparents were in their bedroom upstairs and Dad, who as the educated son had a special status in the household, had the other bedroom for our family to share. My parents and sisters were up there taking an afternoon nap but I was not sleepy. I watched my aunts and the servant in the courtyard kitchen hosing down the concrete floor and preparing the next meal. Then I went to the front room where several cousins and uncles lay napping on the floor or benches.

Mum came into the front room. Daintily stepping around the bodies strewn across the floor, she made her way to the outside porch. I followed her. 'Ping Yu, come!' she called out to the rickshaw driver, who was allowed to park his trishaw on the footpath in front of the house in exchange for free rides. Curled up asleep in the passenger seat, he did not hear her. Half a dozen children in the street started shouting out his name and throwing small stones.

Ping Yu finally woke. 'Where to, Madam?' he asked, manoeuvring his rickshaw closer to the porch where she waited.

'Nam Cheong Street,' she said.

I called out to Mum to ask if I could come with her. She said yes. Unable to believe my luck, I squeezed onto the plastic passenger seat next to her.

We alighted in an old part of town, where it was thick with

crowds, traffic and the acrid smell of open gutters, food frying and car fumes. Shops crammed the streets, their merchandise spilling out onto the footpaths and causing us to edge towards the drains. Mum kept a protective hand on my shoulder. She seemed to know which shops to go to. We walked in and out of one shop after another until it seemed we had been in dozens. Shopkeepers crowded around her. Most of the time she ignored them, except when she wanted to know the price of a pretty item. She reached for bolts of fabric, unfurled them with a smooth flick of the wrist, and yards of shimmering colour would float in front of her. She walked away if she thought the price was too expensive; if it seemed reasonable, she got down to business. She told them how many shops she had been to, how she could go into the next shop and get a better price. In a haughty voice, she told them that their item was not worth even half what they were asking. If they did eventually come to a deal, it was all friendly goodwill – they would then chat about the heat and humidity, how busy it was and how Kowloon was getting too crowded.

Just when I had tired of the heat and the noise, Mum, laden with shopping bags, led me away from the main street down a cool laneway. Up winding stairs was a door with a sign on it saying *Fine Tailor*. Mum seemed to know the lady who opened the door. The tailor stood my mother in front of the mirror and swathed, pinned and tucked the gleaming fabrics around her in a multitude of arresting concoctions. All the while, in a mixture of Cantonese and English, they chatted about clothes, figures, fashion, their husbands and the shop's clients. When they laughed, they covered their mouths with their hands, as though telling secrets.

I never saw Mum so confident and self-possessed in Australia as she had been then. Maybe it was because of the change in culture, or maybe because my perceptions had changed as I grew older. That day, though, I followed her around, dizzy with admiration and feeling the chasm between us deepen.

*

Returning with Mum's cup of tea, I placed it on the side table and sat down in the armchair facing her. She smiled at me, pleased that I was listening to the American preacher. Sitting opposite felt too direct. I moved to the space beside her on the sofa, where we wouldn't have to stare at each other if we were to talk. Mum let out a gassy burp and I caught a whiff of something rancid, the smell of the cancer eating her insides. *Please help Mum, don't let her suffer, and please help me get to know her*, I prayed in silence, and wondered how I would start our conversation. The CD whirred off.

I decided to appeal to Mum's strong sense of family duty. Mike, her highly esteemed nephew, had rung earlier from Hong Kong. 'Mum, did you know that Mike is writing his family's history?' I began. 'He said we should write our own history.' It was true that Mike was writing his family history, but I made up the part about urging us to do the same. 'Since I'll be here for a while, we could spend some time talking about your family.'

'What for ask me? Ask your dad. He is the clever one,' Mum said.

'You are too!'

'What for I need to be clever!'

She had said similar things before. If I challenged her, she would look at me as if there was something wrong with me. Why didn't I understand it was not her job to be clever? 'We have heard all of Dad's stories.' I said. 'Several times! We could repeat them back to you word for word. But we never hear your stories.'

'What for talk about the past? The past is the past. Why don't you —'

'So what were you like as a child?' I said.

She made that high *hmmmph* sound through her nose that she often made when she thought something was a waste of time. 'Just a child. Just like any child.'

'But what kind of child were *you*? What did you like doing?'

'Play, climb trees, that kind of thing, la.'

'What games did you play?'

'Uh . . . Tim Kong Kong.'

'How do you play it?'

'You throw a tin or something and then have to hide. Quickly, quickly hide. When he gets it he will try to see you.' She opened her eyes wide and turned her head slowly from side to side as though searching. 'If he sees you, he says, "Eh, Voon Leong, there you are," and then you are out.'

Thrilled that she should share so many details, even if only for a childhood game, I kept the questions coming. 'Where do you throw the tin?'

'You throw it far, la.' She gestured with her hand.

'How many people play?'

'Can be many children. The more the better.'

'Were you good at it?'

She nodded. 'Yes, I was very good at hiding. They could never find me.'

'Did your sisters play too?'

'No. My mother always told me off for being a tomboy.' She reached for her book. 'What for you need to know about a child's game?'

'Okay, we'll leave the game. Were you a tomboy?'

'I suppose so.'

'In what way?'

'Climbing trees, that kind of thing.'

'What was your relationship with your mother like?'

'Good. I am her daughter. She is my mother.'

'What was she like?'

Mum's hand flapped around her neck. 'A good woman.'

'Did you talk with your mother much?'

'Why not? She's my mother.' She turned around to look at the clock.

'Do you have a favourite sister?'

'All my sisters. Sisters will always be close.'

'Were you close to Monica?' I asked, knowing from another aunt that Monica, the eldest, had been the big boss.

'Of course, she's my sister.'

'What was Monica like?'

'What for ask? You know her.'

'Yes, I know her as my aunt, but what was your relationship like as sisters?'

'Such silly questions.'

I kept pressing her until finally she took up her book and put an end to our session. I told Mum we would spend at least a few minutes every day talking about her life. I could be a bully too.

'HELP! COME NOW!'

I jolted awake. Flinging off the bedclothes, I sprang to my feet. Mum called again, her voice, distressed, coming from the bathroom. I raced to the bathroom and threw open the door. Her wheelchair was empty, parked beside the closed shower curtain. I pulled aside the curtain, fearing she had fallen on the floor. Instead, she sat wet and naked on the shower chair. She gasped and her hands flew to cover herself.

I snapped the curtain shut. I struggled to compose myself. Perhaps it was the fact that this was the first time I had seen my mother naked, or that I had not seen her when she was healthy and now that time had passed forever, or that the only part of her tired body that looked taut and vigorous was her swollen stomach where the cancer grew. Passing her a towel around the curtain, I asked if she was all right. She exhaled heavily.

'Where is that girl?' Mum said. 'Rosa left, so this new girl comes. The new girl is no good! She has to wash dishes in the kitchen and wait where she can hear me call!'

'I'll help you onto the wheelchair.'

'No! *The girl* is supposed to help me!'

'But you're cold. Let me —'

'Caroline! Caroline! Come here!' Mum shouted, her voice quavering.

Sticking my head out of the bathroom door, I also called, 'Caroline! Caroline!' When there was no answer, I went to find her.

Two voices could be heard in my father's studio. As I approached on the stairs, they did not notice me above their talking and laughing. Through the studio's doorway, I saw an attractive woman around my age standing with Dad in front of his large worktable. She wore the Red Cross uniform tight and short. Dad said something, his eyes rolling sideways towards her. In response, her shiny blonde ponytail bounced and swung, and her shoulders shook with laughter. He pointed to a print still wet on the table. Leaning over, she gasped, 'Oh' and 'Wow.'

They looked the part, I had to admit: old male artist wearing a black beret and paint-streaked shirt with nubile woman, poring over artworks on a worktable strewn with brushes, photochemical trays and rollers in a high-ceilinged studio decked with large dramatic works. The scene brought to mind other young women I had seen in the studio being regaled with stories by my father. They were models, my sisters' friends, my friends, the eager-eyed girls from the Charismatic groups, and, of course, Bonnie.

'Oh, Natasha!' he called out when he saw me. 'Meet Caroline! Caroline, this is my daughter, just down from Darwin where she is a crusader for the disadvantaged and the sick. And Caroline is a most wonderful artist.' His face and voice were animated and warm.

'No, I'm not, Paul,' she protested, laughing.

'But you are,' he insisted. 'It is self-evident from the inspired comments you have made about my artworks. I must say you have an eye and an aesthetic that I find truly —'

'My mother was calling you,' I said, glaring at her.

Caroline stopped smiling. 'I didn't think she'd need me while she was having a shower. I've only been up here a few minutes!'

'Never mind, Caroline,' Dad said. 'Time spent on art is never wasted. I'm sure Irene doesn't mind —'

I continued, louder. 'Next time, wash the dishes while she's in the shower. From the kitchen you can hear her call. Now you need to come downstairs and help her out of the shower.'

'Uh-huh,' she said.

Suddenly embarrassed by my bad temper and the baggy tracksuit I had slept in, I led her back downstairs in silence.

The bathroom mist had cleared and the shower curtain had been pulled back. Wrapped in a towel, Mum perched on the shower seat. Her jaw was tight and the skin on her arms and legs was tinged grey and pimply with cold.

'Where were you?' she said to Caroline.

'Sorry, Mrs Chan,' Caroline said, 'I didn't realise you needed me. Your husband was showing me his art.'

Dad had followed us down and stood outside the bathroom, peering in. 'Everything okay, Irene?'

'*Cho meeyah?*' Mum asked him.

'I came to help,' he answered.

'We're fine,' I said, shutting the door on him.

'I'll lift you on the count of three,' Caroline said. 'One, two, three!' She curved her long, supple back, flexed her shapely arms and legs, and in a fluid motion, hoisted Mum off her feet. Mum flopped against her like a dead weight.

After she left, I heard Mum and Dad arguing in the bedroom.

'Why talk to her? She is here to work, not look at your art!' Mum said.

'We are Christians, Irene! We have to be generous with everyone.'

'Then how come you never show your photos to Rosa? How come only this girl?' she cried in a shrill voice.

'Why do you have to be so suspicious, Irene? She was nervous because it was her first time here. We must show her some Christian kindness. Reject such bad thoughts, Irene, so Jesus can heal you.' He walked out of the bedroom with an injured look on his face.

I went in to Mum and wheeled her in front of the dressing table so that she could do her hair and face. 'We don't need a replacement for Rosa. I can do the mornings,' I said. 'Shall I ring the agency to cancel her?' She nodded. Waiting on the phone, I watched her stare at herself in the mirror. Her troubled eyes scanned up and down, and from side to side. With jerky hands she pulled at her hair, then took the brakes off the wheelchair and turned herself to the window.

As a girl, I had often watched Mum checking her appearance. She did this with scrupulousness and regularity, as though it were her job. The mirror on the dressing table and the one inside the wardrobe door were used for long, careful scrutiny. The hallway mirror was for last-chance checks before stepping out the door, and compact mirrors that popped out of her handbag, car mirrors and reflecting shop windows were also frequently consulted.

One day, when I was about fifteen years old, she held me by

the shoulders and forced me to face the full-length wardrobe mirror. 'Just look at yourself and enjoy it,' she ordered. My reflection scowled back as I pulled away from her. Mum remained in front of the mirror. 'When I was your age,' she said, 'I always peek at myself and say, "Hey, who is that pretty girl in the mirror? Is it really me?"' With one hand on her hip, she spun from side to side, swishing her skirt around her legs.

A woman from the agency came on the line. After some discussion, she agreed to cancel services and we ended the call. I walked towards the sombre woman staring out of the window. Taking her wheelchair handles and turning her to face the dressing table, I said, 'Look at yourself, Mum – you still look so young!' I was searching for something comforting to say, too embarrassed to say what I was thinking – that she really was beautiful, even more beautiful, in a way, than she had been as a young woman. Her cheekbones were high and thin, like a bird's wings, and her eyes were dark and dramatic in her face.

'I am sixty-two years old, my dear. I am a grandmother!' she said. 'Who cares how I look! Don't think of me, think of yourself!' Her face brightened. 'We must always try to look our best, but so what? Only God matters.' She raised an open hand to the ceiling and flashed a smile. 'Alleluia. Jesus is Lord!'

Standing behind her I saw my own face look back from the mirror – serious, round and taut, unsubtle in its even proportions.

*

I took my dishwashing gloves off and opened the front door. Patsy's stick of a body was bowed over to one side, dragged down by her guitar in its angular hardcase. I pulled the guitar off her as she came in the doorway and scolded her, as Mum would have done, for carrying something so heavy. She had come straight from the conservatorium where she studied music, and wore a blue corduroy pinafore over leggings.

'You look like a schoolgirl,' I said. She raised her eyebrows and walked away to see Mum in the kitchen.

Doing housework always put me in an irritable state. For the past two hours I had stomped from room to room with my bucket of sponges, scrubbing brushes and detergents. Who could have left that piece of biscuit to be crushed into the carpet? Are they blind to the mould growing on the kitchen bin lid? How many weeks of scum have been allowed to build up under the taps? It's disgusting that anyone could leave their shit stains on the toilet for others to clean! I recognised this irritation at housework as a trait of Mum's. I had an image of her squatting on the floor, flushed and scowling, muttering about the filth as she scrubbed at the carpet. But that was when Mum worked on her feet from 8 a.m. to 4 p.m. every weekday at the Arnott's biscuit factory, and I had no excuse for not helping.

My final task was to wipe down the tables in the lounge room. Mum's medicines, cups and cloths had piled up, leaving rings and stains on the coffee table by the couch where she lay during the day. I cleared and cleaned the table so that it looked barely used. Then I removed Mum's pillow and blanket from the couch and straightened the cushions. All was looking fresh and gleaming, ready for the ladies' cell group.

For a few years after becoming Charismatic, Mum and Dad had led the St Joseph's Catholic Charismatic prayer meeting.

Perhaps Mum was too reserved and Dad too unorthodox, or perhaps some felt uncomfortable that the majority of the group were Chinese, but it never took off like the other Charismatic prayer groups. Mum would count the number each time – for us, twenty-five was a good turnout, whereas the other Catholic groups like Oakleigh had 150. Dad, Mum and Maria would go to great lengths to lift the numbers, preaching to any person they met, ringing them to remind them to come, offering to pick them up. There was a creep who lived in St Kilda whom my parents saw as their project. They would drive forty minutes out of their way to pick him up from his hostel. Once, sitting in the back next to me, he put his hand up my dress. I was too ashamed to do or say anything.

At these meetings, Maria, Patsy and I quickly learnt the easy guitar chords and beat of the hymns and became the 'music ministry'. Patsy, we discovered, had the gift of an unusual voice, and she threw herself into the music ministry role.

Today's cell group was an offshoot of the old prayer group. It met for morning tea once a week at the parish house, but since Mum's cancer the ten or so ladies, including Patsy, had been meeting at my parents' house instead.

In the kitchen, Patsy and I laid out the cups, saucers and cakes on a trolley that we kept under the stairs for entertaining. We were to wheel it out when the ladies arrived. Mum sat at the kitchen table, watching us and smiling. 'Everything is just right! Sit down and rest now. Why don't you two start on the cakes?' she said. 'Come on, take your pick. They all look so nice.' She was looking at Patsy.

I picked up a sticky pink-and-yellow vanilla slice and took a big bite. Custard squirted out on both sides. 'Yum,' I said.

Patsy, not moving, stared at the cakes. She got up. 'Anyone want a glass of water?'

'Sit down and take a cake!' Mum ordered.

Patsy selected the smallest – a mini fairy cake in a paper patty. She played with the paper, picked up a crumb with one finger and put it into her mouth.

'Put it all in your mouth,' Mum said. 'Eat it and enjoy it, like Natasha.'

'I'm sorry, Mum, I just don't feel like cake. I'll have an apple,' she said.

'Apples, apples, that's all you eat. Did you have breakfast this morning? You didn't, did you! You want to go to hospital?'

'I'm fine, Mum.' Patsy put the fairy cake back and pushed the trolley into the lounge room.

I picked up the plates and followed her. Out of earshot of Mum, I said, 'Go back and have a bit of cake. Can't you at least pretend for Mum?'

'Like you?' Patsy said.

We arranged the trolley and plates and returned to the kitchen. Patsy pulled up a chair next to Mum. 'Do we have time to say a prayer before the ladies come?' she said.

'Yes, let's pray. Natasha, you too,' Mum said.

I told Mum I had to get ready to go out shopping with Dad. As I left the kitchen, Patsy opened a bible and started to read a verse from Mark: '"And these signs will accompany those who believe: In my name they will drive out demons; they will speak in new tongues. They will . . ."'

Some minutes later, I was drawn back to the kitchen by the

sound of Patsy singing in tongues. She stood behind Mum with her hands laid upon her head. Both faces, so enraptured that I could not say which was young or old or beautiful, tilted upwards as though bathing in life-giving sun. '*Ushti, kasha, unak-unay-unay asti, shaya*,' Patsy sang in a minor key. I shivered at her voice, which was soft yet piercing, angelic yet eerie.

*

Dad was still driving the yellow Holden station wagon he had bought thirteen years earlier, soon after we arrived in Australia. The four of us sisters would sit shoulder to shoulder in the back, and since there were only three seatbelts, none of us wore them. The paint was faded and rusting in places, but it was in good shape for its age. He had it serviced on time and treated it well – not out of any interest in cars, but out of fear, since he had no mechanical knowledge. Only he drove the car. He had discouraged Mum from getting her licence, and my sisters and I, who did get ours, had not been allowed to drive it. The bottom of the rear window was lined with three stickers. One said *God is Life* above a picture of a foetus in a womb. The middle sticker said *Pray the Rosary*, and the one on the other side, *Honk if you love Jesus*. Dad had also painted a fish symbol in red on the bonnet and the boot of the car. The same symbol appeared on some of Dad's clothes, hand-painted on his shoes, hats, lapels and breast pockets.

I got into the back seat and waited. Even if the front passenger seat was vacant, my sisters and I, with the exception of Anita, always sat in the back. I wondered if I should move to the front, but just the thought of sitting next to him made me uncomfortable.

Dad came out of the house and got into the driver's seat. 'Natasha, mass first before the shopping. Right?' he said, starting the car. I didn't answer.

In the church, the air was even more frigid than the thirteen-degree chill outside. Father Robertson's dull words were absorbed into the high ceilings and cold bricks of the large, almost empty building. Only a few attended mass at St Joseph's on a weekday, and Dad appeared to be the most devoted of them all. Removing the cushion from the kneeling bench, he knelt down directly on the hard wood. When others sat back down, only he remained on his knees with eyes pressed shut, hands clasped, and mouth moving soundlessly.

Seeing him pray with such fervency, pity rose in me. I thought about his brother in the cage and the stories Dad had told me about his family. You had to be a survivalist, he said. At any moment of the day or night, a fight could break out. It might be his brothers bashing each other, or they could be meting out punishment to his sisters for not ironing their shirts right, or for any imagined slight. His brothers would punch or kick or cane his sisters, leaving them bloodied and bruised. And the worst of it was that their mother encouraged them. Only Dad tried to stop them, but he was the intellectual and not big or strong enough.

Once, Dad had shown me his knees – knobbly, he said, from hours of kneeling when he'd converted to Catholicism at the age of nineteen. Seven years later, he lost his belief. The period in the wilderness lasted twenty-six years, until we came to Australia and he found Jesus again. Dad became a born-again Catholic Charismatic and the family was expected to follow suit. All of us except Anita, who had already moved out, were obliged to go to mass every day. He also made it compulsory to go to three or four Charismatic meetings each week. I would often think that if I were allowed to choose between the two, I would choose this sterile church service any day over the loud crashing emotions of the meetings.

We were in the second pew, in front of the altar and raised sanctuary where Father Robertson and the altar boy were seated. Recognising me next to Dad, Father Robertson nodded. The altar boy sat stone-like, except for the sneakered foot fidgeting below his gown. In the pew in front of us was a preschool girl next to a thin old lady. The little girl kept turning around, staring at Dad and me with her round blue eyes and giggling. She wore a woollen poncho with a full denim skirt and lacy knee-high socks.

Each time the girl tried to escape from the pew, her grandmother grabbed the back of her skirt and pulled her back. When it was time to kneel, however, the little girl broke free. She ran up the steps to the sanctuary and sat on the top step, looking pleased with herself, and ignoring her grandmother's urgent entreaties that she *come back now*. Falling on her back, the girl lifted her legs up. Her skirt opened, showing pudgy white thighs and polka-dot knickers. While we said the Eucharist prayer, she lay on the floor in front of the altar, waving her legs in the air.

After mass, two lady parishioners came over to ask how Irene was. One of them, with sympathetic, watery eyes, patted Dad's arm. I remembered them as everyday churchgoers, not Charismatics. Dad thanked them for their concern. He explained that Jesus had healed Irene, and invited them and their families to the healing party. The first lady blinked her watery eyes a few times and folded her arms. The other one took a step back, then both quickly excused themselves.

*

Missionaries for Christ Men's House was a household of nine young, single Charismatic men who had taken a vow to spread the message of the Holy Spirit. Mum and Dad had the voluntary job of buying groceries for them and picking up donated items from businesses every fortnight. They had stopped this when Mum was diagnosed with cancer, but last week, after it was prophesied that Mum would be healed, Dad decided he would resume the work. Dropping me at the supermarket, he gave me 200 dollars to spend.

'Mum told me not more than 150 dollars,' I said, holding out a fifty.

'Never mind. Spend it,' Dad said, pushing the money back into my hand. 'They do such good work for the Lord. Get them nice chocolate, ice cream, cashew nuts, treats! Spend it all on them.'

Dad liked to go out with a full wallet. It would bulge with two-dollar coins in readiness for any buskers, collectors or homeless people who crossed his path. Five, ten and fifty-dollar notes overflowed from it for donations to Christian causes. After mass, he had handed a fifty to Father Robertson. When we delivered the groceries to the Missionaries for Christ, Dad pressed another fifty into the hand of the leader of the household. As the day progressed and we performed our errands, Dad's wallet steadily emptied.

It was not that my parents had a lot of spare cash. Except for the parties, they lived and brought up the family abstemiously on Dad's photography jobs and, in the early years in Melbourne, Mum's wage as a factory worker. Dad had left his job at the National Photo Gallery last year. Now they lived on the intermittent money he made from selling artworks. 'Acting like a big shot!' Mum would say of his donations. Anita, the only one of our family who understood money, lectured Dad on the dangers of having no savings at retirement. He always ignored these warnings, and this morning, as I watched him, it seemed he was giving out the money at an even faster rate. He told all the Charismatics we met along the way of the prophecy of Mum's miracle. They thanked the Lord and praised my father for his faith, and promised to come to the healing party.

So far the errands had broken up our journey, but now we were heading home. That would mean an unbroken stretch of about forty minutes in the car with Dad. He started singing. It was the kind of singing he did for an audience, with trills, staccatos and gasps. I pretended to be asleep in the back seat, but this did not deter him.

He started to speak. 'There seems to be a change in you, going to church and praying with the family. That makes us happy. I'm not going to question how deep it goes. For a start, you are doing it for your mother, which is an unselfish thing. But do not doubt the miracle. For if anyone doubts, there will be no miracle. Jesus will not force a miracle on anyone. It has to be courted. That sounds like a coy word, and it is, in a way. Jesus has so much respect for each one of us sinners that he would stand back though he hungers to shower us with his love. He is waiting to be invited.

'I know you have travelled overseas and now live in a young group home. When I was your age, I was feted in London and New York as the new young exciting artist. A newspaper article said, "This *enfant terrible* has talent to burn." I know the temptations of the world, the hedonism, and the ego. I have no ego now. I am just here to be a servant to the Lord. Lord, I say, my talents are for you to use. I am ready to be persecuted for Christ. The other photographers say insulting things about me, but I am ready to be a fool for Christ. Can you believe that they are afraid to speak about Jesus? It threatens them to know the real love of Jesus and what it is to live in His footsteps.

'There is nothing that threatens the so-called intellectual more than to see the vacuity of his soul. How can we call ourselves a freethinking nation when there is one thing we are afraid to talk about? Guess what it is. Aussies will all happily talk about the footy for hours but one mention of Jesus and they are running scared. That's what I said in my manifesto to each of my colleagues at the National Photo Gallery. I wrote it and printed out a copy for each one and put it in their pigeonholes. They complained and the director asked me to tone it down. Tone it down! He said it was unprofessional! I could have been represented by the most important galleries in Australia, but they want me to tone it down!' His voice droned on. He kept his eyes on the road, never turning around to look at me. The pattern had been set since childhood – Maria, Patsy and I would sit, mute, in the back while Dad talked in the driver's seat. I would try not to listen, but most of the time I did, transfixed. He would talk of how God tested him, and, if Mum was not in the car, of the trials of being married to her. He told us how Satan tries harder the more you turn to Jesus, how he suffered as a child, how he gave up fame and the temptations of the world for Jesus, how the world will persecute you for this. He talked of great truths, and wisdom, he taught us a new word for the day guaranteed to enthral, he quoted the bible, himself, poetry; he shared his visions. Once, when we had stopped at the lights at the intersection near our local supermarket, he told us that he saw a devil standing by our side, as tall as the power pole in front of us.

How long had Dad been talking now, I wondered. I tried to focus on the passing scenery. We were back in the broad streets and hills of the eastern suburbs. In front of us the six-lane bitumen road rolled up and down in a black band out to the horizon. When we first came to Australia, Dad would, to our delight, turn off the engine when we reached this road and let the car cruise all the way home. Coming up each rise, the car would go slower and slower until we feared it would not make it. Going down again we went faster and faster until we feared the car could not stop. 'Where else in the world can you do this?' he would say.

Something he said drew my attention back. 'The behaviour of the little girl in church this morning was 100 per cent natural,' he said. 'You see, Natasha, even at that age, they are very aware and know how to seduce.

'It's been very difficult, Natasha. Your mother is a saint. I cannot bear to see her suffering. She stays awake at night with gas in her stomach. All the time I have to be ready to get her a drink, pull the blankets up, turn the heater off, talk to her and hear her complaining. Her suffering is terrible. It has made her illogical. Your mother must ask God for forgiveness for her jealousy. There can be no interference with the great miracle that will happen. Did Caroline say anything about me? You see, even at my age, many women find me attractive. I am not a young, handsome man. I am not slim and strong. You know what it is? It is my intensity they find attractive.'

He had stopped talking and I realised he was waiting for me to answer his question about Caroline. 'No, she didn't say anything,' I said.

'She was moved, I know it. You know, we all have the power to touch each other's lives,' he said.

What was it about me, I thought, that made him feel he could talk at me like this? I felt sickened. The car entered our driveway and Dad braked. I scrambled out of the car and took a deep breath.

Inside the house, Mum, Patsy and the ladies were still praying. Mum called from the lounge room for me to join them. Maureen, the formally dressed and perfumed leader of the group, bade me to sit. 'We will finish up by reading from the words of the evangelist Katherine Kuhlman,' she said.

Maureen opened the book and read aloud, '"What is in the mind of God? There comes a time when we love Him so completely that we do not say anymore, there is God's will and there is my will. There comes a time when it will be impossible to miss the will of God. When you do not have a will separate and apart from God. When you have no will of your own. The very son of God had to give up his will . . . Not my will, but Thy will." Now repeat the last sentence with me three times.'

'Not my will, but Thy will. Not my will, but Thy will. Not my will, but Thy will.'

*

The ladies had left, Patsy had taken the bus back to her student lodging, Dad was in his studio and Mum had woken up from her nap on the couch. I handed her a cup of tea.

'Isn't it great you joined us for prayers?' she said. 'The ladies were so happy to see you again.'

'Can we talk again about your childhood?' I asked, taking out my notebook.

'My father was a very good man,' she began, without any resistance. She seemed to want to talk.

'Mum, you've talked about your father before. How about your mother?' I said. Her stories of her father seemed to be the only childhood memories she would volunteer.

'He was so holy,' she continued. Her brow softened, her eyes lit up and she smiled. 'You know the first thing he did when he got home from work? He knelt down and prayed. On the staircase landing, we had a little altar and crucifix. He knelt there for at least one hour.'

'You and your sisters had to kneel there too sometimes for punishment, didn't you?'

She did not even pause. 'You know the war? The Japanese came to Hong Kong. The British ran away. All their houses and shops just empty. Everyone stole from them. But not my father. He tried to stop people from going into their houses. My dad was ARP. You know what that is?'

'Yes, Air Raid Precaution. You've told me. Did you talk much with your father?'

'He was my father, of course we talked. Some ARP were bad, take bribes. But never my father. Everyone looked up to him.'

'What was your parents' relationship like?'

She sighed. 'They were husband and wife all their life, why ask silly?'

'Your sisters said your mother spent too much time playing mahjong for money.'

The smile stayed on her face. 'My father liked your dad very much. You know I had too many suitors. It was so hard to choose.'

I had heard Mum's relatives tease that every second man in Hong Kong had proposed to her. Her sister Monica's husband had first proposed to Mum and been rejected. So too her cousin's husband. Whenever Dad boasted that he had married the belle of the island, she told him to be quiet, sensitive to how it would seem to them.

'I met your father at church after he became Catholic. He was at every mass, always kneeling. He sang in the choir, so loud and so out of time! He was very funny too. You know what he did? Other boyfriends give me jewellery and flowers – but not your dad. One day the postman came to my house. He is laughing loud. All the neighbours too are laughing. The postman gave me a big picture – this big.' She stretched her hands out as wide as they would go. 'It was from your dad. He made a cute picture of himself carrying a big bunch of flowers!'

Mum laughed and her eyes grew wistful. She loved him. There was no doubt about it.

'I didn't know whether to marry your dad. When I met his family, I thought, "Oh dear! What ruffians!" But I prayed and prayed. One night Jesus put it on my heart to marry him. I heard the name Paul in my heart. So isn't that good, Natasha? Praise the Lord.' She paused. 'Not my will, but the Lord's will. Like we prayed today – not my will, but Thy will. Not my will, but Thy will.'

SIGNS OF THE TUMOUR IN MUM'S SPINAL CORD had appeared about nine months before it was diagnosed. She and Maria had been with me in Darwin at the time. It was Mum's first visit there.

Maria and Mum stayed in my bedroom while I moved onto a bed set up on the verandah. My housemates were kind about the visit and agreed to be discreet about drugs and partners for the ten days.

When we plonked Mum's suitcase on my bed and opened it, slippery synthetic blouses and skirts frothed out and the fragrance of her floral perfume tinged with mothballs filled my room. Digging underneath the clothes, Mum pulled out a round pink tin of Quality Street chocolates, three packets of Emperor herbal chicken spice and a plastic drink bottle filled with clear liquid. She handed them to me. A piece of masking tape stuck to the bottle had *Holy Water* on it in purple texta in Dad's handwriting.

'The holy water was blessed by Father Lachlan for you. We can bless your house with it,' Mum said.

I returned the bottle to the suitcase. 'Thank you, Mum, for the presents, but you keep the holy water,' I said.

'No, take it. What did I bring it all the way here for?' She took it out again, walked over to my bookshelf and placed it there.

'No thanks, Mum.' I put it back in the suitcase.

She sighed loudly and turned her back on me to unpack. Then she swung around. 'It is time you came home. It is the family's home. This year everyone must have Christmas there together.'

'I am coming to see the family at Christmas. Just not in your home.'

'So silly. So stubborn. What for like that?'

'I've told you before – it's just better that way between Dad and me. His house, his rules.'

For the first few days, we did the kinds of things she enjoyed. We took early morning walks along the foreshore before the sun grew strong; we went several times to Darwin's only shopping centre, where for hours she was content to wander in and out of the same shops as in Melbourne, only smaller; and I dropped Maria and her to the Darwin Charismatic meetings they knew about through their links in Melbourne, although I didn't go in myself. I spent those hours with Jason, making up for the nights we couldn't sleep together while they stayed.

It was the first time Mum had met Jason. We had been going out for eighteen months, the longest by far that I had gone out with anyone. I sometimes wondered why it had continued when all my other relationships had ended after a few months. It took Jason about six months, and a lot of agonising about what he truly felt – whether it was just attraction, infatuation, or a mutually beneficial relationship, and what was the meaning of it all anyway – before he said that he loved me. His whole body shook when he told me. I felt that I could trust him. That when he was no longer interested in me, he would tell me.

Mum did not want to be overly friendly with him, or encourage our relationship, because she knew he was an agnostic. Still, I thought she liked him. 'He seems a nice, quiet young man,' she said. 'Very simple.'

'What do you mean by simple, Mum?' I said.

'You know, look how he dress, that kind of thing.'

Jason spent a few days with us, and it must have seemed as though he was just hanging around aimlessly. He'd turn up in a torn, sour-smelling T-shirt, cut-down jeans and thongs, and not say much all day. He had taken time off work to spend time with Mum and Maria, but he wasn't one to tell them that he had so much work as a graphic designer he had to turn clients away.

For the last days of their Darwin visit, I had in store a special trip out to the bush. Although I had planned the visit to Daly River weeks earlier, I told Mum about it only the day before, in order to minimise the time she had to worry. The drive was only three hours, I said. I described the beautiful virgin bush and termite mounds that we would see on the way, the hot spring that only the locals knew, and the Daly River Aboriginal community where we would stay for two nights with my friend who worked in the art centre.

Mum pursed her lips and frowned. 'Are you sure?' she said. That's all she said: *Are you sure?* If she didn't want to go or had concerns, why didn't she just say so? I could have grabbed her by her synthetic blouse and shaken her.

Jason started laughing as soon as we were out of earshot. 'You don't really think she's going to like it out bush, do you?'

'It will be good for her to see the real bush,' I said. 'She might just love it. It might be a revelation to her. You have to give these things a chance.'

'Ze vill go and ze vill love it,' Jason said, giving me a Nazi salute.

The next day, Mum, Maria and I turned off the highway towards Daly River. Bitumen soon ran out into dirt road and then there was nothing but dirt, trees and sky. Twisted scrub continued in a monotonous line below an empty blue expanse. The occasional gum tree raised itself over the scrub, its thin, old branches forming a spindly calligraphy against the sky. I drove on further and absorbed the surroundings. They did not manipulate with grand vistas, spectacular heights, majestic trees or verdant colour. My spine loosened and my breathing deepened in deference to this harsh, low land.

I looked at Mum in the seat next to me. Although our windows were up, the fine dust of the road was swirling through the door gaps and air vents. We could not talk above the hammering of the van over the ruts in the road. Passing cars threw up clouds of dust so thick that I had to stop the van or else continue blind. Mum's jaw was clenched shut, her eyes bloodshot and tense.

It would be okay. The clearing was a few kilometres away. We would stop there and I would show Mum. I imagined how I would bring her up close to the small hidden treasures: she would see the delicate uncurling fronds of the cycad, the fresh yellow of the kapok flower, the textures of the woollybutt tree and the stone-age presence of the termite mounds. I pressed on the accelerator to get to the clearing faster, but the banging over the ruts only became more violent. I was forced to slow back down and let the ruts resume their rhythm.

We finally reached the clearing. None of us moved for some seconds after the van had stopped, mesmerised by the silence and stillness. I opened my door and suggested we take a look around.

'No, you go. I will just sit here. I don't feel well,' Mum said. Maria and I tried to help her out of the van to get some air. It was when she stepped out that she suddenly shrieked and bent double.

We turned back for Darwin immediately. The trip back was hellish, every rut in the road a punishment, every piece of bush a menace. She writhed in pain the whole way, her eyes shut tight, her face contorted. Her mouth moved and I knew she was praying, though I could not hear her words.

When they returned to Melbourne, the pain in Mum's back receded, leaving a numbness in her arms and legs that wouldn't go away. The doctors decided it was a pinched nerve. Eight months later, the pain came back and one morning she woke up unable to move her legs. This time they found the tumour and a spinal biopsy confirmed that it was cancer. Cancer cells were also found in her large intestine and liver. The cancer had metastasised. Four weeks later, I quit my job and left Darwin to be with her. She was treated urgently with steroids and radiotherapy to relieve the pressure on her spinal cord. This was to be followed by three cycles of chemotherapy. Surgery was not an option. The cancer had spread too far.

*

Mum was to have her second dose of chemotherapy at 12 p.m. today. She was quiet after breakfast, pursing and unpursing her lips, frowning into the distance. She took up a pen and laid a piece of paper on the kitchen table. Hunched over the page, she scratched out one painstaking letter after another.

She seldom wrote, not even shopping lists. I knew her writing from the birthday cards I'd received each year in Darwin. Dad's blessing and call to surrender to Jesus would flow in a stylish and bold script over both pages on the inside of the card. In the bottom-right corner a childish, shaky hand would say, 'Love from Mum'.

'You must do what it says,' she said handing me the piece of paper. I glanced at it. She had written: *1. Vomit bucket must leave on chair next to bed, not floor or how I can reach it? 2. Take plants outside house at night. 3. Throw out leftover food – otherwise* sun voo kay. *4. Soak dried prawns for Dad's noodles. 5. Open all windows before sleep.*

'Make sure you do it, okay?' she said. 'Last time after chemo I was too sick to remember. You must take the plants out at night, okay?' When I nodded without enthusiasm, she glared at me. 'Don't you know they suck up the oxygen? Don't tell me you don't know that? Don't you know?' she said, and would not leave it alone until I agreed.

The Come To Jesus drama group was arriving in half an hour for practice. The CTJ performed evangelical plays written by Dad, who was also the director, choreographer and music composer. They had performed in community theatres, in churches and in the Bourke Street Mall. Two years ago, CTJ dissolved. No one in the family would tell me why, but I remembered the arguments Mum and Dad had, even before I left, about his attentiveness to the prettier girls in the group. When the cancer was diagnosed, however, Dad had persuaded Mum to let him revive the CTJ. He said that the Lord was calling on our family to serve Him sixfold, even tenfold. That way we could show the world that in hardship our faith would not only continue but strengthen, and we would be a testament to His power. The group was to perform at the healing party.

Maria arrived at the front door, wearing baggy jeans and a shapeless windcheater. She was Dad's helper on the CTJ, recruiting members, picking them up, and doing the general running around. She was also one of the actors. Something clicked over when Maria was performing – she would be loud, excessive and funny. She turned sideways to get in the front door, her arms laden with shopping bags.

'Aiya, why can't you dress better?' Mum said, as Maria came into the kitchen. 'Go and get changed. You look like Vietnamese.'

Maria dumped the bags on the table and started pulling out the contents item by item. 'I've got the manuka honey, Mum. It's a natural antibiotic. I was looking for the 75 per cent but could only find the 50 per cent – it should still be effective. This here is olive-leaf extract, which is really good for immunity.' She pulled out a brown bottle. 'This one's a liver tonic. Here's an iron tonic for your blood cells.' I didn't bother asking her how she knew any of this was appropriate for Mum, and she didn't offer an explanation.

'Thanks. Wah, so many things,' Mum said, but looked uninterested.

Maria got a call and left to pick up some new recruits. She returned with a homeless man and an international student she had converted through her street witnessing. At the same time, a stream of members began to arrive. Soon there were about twenty in the lounge room, most of them young, and recruited from church youth groups and Christian ministries. Only one or two looked familiar from the time I lived in Melbourne. I recognised the types, though. The pleasing young women who glowed with love and vulnerability. Young men with stiff mouths, mannered movements and holy airs. And also a few old men having fun, crackling with newfound vigour. We become *childlike*, not *childish*, the more we give ourselves to Jesus, they testified. The older women, who exuded benevolence, did not come to CTJ, though they sometimes dropped in cakes or sandwiches.

As usual, the homeless and the sick had also been brought into the fold. Sitting on a chair with a bulging plastic bag on his lap was the bearded man Maria had picked up from a Salvation Army hostel. One earnest young man sat next to him, telling him the story of how he had found Jesus, but the bearded man's eyes were on the young women.

Jessie, the daughter of one of the actors, must have been about twelve years old now. She thumped backwards and forwards in her wheelchair, whacking against the restraint strapped across her chest. Mouth open wide and tongue lolling, she laughed out loud at the young woman who knelt in front of her, clapping her hands and singing, 'Does Jessie love Jesus? Oh yes, she does. Jessie loves Jesus.'

They moved around the house as though they had the right. I had closed the kitchen door, but they entered without knocking. Several of them came in to greet Mum. They smiled kindly at her, stooping down and saying things like, 'Wow and wow backwards,' and remarking how inspirational our family was. Mum wore a strained smile.

A tender-eyed young woman came up to me, smiling blissfully and opening her arms to hug. Then she saw my face and took a step back. *Losers, losers*, I was thinking. But when I saw the joy drain out of her eyes, I felt ashamed.

Dad called them all into the lounge room. I stood at the side of the glass doors, where I could watch them. Dad was working the room. He was magnanimous and charming and he found a special compliment for everyone. He patted men's shoulders, he kissed the women and he looked down at his feet with a delighted, cheeky expression after telling a joke. He lingered around the girl with the alluring Irish looks. Maria, too, was working the room. She was getting chairs, serving soft drinks, making sure that everyone was comfortable.

Now a middle-aged man in a blue suit and a paunch came to the front door. Dad rushed to welcome him. 'Make way, make way!' Dad shouted. 'Here he is, Geoff Atkins! Make way for the prophet Geoff! Everyone, this is the man who prophesied Irene's miracle.'

Dad gathered the group together and asked Geoff to say a few words. Geoff licked the lips on his pug-like face. 'Well, I was in the middle of work. I own the Retravision store in Chadstone – by the way, if any of you want a discount, just turn up and yell out, "Jesus is Lord!"' Laughs and shouts of 'Jesus is Lord!' came from the group. 'Anyway,' Geoff continued, 'Paul told me to come down and take a look at you. So here I am. He said we need to sponsor some of you. So I said, here's my cheque book. And I'll tell you something you already know: Paul Chan is a saint! And he wasn't born yesterday either. He was – what was it again, Paul? The Renaissance Man of Hong Kong! He was on his way to becoming famous in Australia too. And he gave it all up. Sacrificed it all for Jesus!'

The group clapped and called out, 'Alleluia'. Maria saw me peeping through the glass doors. I rolled my eyes. She smiled.

Geoff was getting so excited now that his jowls were shaking. His watery eyes bulged. 'Satan hates Paul Chan. He friggin' well does. When the devil sees Paul coming, he says, "Fair suck of the sauce bottle, eh! Not Paul Chan! Aaarrrgghhh!"' Geoff jumped backwards, with his hands shielding his face. Everyone laughed. Dad shook his head and beamed.

Mum called me to help her in the bathroom. When I returned, I continued to watch. Geoff had left, the furniture had been cleared aside and the drama class had begun. Dad stood in front of the staircase. All eyes were on him. 'And now . . . I will teach you the theatre of Kabuki,' he said. 'We will use the Kabuki technique for our performance at the healing party. What is Kabuki?' He paused. 'Watch!'

By now, all age and weariness had vanished. Dad bristled with energy. He crouched, ready to spring. His head jerked forward, his neck stretched out, long and sinewy. He pierced the audience with his eyes. His arms shot up towards the sky as though they were being pulled. He dragged each arm down, fell to his knees, clasped his hands together, opened his mouth wide and wailed. The long, pained cry grew louder until it was a scream. He stopped abruptly. He moved into crouching position again, his head and neck strained forward. His eyes searched from one end of the group to the other. Then he repeated all the same moves. When the sequence was complete, he started again from the beginning. He did this again and again, each time with more anguish. Spittle fell from his mouth. Tears rolled down his face. His face turned red, then crimson, now purple. I could hardly bear to look at him, but I was riveted.

He stood upright and pushed his hair back. 'This is the theatre of Kabuki,' he said, his voice hoarse, 'where you repeat and repeat and repeat. Until you feel the agony. Until you feel you can't take it anymore. Until you become the agony and the ecstasy!' He bowed. Everyone broke into cheers and applause.

'Okay. Now you try it. I will call this exercise the three stages of worldly ecstasy. Remember, take two or three movements and repeat and repeat. Stage one: you are on cloud nine. You have got that promotion, won that prize you were fighting for. You've met the man or woman of your dreams. Or you are on a heroin high. How do you act? Let the show begin!'

One by one they started to move. Soon there was a lot of reaching into the air, thumping, jumping and crazy laughter. With a manic expression on her face, Maria fell to her knees and prostrated herself. A man punched his chest over and over again. Two boys wrestled each other. The homeless man pulled up a chair, sat and looked around, nodding. A tall thin woman pranced around like a horse and called out, 'Money, money.' Even as they performed, they kept their eyes on their director.

Dad responded to each of their movements, bounded from one person to another, filled the room. 'Keep going. Keep going!' he shouted. 'Now, the ecstasy has worn thin, you are starting to search,' he said and started to stumble in his step. 'Search everyone, search!'

Maria groped with arms outstretched. A young woman flung out her arms and jerked from side to side like a robot. The boy with the crew-cut lifted up the cushions on our couch and looked underneath.

'Now you see the pathos of life.' Dad hung his head. Slowly he raised it again, gazing into the distance with a deep mournful stare. He bayed like a bear. 'Now moan, everyone!' he shouted. Maria did not hesitate, others joined in and then they were all moaning and groaning. On and on it went until the sound was a bath of human warmth and suffering, filling ears, choking throats and drowning the senses.

'Stop!' Dad yelled. 'Everyone quiet. Now just listen to Bridie.' He turned to the pink-faced young woman whom he had been giving extra attention to. 'Moan,' he told her. She pulled back the hair that had fallen around her face and breathed in, concentrating hard. Sweet, high sighs came from her lips. 'More breath,' Dad commanded. 'Open your mouth!' Her lips parted, and she started to moan. Her cheeks went from pink to a hot crimson. 'More breath! From deep inside you!' he urged. She breathed in and out, each breath deeper, her shoulders and breasts heaving. 'More!' Dad shouted. With each moan, she became more loud and guttural, her body shook and her mouth hung open. 'Beautiful,' Dad whispered.

I kicked the glass door hard so they would hear. 'Mum, are you ready for the chemotherapy?' I shouted. Everyone turned. I moved away from the door and went to her bedroom.

Mum's hair was pinned up, her face pale and powdered and her lipstick subdued. She wore a black skirt and a blouse with a bow-tie neck – a modest outfit she had often worn to church to give out holy communion. I imagined how she might have thought through what to wear for chemotherapy. It was too weighty an event to wear casuals, it was not a social occasion and it was not work . . . church wear seemed right.

I picked up Mum's bags. We waited at the lounge room door for Maria. Dad stopped in the middle of directing the next exercise and signalled for us to come over. He took the wheelchair handles and pushed Mum into the centre of the room. He gestured for a chair. One was placed next to Mum. Dad sat beside her, taking her hand in his. Mum gave a wistful smile.

'Come closer, everyone. Please, we need your prayers,' Dad said.

They encircled her, those closest laying a hand on her head, shoulder or arm. Those in the outer circle held the person in front of them, and all reached towards Mum, the focus of all that radiant energy. I stood apart. Maria saw me, gripped my arm and pulled me closer until I could feel their heat, hear their breathing and smell the perfume and the sweat from their exertions.

Dad waited for the group to settle. 'Dear Lord, we praise you for your healing of Irene,' he said. 'Today Irene will be undergoing chemotherapy, man's medicine. Why should Irene subject herself to the needles, the chemicals coursing through her veins, the administrations of mere men when you, the divine healer, have touched her? Why?' He paused and looked around at his faithful team. 'Because the Lord God is so great, yet so full of humility and love for mankind, that He stands back and will not interfere with man's work. The Lord will do His work and man will do his. And the Lord will bless man's work where it is good. All we need to do is to ask Him.'

Dad's voice rose in pitch. 'So we pray, O Lord, that this chemotherapy will be your holy water flowing through Irene and part of your healing plan. May man's work be part of your greater glory! We visualise Irene fully cleansed of the cancer, her body fresh, glowing and vital.' He was charged up from the drama session. Now he shouted, 'We claim the miracle!' A shiver of electricity shot through us.

Cries of 'Amen!' 'Praise the Lord!' 'Yes, Jesus, alleluia, praise you, Jesus!' came from the group. Some started praising in tongues. It began as a cacophony. Then Maria picked up a guitar and strummed some chords and the tongues slid into tune. When the tongues quietened, Dad started to sing, 'In the name of Jesus, in the name of Jesus, we have the victory!' Everybody joined in.

Still singing, Dad released the brake on the wheelchair. He pushed Mum out the door and towards the car. The group followed, singing, some skipping, some dancing, surrounding the car as we helped Mum in. We slammed the doors. Inside Maria's small Toyota, we wound down the windows and looked up at their joy-filled faces. Maria started the engine, but we could hardly hear it above the fervent shouts of the victory song. We pulled out of the driveway, laughing and waving.

On the road, the drama group left behind, Mum, Maria and I continued to sing. Our voices now sounded thin and lonely. When the grey block of hospital buildings came in sight, Mum stopped singing. By the time the car was parked, we were silent. Mum was not listening when I took her wheelchair out and asked whether she needed her coat.

The lift doors closed. We were taken up to the ninth-floor waiting room, where it was quiet and the air was cool and bitter-smelling.

Maria and I sat on either side of Mum and waited for the chemotherapy mixture to be prepared. Maria handed Mum a *Women's Weekly* magazine, which she held shut on her lap. A well-dressed Greek couple sitting on the opposite bench smiled at us, then looked away. I wondered if we looked as vulnerable as they did. I guessed that it was the man who had the cancer from the solicitous way the woman had her arm around his shoulder. Maria stood up to get a cup of water for Mum from the dispenser and offered to get one for them too, although they already had paper cups in front of them. They politely declined and Maria followed up with, 'Been here before? My mum is here for chemotherapy.' They did not want to talk. I shook my head at Maria and silently pleaded with her not to start evangelising.

A nurse came up to the woman and said, 'Are you ready, Mrs Bakas?' I realised it was she who had the cancer. As they walked off, they smiled kindly at us and said good luck.

Another nurse led us into a ward partitioned by white curtains and directed Mum to sit in a grey reclining armchair. A steel hook hovered next to the chair, hanging from a tall metal frame. From compartments in her trolley, the nurse pulled out a fluid-filled tube, needle and swabs.

'Can you please give me the butterfly needle?' Mum asked. 'You know the baby needle – it's very thin?'

'You're Chinese, aren't you,' the nurse said in a loud voice. 'We often get that request from Chinese on account of your thin veins. Don't worry. I've got another needle here that will do just as well.'

'Doctor Richards recommended the baby needle for her,' I said.

'The last time they couldn't get the needle in until we got the baby needle,' Maria said.

The nurse ripped open a sachet. 'Listen, for blood tests we can use the baby needle, but for drips we use a different needle.'

'Okay,' Mum said quietly.

The nurse took her arm. She shook her head when she saw the bruises from previous needles. 'You've been in the wars, Mrs Chan. You poor dear.' She took Mum's other arm. 'I see they had a go at this one too. We'll have to try somewhere else.' She picked up Mum's hand and traced her finger on the back of her wrist. 'They're hiding. Here's one!'

She pulled on the plastic gloves. 'Don't worry, I'm a pro,' she said. She slapped the back of Mum's hand a few times, then repeatedly flicked her finger at the spot until we could see the faintest, thin blue outline of a vein appear. 'Just a pinprick,' she said, and slipped the needle in. No blood. Mum's eyes were trained on the spot. The nurse manoeuvred the needle around under the skin. Mum's face screwed up with pain.

'Shoot, I hate it when the veins wiggle away,' the nurse said. She pulled out the needle. She pierced again, moved it in deeper, to the left, to the right. 'I'm sorry,' she kept saying. She tried a new needle. Again she fished around with it under her skin.

'Are you all right, Mum?' I said. She did not answer. She was white, stiff, hardly breathing.

'Take deep breaths, Mum,' Maria said. 'Let's pray to Jesus.' She massaged Mum's forehead.

'This is my last go,' the nurse said, 'and then it's another nurse's turn.' The nurse pierced Mum's hand where it was already darkened by a bruise. Bit by bit she moved the needle under the skin and then held it. A slow dark-red trickle filled the thin tube.

'Thank you, God!' Mum said.

The nurse hung a plastic pouch of clear liquid on the hook and connected it to the tube in Mum's wrist. We watched the pouch release its poison, drip by drip. Each clear bead formed until it broke with its own weight and fell down the tube.

'How are you feeling, Mum?' I asked. 'Does it hurt?'

'No,' she said, 'it only feels cold.' She stared at the liquid slide down the tube and enter her vein. For a moment, she screwed her eyes shut and we were silent. Then tossing her head, she opened her eyes again. 'Maria, get me my rosary beads. And stop hunching, will you? Sit up straight.' Maria handed the beads to Mum. Mum put the crucifix to her mouth and kissed it. 'Let's say the rosary. In the name of the Father, Son and Holy Spirit' – she made the sign of the cross – 'we offer the first decade to baby Vincent with you in heaven. We pray Maria will find a good husband and Natasha will find you, Jesus.' I wondered whether Mum had thoughts of death and was thinking about seeing Vincent again in heaven. He was born two years after Anita, and lived only for a few hours because of a malformed kidney. There was no photo of him.

We proceeded through five decades of Hail Marys in hushed but insistent voices. During the final prayer, the drip started beeping. A nurse came to change the pouch. 'Don't stop on my account,' she said, so we continued.

'O my Jesus, forgive us our sins, save us from the fires of hell, lead all souls to heaven, especially those who have most need of your mercy.'

Maria tried to arrange Mum's seat so she could lie back, but Mum would have none of it. Her eyes were glazed and tense. She wanted to talk. 'We called him Vincent after my father. Because my father was a very good man. A very good man. They are now in heaven together. Your dad was very disappointed. Of course we wanted a son. One thing we did that was very bad, Jesus forgive us, we took the herbs the *wu* gave us. That witch said it would give us a boy,' Mum strained forward in the seat. 'Such rubbish. Your dad changed after the baby boy died. That's why he became modern, no good. You should have seen how terrible he was before the Charismatic. *Tsk tsk tsk.*' She shook her head.

'Do you really think it's because you lost Vincent?' I said. 'I thought there were issues before that.'

'Don't be silly. How do you know? You weren't even born. Anyway,' – she lifted up the hand without the drip – 'Jesus will heal me to help Dad. And also to bring Natasha to Him.'

The drip beeped. The nurse came in, chatting with Mum while changing the bag. She told Mum it would be another hour or two and she should try to rest.

Once, in front of a bonfire in our backyard, when I was twelve years old, Patsy and I had heard Dad shout out his sins to God. After being baptised in the Holy Spirit, he had rampaged through the house. He grabbed CDs, books, pictures, fabrics, an antique vase with a dragon painted on it, anything that the demon could use against us, and threw them in the fire. Mum was out, or she would have salvaged some of our possessions. He prayed out loud to the sky, he asked for forgiveness. At one point he fell to his knees and sobbed, 'Irene and I were newlyweds. But still I went to that woman. Every time I came to her door, she said to me, "You've got the Devil in you, Paul." But I couldn't stop. "You've got the devil in you." I renounce her words! In the name of Jesus, I reject Satan!' he shouted over the roar of the fire.

'Try to sleep, Mum.' Maria stood behind her rubbing her shoulders. Mum closed her eyes but kept opening them again to look at the clear drops sliding down the tube.

'Do you want to do some meditation?' I asked.

'What type?' Mum said. 'Don't tell me you do all those bad Buddha, Hindu things.'

'No, this is Christian meditation,' I lied. I had learnt the meditation at a ten-day Vipassana retreat with a Buddhist monk. The words could be adapted so they referred to Jesus, I thought.

I asked Mum to sit straight and relaxed and to hold her palms open to Jesus. Maria sat on the floor and crossed her legs. I made my voice slow and resonant. 'Sit comfortably and concentrate on your breathing. Breathe Jesus in and breathe the illness out,' I said. 'Feel the air passing through your nostrils and passing out again. Focus only on the air moving in and out, until you are fully aware of your breath.' I reminded Mum to breathe out of her nose, not her mouth. After a few minutes, Mum's and Maria's breathing slowed to a gentle rhythm. 'Now focus on relaxing each part of your body. Start from the crown of your head and move slowly down your spine.' I talked us through each part of the body.

In silence, in my mind, I visualised the cancer in Mum's body. I made myself imagine the tumour on her spinal column below her neck, three centimetres wide, the doctor had said, compressing the nerves. I imagined the growth a lurid green. I imagined the hateful lumps in her liver and in her bowels. I saw the sickly fluid collecting in her abdomen, making her belly bloat. *Stop . . .*

Don't loathe it, don't fear it, I told myself. *It will grow if you do that. Just see it and imagine it dissolve, dissipate, leave.*

I forced myself back, shook my body and opened my eyes. 'Imagine the medicine going into Mum's vein as the healing power of Jesus flowing through her,' I said fervidly. 'Cleanse away the bad cells and strengthen the good cells. Visualise the medicine of God's healing as a shining purple light, the colour of healing.'

'Good, Natasha. Enough,' Mum said. 'Now you two go and eat your lunch. I'm going to rest.'

*

We walked out to the waiting room.

'That was really good, Natasha. Where did you learn it?' Maria said.

'I did a meditation course. I adapted it to be Christian.'

'You sounded like Dad.'

I looked at Maria to see what she meant by this. Her face was innocent. She left me in the waiting room to go to the toilet.

Lying on the table next to the magazines was a stack of pamphlets. I picked them up. The blue pamphlet said *Choose Life, Choose Jesus* above a picture of a baby in a womb. The other pamphlets were information about the Charismatic renewal.

When she came back, I waved the pamphlets at her. 'You can't put these here, Maria.'

'Oh, sorry, they must have fallen out of my bag.' She wouldn't meet my eye.

'That's what you said in Darwin when I found your pamphlets on the reception table at my work!'

'I really didn't realise. There are so many things in my bag.' She took the pamphlets from me and walked quickly towards the lifts.

I ran to catch up with her but she went faster. What was the use anyway? In Darwin I had tried to make her admit the truth about the pamphlets, and when I'd finally got through to her enough to make her upset, she turned around and said, 'You think I'm a loser, don't you, but I'd be much worse without God.'

The lift doors opened and it was Dad. 'Ha ha!' he said, beaming, and patted our shoulders. 'How is she? I made the drama group leave early so I could come as soon as possible. The chemo went well?'

'She's fine. One hour to go,' Maria said.

'Thank God. Praise the Lord. Same room?' he said.

'Yes,' said Maria.

'She's resting,' I said. 'We're just going down to the café to get a coffee.'

'Yes. Good girls. You must have something to eat and drink.'

*

When Maria and I returned from the café, Anita was standing at the reception desk, talking to the nurse.

'So, let me clarify. The drugs that we got after the first session of chemotherapy need to be discontinued and replaced with these ones. Is that correct?' She wore a suit I had not seen before. The nurse was giving Anita her full attention.

When she had finished with the nurse, Anita walked with us towards Mum's room. 'The traffic from the city to here was terrible.

How's Mum? How did it go? Did they do better with the needle this time?' she said.

'They couldn't use the butterfly needle,' Maria said.

'What? How many stabs?'

'About five,' I said.

'Unbelievable! I told you to make sure she got the butterfly needle!' She strode back to the desk. We could hear the nurse repeat the explanation she had given us. 'That is not what Doctor Richards told me,' Anita said. 'We will certainly take this up with him.' *Clack*, *clack*, *clack*, her heels came back towards us.

Anita, Maria and I walked into the room. Mum was lying back. Dad had pulled up his chair alongside hers. He sat with his head inclined towards her serene face. One hand held hers. Lost to the world, mouths slack, they snored in tune. The fluid continued to drip down the tube into Mum's vein.

'Ohhh, aren't they cute?' Maria whispered. She started to giggle.

'Shhhhh,' I said, and started giggling too.

'What are you both laughing about!' Anita said.

Soon the three of us were laughing so hard we had to run out of the room.

FOR THE FIRST WEEK AFTER THE CHEMOTHERAPY, Mum was nauseous and weak. Still, she made sure we held to a strict morning routine. At 7 a.m. each day she rose – her face grey, her eyes dull and her lips pronouncing faith in the miracle.

I had taken over from the morning carers. By the time I entered Mum and Dad's room, Dad would be up and eating breakfast in the kitchen or working in his studio. I would pull away the bedclothes, raise Mum to a sitting position and help her shift onto the wheelchair and into the bathroom. She was careful to choose clothes that were easy to wear but kept her looking trim and fresh. The steps for ablution, hygiene, dressing and grooming followed an order from which she would allow no deviation. By 9.30 a.m. I was ready to tidy and air the bedroom and bathroom, prepare breakfast and lay out her medication for the day. It was important to have the orderly start, because from there on she struggled to stay awake and keep track of the day. Each vomit was a minor catharsis. Her body, which was so passive and feeble, would lurch forward with a violent energy. This happened about six times a day at first. She moved between lying on the couch and lying in bed, the bucket beside her still wet from being washed out after its last use.

After the first week she stayed awake longer and ate without vomiting. I wanted to tempt her with her favourite foods but had to ask her what these were.

'Fry some noodles for your dad,' she replied.

'But what do *you* want to eat? What are your favourite foods?'

She pursed her lips. 'My favourite foods . . .' she said, concentrating and trying to oblige. 'Anything,' she eventually said. 'I like anything, la.'

We all knew Dad's favourites. He loved fried noodles glistening with black soya sauce and oil. They had to be the broad type of rice noodle, covered in gravy with fleshy prawns and slivers of pork. Or else yellow curry chicken, so deeply cooked, he said, that you could chew into the bones and marrow. *Char siu,* sweet, salty red barbequed pork, must be moist inside and a little burnt on the outside. Since coming to Australia, he also loved 'finger lickin' good' Kentucky Fried Chicken. He couldn't stand the way Australians put beans or corn in savoury foods – they were for dessert, cooked in sweet coconut milk. And lamb, he said, smelt like human armpit.

Soon after I arrived, Mum asked me to cook Dad's noodles each day for his lunch. 'Very easy,' Dad said. 'Just cook fast – *shah, shah, shah.*' He flung his arms around as though handling a spatula and wok over a fire, then spread out his hands. 'Done!'

It wasn't easy. Each ingredient had to be thinly sliced, marinated and fried separately before being mixed together at the end with the noodles. 'No, no, no,' Mum cried when she saw me poking into the rice noodles with the steel spatula. 'You will break them up!' She showed me how to dig down and hard into the wok and then lift in one swift motion. I copied her a few times and it was only when I shoved with my elbow behind it and the spatula scraped loudly, steel against steel, that she said, 'That's it. You must hear it.'

Since replacing the carer, I grew resentful of having to cook Dad's lunch every day when there were so many other tasks to do. He was always appreciative, however, and ate everything. I also found myself cleaning up after him and climbing the stairs to bring cups of tea and other things he might call out for. Dad was the kind of man who had to be served. We all knew that. Now we had to make up for Mum being ill. He sensed, however, that I would not massage his neck and shoulders as Maria and Patsy did, and never asked me to do this.

One day, while preparing dinner with Anita, I complained about having to make Dad's lunch. She said nothing to me, but fifteen minutes later, as Dad was walking through the kitchen to the family room, she stopped him.

'Dad, you can't have Natasha cooking lunch for you every day when she's so busy with Mum,' she told him. I overheard her while washing the dishes, too mortified to say anything.

'What are you talking about? Everyone is busy,' Dad replied.

'Make yourself sandwiches or have leftovers for lunch,' she said.

'Nobody asked her to cook for me,' Dad said, miffed.

I rushed towards him. 'It's okay, Dad, I don't mind cooking.'

'No big deal. I can go to the Chu anytime.' He waved his hand dismissively and left the kitchen.

I turned to Anita. 'Why did you have to say that?'

'Don't complain if you're not going to do anything about it,' she said.

'It was not for you to say anything.' My voice shook.

'He'll get over it. What are you getting so upset for?'

A familiar feeling pickled in my stomach. I wanted to run after him and beg forgiveness. Even though he told people he had the most marvellous children in the world, I always disappointed him. I did not praise and admire him, support his drama group, devote myself to selling and promoting his artwork, or follow his beliefs. I didn't even want to cook his lunch!

After this incident, Anita started to bring noodles and other dishes for Dad when she came over. She put a number of his favourites in the freezer for me to thaw out and heat for him. She was always looking after him even while she was telling him off for something. She was like Mum in that way. However, Anita never seemed to talk with him unless it was for practical reasons and most of the time would avoid even looking at him. In fact, among my sisters and even me, she seemed the only one whom Dad couldn't reach with his charm.

My sisters came over every day, flocking in like angels to Mum. If there was time before they arrived, Mum and I would meditate using the method I had started in the hospital. As she gained more energy, she would tolerate some of my questions about her life. Mostly she asked me to read aloud or listen to a preacher on a CD with her.

Dad worked in his studio, held drama rehearsals, prayed with Geoff and his cell group, and made arrangements for the healing party. Every day he went to mass. Sometimes he ate lunch elsewhere. He and Mum often sat together on the sofa in the lounge room, praying, reading or talking, and sometimes napping together. Each evening the family gathered for prayers.

The first three weeks in Melbourne, I had continually been communicating with Jason in my head, wondering what he was doing, and how he would respond to the things I was experiencing. I could still feel him next to me – his shy sideways glances, his overheated body. But now I was beginning to think about him less. We still spoke on the phone every day, but the conversations had become increasingly distant and frustrating. Sometimes I felt we were on different planets.

My world had narrowed to my parents' home and the local supermarket, the care and cooking routines, the prayers and meditation, and my daily attempts to get Mum to talk to me about her life. The healing party loomed before us. My head felt woolly, my thoughts and reactions seemed at a remove. Sometimes I forgot to eat. My whole body had slowed down, had become contained.

*

After I had been in Melbourne for four weeks, Dad came running down from his studio. 'Good news, good news, Irene!' he called out. 'Anita's property colleagues are going to buy the triptych of tigers for 6000 dollars. It will pay for the healing party. Praise the Lord.'

They rejoiced. It was proof that Jesus wanted the party to go ahead. Mum's smile was like the sun coming out. 'We must celebrate,' Dad said. 'We must invite Geoff and Father Lachlan to a slap-up meal with all the family!'

That Saturday afternoon we piled into the Holden: Dad and Mum in front, and Maria, Patsy and me in the back. Within ten minutes, we were at the commercial centre of our suburb. Brown brick shops with faded signs – Milk Bar, Sunny Boy, Normans Newsagent – lined both sides of a six-lane highway, full of trucks and noise, even on a Saturday afternoon. Among the functional row of shops was one small piece of red and gold exotica, the Ting Chu Chinese Restaurant, or 'the Chu'. When we had first moved to Melbourne, the Chu was the only Chinese restaurant in this part of the eastern suburbs. The Cheahs, who owned the restaurant, had been the only other Chinese people for miles around. People assumed we were related. While my schoolfriends got casual jobs at the supermarket, my sisters and I waitressed at the Chu. Children at school teased us, saying we put cat food in the dim sims. I would have taken all the waitressing shifts that clashed with prayer meetings to avoid going to them, but my father made me alternate with my sisters.

Mr Cheah's daughter, who now managed the restaurant, held the entrance door open for us. Hanging in the windows were the same golden lanterns and red polyester curtains that my sisters and I would brush the dust off once a fortnight when we worked here. We walked past the front counter and the handful of people sitting against the wall waiting for takeaway. I imagined I saw Bonnie sitting there, waiting for my shift to finish.

Anita, Charles and Will, Father Lachlan, and Geoff Atkins and his wife had already arrived. They sat at a big, round table near the back of the overly large and empty room. Only two other tables were occupied by diners. Covering the back wall from floor to ceiling was a faded wallpaper print, in traditional brush-painting style, of a misty mountain Chinese landscape. I was glad it was still there – I loved its sometimes soaring, sometimes meandering lines and the luminous spaces.

Father Lachlan and Geoff and his wife rose from their seats to greet us. Father Lachlan, stooping from his great height, took our hands in turn and looked into each of our faces as though he really saw us. He had big hands and a broad, deeply furrowed face. Seeing his beatific smile and hearing his brimming-over voice, I remembered why I liked him. He still led the Saint Mark's Charismatic meetings that we had attended every Tuesday night for years. He was almost my parents' age but had a shyness about him that made him look younger. People would gather in their coats in that cold church, and were soon warmed by his rejoicing and his singing in tongues. Father Lachlan was one of a few Catholic priests who had embraced the renewal, and the only one to lead a Charismatic prayer group.

It was the first time I had met Doris, Geoff's wife. She was poised and upright, and almost a head taller than Geoff.

Dad, directing everyone to seats around the table, positioned Mum's wheelchair next to Doris. Pride of place went to Father Lachlan, flanked by Dad on one side and Geoff on the other. 'Father, Father, these girls have not heard your wonderful testimony,' he said.

'And which testimony is that, Paul?' said Father Lachlan.

'How you came to the Lord. You know. You were stationed as a missionary priest in Bogota, sickened by the corruption and mindless suffering. One evening, questioning the existence of God, you reached for the *Playboy* magazine that another disillusioned priest had left in a drawer, but grabbed a bible instead —'

'Well, Paul,' Father Lachlan said, taking up the story, 'the gist of it is, Jesus spoke to me through a message in the bible. It was a verse from James: "Count it all joy, my brothers, when you meet trials of various kinds, for you know that the testing of your faith produces steadfastness." Count it all joy,' he said. 'I love that.' Laughter and joy trembled in his voice.

For some minutes, the men bantered about the verse, bright and jovial. Geoff caught me looking at them. 'We've not properly met you before, young lady. You're the one from Darwin, aren't you?' He pointed at me across the table. 'There's just one thing I need to know. Do you love Jesus?' Geoff leant over and held a pretend microphone to my face. Dad chuckled.

'Oh yes, she does,' Mum said. 'Don't you, Natasha!'

I nodded, but didn't smile.

'Don't worry about him, darling,' Doris said. 'He's a josher! What an inspirational family you all are.' Geoff and Doris were smartly dressed, Doris in a linen day suit. I felt embarrassed that the restaurant was not more grand.

'Look at all these gorgeous daughters,' Geoff said. 'You'll be fighting off the blokes, heh heh! And look at the young fellow. He's a little prophet Samuel in the making, aintcha?' Geoff poked his head towards Will. Will turned down his mouth, folded his arms and swung his back to him. I felt like doing the same. 'Praise the Lord for this blessed family!' Geoff clapped his hands.

'We must order! Call for anything you like. Father, Geoff, Doris?' Dad said.

'I'll have Peking duck,' said Geoff.

My sisters and I exchanged a look – there was no such thing here.

'Okay,' said Dad, 'it's not on the menu – but let's ask Mrs Cheah to cook it specially for us. I'm sure she will.'

'No, Dad. For a start you have to have a duck,' said Anita. 'Sorry, Geoff, no duck, we know the menu well. We used to waitress here. What else do you like? They do good pork.'

'Yes! Forget the quack quack and let's have some oink oink!' said Geoff.

Dad laughed, and the conversation continued in this vein until the first course started to arrive. The waiter plonked down on the lazy susan the Chu's jumbo spring rolls, each one thick and long enough to cover a dinner plate.

'Before we start on this feast,' Dad said, 'I want to thank you, Jesus, for sending Father, Geoff and Doris to share our table. Bless us, O Lord, at this pre-miracle meal; it is the celebration to precede the main celebration – the healing of Irene. Father, please say grace.'

'Bless this meal we are about to receive through your bountifulness, O Lord.' Father Lachlan closed his eyes and opened his hands. 'We praise you, Jesus, for this wonderful, loving and faithful family, the Chans. We lift up Irene, your devoted daughter, especially to you in prayer. We ask for joy and readiness for Thy will to be done.'

'Amen.' Everybody now began to eat.

'Eat more, Father! You must build up your strength for the night of nights coming up. Once they witness the miracle, hundreds more will be lining up for healing,' Dad said.

Father Lachlan pursed his lips. 'As you know, Paul, on the night of the party I have a seminarian training session and won't arrive until about 9 at the earliest.'

'Not to worry,' said Dad. 'You arrive, have something to eat, and then around 9.30 or so, when you are ready, we will ask everyone to gather round, and you will lead the healing and the laying of hands.'

'Please don't wait for me to start praying over Irene.'

'Oh, but we must, Father,' Dad said.

Father Lachlan stopped eating. 'It would not do to place too much importance on the healing being conveyed through me, Paul.'

Dad smiled. 'It was prophesied, Father, that it would be through your laying on of hands.'

'Never mind, la, Paul. After all, Jesus is the one ...' Mum, shy, trailed off.

Father Lachlan pushed his seat back into the Chinese landscape wall. We stopped eating and looked at him. 'God's mystery and will transcends us,' he said. 'We must be prepared for anything. Readiness is all.' In his black clerical gear, waving his long arms, he blended strangely with the black-ink brushwork of the wall behind him. For a moment, no one said anything. 'Readiness is all,' Father Lachlan repeated, shooting his arm out, his face suddenly passionate. My thoughts jumped to the jungles surrounding Bogota, the drug wars, death and poverty that he had described at prayer meetings and I imagined what those words would have meant to him.

Dad broke the silence. 'You are absolutely right, Father. You, like all men, are but a vessel for Christ. But it is through man, through humble and foolish man, that God performs his miracles!' Dad said.

'Fools for Christ!' said Geoff. 'That's what we are! One Corinthians four!' Geoff raised a hand heavenwards. 'And by the stripes of Jesus, we shall have that miracle!'

*

After lunch the guests departed, as did Charles and Will, and the rest of us returned to Aquarius Court. Dad went straight up to his studio. Anita helped Mum into bed. Maria, Patsy and I put on old shirts and commenced work in the kitchen. The aim was to wrap 600 wontons and freeze them for the healing party.

It was a routine we knew well. Without talking, we dodged around each other, taking out ingredients from the fridge and choosing our implements from the cupboards. I gave a final stir to the basin of sticky pink pork mince mixed with chopped herbs and placed it in the centre of the round kitchen table. Scooping up a handful of flour, I swiped the section of table in front of me, then set out the small squares of wonton pastry in close rows. With thirty squares laid out, I proceeded to spoon a lump of pork mince into the centre of each one. When I looked up, Patsy had only started to flour her section of the table and Maria was still looking for implements.

I was determined to say something before Anita came back from helping Mum. 'Father Lachlan seems to have cold feet about the miracle,' I began.

'No, he doesn't,' Patsy said.

'He said that it depends on God's will – whether Mum will be healed. He was basically saying it might not happen!'

'No, he didn't say that,' Patsy shot back. 'You don't understand. Yes, it depends on God's will and God has shown *it is His will* that

Mum be healed. The Lord has promised it through the prophecy.' She paused and said more softly, 'He put it on my heart too.'

Maria opened the fridge door and stood in front of it, frowning. She was building up to say something, I could tell.

'Are you just going to stand there with the fridge open, Maria?' I said.

She closed the fridge and took a space at the table beside me. 'Do you believe in miracles, Natasha?'

'Do you?' I said.

'Yes, I do,' said Maria.

'As Dad says, miracles happen only to those who believe,' Patsy said.

I didn't like her righteous tone. 'So you think that Mum will be completely healed of cancer,' I said, 'that she will leap out of that wheelchair and live into old age, just because we believe it?'

'Yes, I do,' Patsy said. She stuck her chin out but I saw her bottom lip tremble.

I tried to make my voice gentler. 'In all those years we were going to prayer meetings together, I never saw a miracle. I mean a real miracle.'

'Well, if you're looking for proof, you're taking the wrong approach. You either believe, or you don't.' Patsy's voice took on a stridency. 'It's a gift. You could pray for the gift.'

'Right,' I said, 'so you're saying that's all there is to it – you're blessed and I'm not.'

'You don't have to put it that way —' Patsy started to say.

'Nat, I can tell you about real miracles,' Maria interrupted. 'They happen all the time. What about Janice Samuels, who converted

Dad? Didn't you read her book about being healed of cancer?'

'She's dead now, isn't she? What did she die of?' I said.

'Not cancer!' Maria said. 'I witness miracles all the time. Just last week my housemates and I prayed over Bronwyn to be healed of cysts on her ovaries. The cysts disappeared! Dad prayed over Mei to become pregnant. She has a baby now! That meditation you do with Mum – you pray for healing.'

'I'm doing it for Mum,' I said, but as soon as I said it I realised it wasn't true. Each day, the meditation was what I looked forward to.

My hands were busy all the time we talked. I dipped my index finger into the milky water and cornflour mixture and wet the sides of the tender pastry. It was like touching skin. With both hands I picked up the wonton package, folded the pastry over the meat and formed the wings in a simultaneous tuck and twist of thumb and fingers on each side. I placed the wonton on the tray. Without pause, I started on the next one.

Maria looked at me with her concerned counsellor face. She wasn't even pretending to work on the wontons. 'We all have doubts sometimes,' she said. 'It doesn't matter. Just by wanting to believe, you will believe. Sometimes you need to just say it and your heart will follow. Even if you don't feel it now, if you declare with your tongue, the rest will follow. That's what I do.'

Maria took a step closer to me. 'You had faith, Nat. Remember when we were kids, when I made the picture of Jesus light up? You fell asleep during prayers in the family room. We woke you up and said, "Look, the face of Jesus is glowing! It's a miracle!" You believed it. I can't forget how your mouth and eyes opened so wide,' she said.

'You got down on your knees, poor thing,' said Patsy.

Maria put a hand on my shoulder. 'I've always felt bad about tricking you with that light. Have you forgiven me?' she said.

'Don't be silly, Maria, that didn't mean a thing,' I said.

The phone rang. We heard Anita pick it up and call out to Dad in his studio that it was Geoff. She came into the kitchen and started counting the wontons.

'Not Geoff again,' I said. 'They just saw each other and he's already ringing. Dad and Geoff meet for breakfast, then keep on talking on the phone every day. Mum doesn't like it.'

'He's funny,' said Patsy.

'Funny strange, or funny ha ha?' I asked.

'Maybe both,' said Patsy.

'He's creepy,' I said.

'Don't just come here and start criticising people,' said Anita.

'Well, what do you think of him?' I said.

'It's not about what we think of him. He is having a good effect on Mum and Dad. You should have seen how miserable Dad was before. Now they have hope,' Anita said.

I had nearly filled my tray with wontons, fifteen per row, twelve across. Patsy's was one-quarter full and Maria had barely started.

His phone call over, Dad came into the kitchen. 'Wonderful girls. Praise the Lord. Your mother will be proud of you, keeping up the Chan hospitality. We will not only feed their souls at the healing party, we will fill their stomachs!' He picked up a wonton from Patsy's tray. 'Look at these beautiful shapes. Classic Cantonese-style, with folds and crevasses like the craggy mountains of Huangshan! Which of you artistic girls crafted these?'

'I did,' Patsy said, and meekly cast her eyes downwards. Her shoulders, however, pulled back in pride.

'I should have known,' Dad said.

*

When we had made 440 wontons and there were no more pastry wrappers left, we cleaned up and went to Mum's room. She had woken up a few minutes earlier, but the room was still dark.

Mum lay on the bed, wrapped in the quilt. 'Open the curtains,' she called out. Light flooded in through the glass panels that swept from one corner of the room to the other. 'Hello, hello!' She looked happy to see us and tried to sit up on her elbows. I took one arm and Anita took the other to pull her up.

'Open up the windows, Maria,' Mum said. 'Wider. Let all the bad air out.' Her skin felt chilled, but still she wanted the window open. It was always the same. She liked it cold. Cold meant clean.

Anita pulled a chair up to the bed. 'How are you feeling?'

'Better and better. Praise the Lord,' said Mum. 'How are the wontons?'

'We made 440,' Patsy said, sitting cross-legged next to me at the foot of the bed.

'So many,' Mum said. 'I hope you didn't put too much meat in each, or else they burst open.'

Maria, leaning against the bed, kneaded Mum's shoulders. 'The wontons are fine,' she said. 'We would have made them quicker but were chatting too much.'

'Nice to chat. Sisters are the closest thing. Was Natasha asking you her questions?' said Mum.

'Mum and I have been talking about her childhood. I ask her questions,' I explained.

'What kind of questions?' said Anita.

'Last time we talked about school. Mum said she missed a lot of school because she was always sick or pretend-sick,' I said.

They laughed. This encouraged me. 'We also talked about Mum and Dad's courtship. Next I was going to ask about motherhood – what it was like to be a mother.'

Anita raised her eyebrows and turned down her mouth. 'Such deep questions!' she teased.

'So silly,' said Mum. 'A mother loves and looks after her children – that's it!'

'You know Mum had to stay in bed at the Rowling Road house for two weeks after I was born because of Chinese tradition?' Anita said. '*Agnin* wouldn't even let her go to the toilet – she had to use a bed pan.'

Mum shook her head. 'What a silly tradition,' she said

'Was it two years later that you had Vincent?' I asked.

'Yes. Such a perfect boy. Looked just like your dad. He is with Jesus.' She gave a wistful smile. 'After Vincent I couldn't conceive for many years. I thought Anita will be an only child. Then I had three of you, one after another. No break!'

'Wasn't I only one week old when we went to England?' said Patsy.

'Something like that,' Mum said. We could never pin her down on these details – the little we knew we had pieced together from snippets collected over years of asking.

Anita said, 'I was about eleven, and Patsy, you had just been born.'

So Maria would have been three and me one. After two years, we returned to Hong Kong. I was too young to remember anything about London, but I knew we'd gone because Dad had secured a residency at a photography institute there.

'Anita was always the little mother,' Mum said. 'Sometimes in England I couldn't stand being stuck in the small flat all day with three babies. I would put Anita in charge just to take a quick walk. Ten minutes only. When I came back I'd see her little face in the window, looking for me.'

Maria stopped massaging. 'Didn't you have to put me into a children's home in London for a few months?' she said, averting her eyes.

Mum grimaced. 'It wasn't that long. You were too difficult to control. The nurse brought you home some nights,' she said. 'There was no one to help us in England, and your dad – always working!' Mum struck the bed with the flat of her hand. 'It was only for a few weeks, la.'

'Look at Maria now – such a saint! Right, who's next?' Anita interjected, glaring at Maria. Mum had had some kind of nervous breakdown then. That was all we knew. Maria wanted to know more about the time she spent in the children's home, but she was never going to find out. 'Mum, tell us what Natasha was like as a baby.'

'Sores. Natasha always had sores on her body, since she was a baby. And too much resentment. But now she's a good girl. Praise the Lord.' Mum said, looking tired.

Anita stood up. 'Okay, enough talking. Let Mum rest now. Sing for her.'

Maria brought out the guitar and she and Patsy started to sing a duet.

Sores and resentment. When I was eight and living in the house on the hill in Hong Kong, a red sore appeared on my belly. Several times a day I checked to see whether it had become smaller or bigger. A blister grew on top of it. I accidentally popped it with my nails and clear pus oozed out. In the next few days more sores clustered around the original sore. After a few weeks there were dozens of sores covering my abdomen. I hid them from sight and made Patsy and Agnes promise not to say anything to Mum, but one day, home from school, I was careless with my schoolbag and it jabbed against my side. Blood soaked through my white shirt. I tried to run away, but Mum saw it. She caught me and lifted up my shirt. Next thing she was grabbing me and crying out, 'Aiya!' and 'My God, my God! How terrible!' and 'What dirty children have you been playing with!' The sores that I had so carefully and gently tended and protected for weeks, she pinched with rough hands, pierced with a needle and wiped with stinking, burning red ointment. The sores dried up and left only scars, which faded away years later. I should have been grateful. Instead, every time I'd looked at the scars, I was furious at her.

My resentment, however, had not started then but a year earlier, in a taxi in Central Hong Kong on the way to a party. I must have been seven years old. The whole family was in the taxi except for Anita, who was old enough by now to go out with her own friends. Dad sat in the front passenger seat, and Mum, my sisters and I were in the back – Mum behind the taxi driver. Usually we younger sisters had to stay at home, so we were excited to be accompanying Mum and Dad to their party. Both of them were reeking of perfume and dressed to the nines. The air-conditioning in the taxi was exhilarating, and we glided along, special, cocooned from the noisy, traffic-jammed road and the crowds of busy, sweaty people.

Dad turned his sleek Brylcreemed head to look at Mum. 'The dress is very striking. It shows off your figure,' he said. Mum made no reply, continuing to stare out the window. He rubbed his hands together. 'You know where we're going, kids? To one of the richest estates in Hong Kong. You will be amazed by the fountain outside their house – there is water dancing up to the sky, lit up by a thousand lights! Everybody there will look at your parents and wonder who we are.' He laughed indulgently and said, 'Look at your big eyes, Natasha!' Dad sparkled in a silk Hawaiian shirt he had bought during his recent visit to Washington.

He reached back to touch Mum's knee. 'You should wear dresses like that more often! So pretty, huh? Like a movie star. We both look like movie stars. My shirt too is not bad – what do you say, huh?' His eyes were wet and shiny, and he had that eager look he got before eating his favourite noodle dish. Through his aftershave I could smell fresh sweat.

At last Mum turned and glared at him. 'Will she be there?' she said.

A pause. 'What are you talking about?' he said.

'You know what I'm talking about. The young model. Will she be there?' Mum shot forward in her seat. Her voice was shrill.

'Always so jealous!' Dad shouted. 'Why do you have to say such stupid things – think, think, *think* before you speak! You just can't help spoiling things, can you?'

There was silence for a couple of minutes. Then Mum said to the driver in Cantonese, 'Stop the car, stop the car. Let me out.'

The driver asked Dad what he should do.

'She is not well,' Dad said. 'Let her out and then keep going to the address I gave you.'

Mum stepped out of the taxi, followed by Patsy. 'Come on,' Maria said on the other side of me. When I wouldn't budge, she climbed over me and got out. Mum bent down into the car, her mouth tight and eyes wild. 'Come out now!'

'No!' I yelled, trying to pull away. 'I want to go with Dad to the party!' Digging her long fingernails into my arm, she hauled me out. The taxi driver shut the door behind me.

Mum lifted me up over the gutter and onto the footpath. As soon as she let go, I ran a few steps and then squatted down with my hands over my head. The heat closed in around me.

She marched over, with Patsy and Maria close behind. 'Stand up and come with me now. What is wrong with you! Don't be stupid!' she hissed.

Patsy and Maria called out too. 'Come on, Natasha, what are you doing?'

A crowd gathered around us. I heard people saying of Mum, *look how beautiful she is.* An old woman crouched down and started to shout in my face in a dialect I couldn't understand. A beggar approached Mum, and then another, hassling her until a man in the crowd shooed them away.

Finally, Mum bent down and dragged me up by the ear. I stood up and followed, my head throbbing with shame and pain. For years afterwards I would see Mum as the one who spoilt everything for Dad. I would replay the incident, remember her claw-like fingernails digging into my arm, grabbing my ear, and burn with resentment.

As a child, I felt special when Dad confided in me that Mum was the cross he had to carry, that she was well-meaning but rough and insensitive and we had to forgive her because of her lack of education.

He sometimes forgot whom he was talking to. 'A man always thinks of another woman while he makes love to his wife,' he said to me in his studio. In those days I often sat quietly watching while he cut, tore, arranged and pieced together his photos. 'He may be a good man and love his wife, but that's the way it is,' he went on. 'Man is imperfect.'

Even when I was old enough to know better and the only time he could get me alone was when he drove me in his car, even then with his words pouring like poison into my ear, I still listened, transfixed, frightened to disappoint him.

But one day when I was about sixteen, I said, 'What would Mum think of what you are saying? Maybe I should ask her?'

'I thought you were more mature. I thought there were things that we could share. My fault. I am too idealistic,' he said. He stopped confiding in me then.

*

During family prayers the night of the restaurant lunch, the phone rang. 'It's Jason,' Maria called out. I carried the phone into my bedroom, closed the door and leant against it.

'Hi.' I pressed the phone against my ear.

'Gidday,' he said. 'What's a nice girl like you doing at home on a Saturday night?' His voice sounded upbeat and velvety, the way it was when he'd had a drink.

He asked me how Mum was, how the lunch went. I tried to be engaging, but we were both awkward, skirting around each other. I concentrated on the textures in his voice, the sound of the clanking fan in the corridor where he sat, and tried to bridge the distance.

'What's the new housemate like?' I asked.

Jason's other housemate, Penny, was in teacher training. She was nice, vague, not his type. But all Jason had told me so far about the girl who had moved in the week before was that she was a Fine Arts student.

'Good,' he said, and hesitated. 'She cleared half the garage to do her painting in.'

I wondered why he didn't offer any more information about her. 'What kind of painting does she do?' I said.

'Largeish scenes.'

'Well, what are they like?'

'They're interesting,' he said.

It seemed as though it was *her* he found interesting. She had to be attractive – I could tell from the way he talked about her, never saying her name or describing her.

'Are you going to tell me her name?'

'Clarissa. She and Penny have gone out to the Dolphin tonight.'

'Why didn't you go with them?' I said, and didn't like the sound of my voice.

'I wanted to ring you.'

'You could have done both.'

'Didn't want to.' He sounded vague, confused.

My heart was beating fast. 'The party you went to last night. Was that with Clarissa?'

'Yeah, she came along to Mick's party.' He paused. 'I'm just going to turn the fan up. It's fuckin' hot in here. Hold on.'

I put the phone down on the floor, shook my hands and feet and rotated my neck. Thuds came from the phone and then his voice. I picked it up.

'Are you there?' he said.

'So, what else is happening?' I asked.

His voice relaxed. 'Yesterday a couple of jokers were playing with a snake down at the rocks. Drunk as skunks, they were. They found it in the mangroves at the mouth of Rapid Creek. King brown snake, deadly one, big one. Anyway, these guys are that off their heads they thought the thing wouldn't hurt them. They pick it up and pass it backwards and forwards to each other, pissing themselves laughing, until both get bitten. Still, they'll have a story to tell next time.'

It was sweet, the way he stored up stories to tell me. But I wasn't interested. I closed my eyes and imagined him on the other side, lying shirtless on the floor with his feet up on the louvred window, his long, slim muscularity, and the fuzz of dark hair on his chest funnelling down his stomach. He would be wiping sweat off his brow, looking restrained and a bit helpless.

'Are you all right?' he said.

'Yep,' I said.

'You sure?'

'My family drives me insane.'

'They are insane,' he said.

'Don't be glib,' I said. 'You don't understand, do you! How do you know that they're not right and that we're the ones who are missing the point? How do you know miracles don't happen?'

'It's possible, I suppose,' he said, trying. 'I'd like to believe it. That's the problem I have if I ever go to church. I'm in an agonised state for days. Like when you dragged me to church at Easter. All those people – they look so sure of themselves, the priest saying all that stuff about Jesus coming back to life from the cross. Do people actually believe it – actually believe? That's what I can't get.'

'My family always say faith is a decision, not an emotion,' I said.

'I guess they've got a point. To be so sure, you've got to be lying to yourself, or blocking everything else out and just deciding to believe.'

'It's not faith, is it, if you have all the proof? I think I understand why they say it's a decision,' I said. We were silent again.

Jason sighed. 'This is torture,' he said. 'I'm worried about you.'

'I'll be all right.'

'Anyway,' he said, 'you should let me come down. I asked my boss if I could have time off to see you and he said yes. Then he said, "You'll be carting your balls down there in a wheelbarrow, won't you?"'

'Do you hear that?' I put the phone out into the corridor so he could hear them singing. *Walking and leaping and praising God.*

'Where are you?' he said.

'In my bedroom.'

'Why don't I come down? Christen that childhood bed of yours.'

I didn't feel in the least bit sexy. I looked at my room. It was like a cell or sanatorium at night. I had not decorated or softened it at all, and had been sleeping with the light on. It made me feel dirty thinking about sex in this room. Their singing rose in the background. He had no idea. He'd been drinking.

'If you need a fuck, why don't you just have it with the new housemate?' I said.

'What the hell?' His voice cracked.

'You're attracted to her, aren't you?'

'What are you talking about?'

'I can tell by the way you avoid talking about her that something is going on.' I didn't care if none of it was true. I leapt. 'You just want to come here because you can't fight the temptation of her in your house!'

'I can't believe this! I am not your father.'

My mind reeled. 'Don't bring him into it! It's best if we break up, at least while I'm down here.'

I could hear him getting to his feet, dragging the landline up from the floor. 'What's this about?' His voice was strangled.

'It's probably just me,' I said. 'I don't feel I can take another thing.'

He breathed hard. 'I want to support you through this.'

'I know you do. I'm just not very good at being supported. I'm sorry.'

'I'm not good enough for you, am I? Never have been.' he said angrily. Then he started to cry.

'Sorry, but I'm not going to start consoling you. It's me, I really just can't take another thing. I love you, goodbye.' I put down the phone, covered my face with both hands, fell to the floor and sobbed.

If I did not join them, they would wonder what was going on. Wiping my eyes, I walked out of the room and down the corridor, and took my place on the couch at family prayers.

In the half-dark, lit only by candle flame and the glowing portrait of Jesus, permeated by the smell of melting wax and fragrant oil, my family gathered in prayer. It was a touching sight. 'Let the mighty love of God flow out through me,' they sang with full hearts. Mum twinkled a smile at me as I sat down. She closed her eyes again, still smiling, her hands gently raised and upturned to God. On bended knee, eyes squeezed shut, mouths open wide in song, Dad and Maria lifted their arms high and contorted their faces in worship. Anita, her eyes open and watchful, sang chin up, loud and clear. As usual, Patsy's voice soared above the others, effortless, her closed eyes fluttering as though in a trance.

Bitch, I said to myself. *You stupid bitch. What is wrong with you, bitch?* I had not intended to break up with Jason. I looked up at the face of Jesus hanging on the wall, lit up, as I now knew, by diodes behind a translucent screen. The likeness was drawn from the markings of the Turin Shroud that had covered his face for the three days and nights before he was raised from the dead. I shuddered. This was the face of a dead man.

Maria had been right. Years ago, when my sisters secretly turned on the light behind the picture of Jesus and declared it a miracle, I did fall to my knees and gasp. I could still remember the sense I had that the light was pulsating, alive, searching for me. I had no reason not to believe. They were wrong, though, to think that it showed I had faith. Miracles, catastrophes, ghosts, poltergeists, resurrections! I had no faith in order. Anything and everything could happen. I believed in utter chaos.

I HAD BEEN IN MY PARENTS' HOME FOR SEVEN WEEKS. The days were full of purpose, but the nights were long and gnawed away at all three of us. Taken in the right dose before bed, the morphine capsules helped to control Mum's pain, but what was there for the fear that at the foot of their bed grew ten feet tall?

Perhaps it was me projecting my own fear. They said they trusted in God. I knew what I heard, though. Each night their sighing, shuffling, bed-creaking and muttered prayer leached through the bedroom wall.

I had bought a lamp for the bedside table and left it switched on. I also had a torch under my pillow in case the lamp failed, or the hair-thin filament fizzled out. It felt as though I had not had a good night's sleep in weeks. When I lay awake, I read the books on coping with cancer and dying that I kept hidden under the bed. I did not contact Jason. I tried not to think of him.

I opened again the sombre grey cover of *On Death and Dying*. 'How sick are you?' the author asked a cancer patient in one of the interviews. 'I am full of metastases,' the patient replied.

I had to put the book down.

Sleep, when it came, was confused by the light of the lamp. Its white energy seared my brain. I felt as if I were under twenty-four-hour observation. I had experienced this before, sleeping out in the Darwin bush under the intensity of a full moon.

The next morning, as usual I rose when it was still dark. The clock said 6.05 a.m. I had taken to walking around the oval before helping Mum up if I woke early enough. How delicious it was to step outside into the blackness. The dark before dawn held no fear for me. It was like velvet over my eyes.

Breathe! Mum had always told us if we were sick. Breathe and pray. She would demonstrate, inhaling through the nostrils until her chest expanded and she could take no more in. Then she would open her mouth and expel her breath with a loud animal hiss. Walking on the road to the oval, I breathed as Mum did. Icy air filled my nostrils and purified my lungs. Ready to burst, I exhaled, sending out warm, moist clouds before my face.

When I reached the middle of the broad oval, I stopped. It was still too dark to identify houses, trees or fences. With only the ground and sky as my reference, this spot could have been anywhere in the world between heaven and earth. There was a stirring and glowing in the purple-black shroud above. I waited for the first rays.

Some mornings I saw the beauty, but it slid off me, unfelt. This morning though, the rays of light pierced me. This morning, I worshipped. What else was the sunrise but a brimming over of hope? I felt the all-ness, the miracle of creation, and my own nothingness.

'My mother's body is full of metastases,' I told the sky.

*

I had stayed out too long. In the powdery light, the wire fence surrounding the oval, and beyond that the box-shaped houses with their bins and cars, started to form. I rushed back to meet Mum's 7 a.m. rise. The light was already on in Dad's studio.

A pungent smell filled the bedroom. It was always present now, around Mum, from the gas that she burped out every few minutes to relieve the build-up in her stomach. After a night's confinement however, it was especially intense. Mum was upbeat when she saw me. Her hair was back, and her face on the pillow looked flat and exposed. Trying to raise her head, she lifted her eyebrows and smiled.

'Today! All the family together at the faith rally! Thank you, Jesus.'

It had been planned for weeks that we would all go to a rally at Dallas Brooks Hall. I had not been to one since my schooldays. *The honeymoon days* or *cloud nine* was how Mum and Dad referred to those early Charismatic years. It didn't matter that we had school or work the next day, how far it was or how long into the night the rejoicing extended; we whirled from one prayer meeting to another, several times a week. On weekdays there were the local prayer groups, on weekends the larger faith rallies, and a couple of times a year the rock concert–sized, international Charismatic conferences that went all week.

'You will go to the rally, won't you?' she said.

'Yes, I'll go,' I said. 'Is Anita going?'

Mum nodded. 'Oh yes, of course. She always goes.'

No, she didn't. But there was no point saying that to Mum. Anita had not been baptised in the holy spirit like the rest of us. She had not joined in the endless round of prayer meetings. She didn't speak in tongues or get slain in the spirit. Somehow Anita had avoided the whole Charismatic thing from the beginning without causing any of the conflict that arose when I resisted going to the meetings in my final years of school. It wasn't just the age gap between us and the fact that she had moved out of home before we became Charismatic. She got away with it because she never objected. She came to the occasional meeting when my parents asked and when it didn't clash with her work. She voiced no criticism, sang when they sang, knelt when they knelt and prayed when they prayed.

Except once. A few weeks after my parents were born again, they arranged a meeting with a Charismatic family counsellor. We sat in a circle of plastic chairs in a side room at the Christian Revival Centre. After two songs and some speaking in tongues, the balding counsellor held Dad by the shoulders.

'Declare in front of God, in front of your beloved family, why we are here today.'

Dad stood up. 'Jesus, I have given you my life. You are the alpha and the omega. Now I give to you what is most precious to Irene and me. I give you my children's lives!'

The counsellor stood in front of my sisters and me. 'Do you, girls, accept Jesus into your lives?'

After some time, it was Anita who spoke up. It was not tongues or praise that came from her mouth, but some plain words. 'Why should I, when Dad always tried to kiss my girlfriends?'

It was so surprising that it was almost as if it had never happened.

*

Dad, hands gripping ten o'clock and two o'clock on the steering wheel, led us in prayers and songs as he drove us to the rally. Mum's eyes, reflected in her visor mirror, were on us girls at the back, smiling to see us together.

Dallas Brooks Hall stood in inner-city Melbourne, a forty-minute drive away. We breezed through our modern suburbs, joined the no-man's land of the freeway and emerged into more intricate, older streets with industrial shopfronts, terrace houses and small corner pubs. I did not realise I had stopped singing until Anita elbowed me. 'Sing!' she said. I complied, shrinking from her strong perfume and angular linen suit.

People and cars collected in front of the hall. A colonnade of columns surrounded the rectangular concrete building, giving it the look of a modern-day temple – a very austere temple, I now thought, though I had remembered it as grand.

The worshippers alighting from the cars were in suits, formal dresses, pearls and shawls. They hadn't dressed like this when I last came to one of these eight years ago. Maria and Patsy had advised me to dress up as well, 'to show the world we are "winners for Christ"'. I wore a woollen skirt and vest of Mum's that she had urged on me.

As soon as we reached the drop-off area, we sprang into action, hauling the wheelchair out, lifting Mum into it, conscious of the long line of waiting cars. Dad drove away to find a park. Anita forged a path through the throng for Mum pushed by Maria. At the entrance, a broad, tiled staircase, two flights high, confronted us. None of us had thought about wheelchair access. We spread out in different directions, searching for another entrance, but all had to return to the foot of the stairs. Mum's face was stretched tight and self-consciously bright. She asked Maria to push her over to the side, where she would be less in the public view. We saw a man, bowed over his crutches, scrabbling over to the entrance. At the foot of the stairs, he dropped his crutches and was hoisted onto the back of another man. Up the stairs he went, his small, twisted body dangling from his companion's neck. Cries of 'Praise the Lord' and 'Alleluia' came from the crowd following their progress.

'This is not good enough! I'm going to speak with management,' I said, and started up the stairs two at a time. Anita followed. The front doors at the top opened onto a packed foyer. There was no manager up there, no office, just volunteers in their 'Faith Ministry' yellow T-shirts.

While I was deciding what to do, Anita approached a volunteer standing behind a pamphlet table and asked him if there was a lift for wheelchairs. 'There's no lift,' he said, with a big unapologetic smile on his face. 'But there are plenty of God's people to help. Just wait here and —'

'That's not good enough,' I interrupted. 'You are required to have wheelchair access. It's the law.'

'Jesus loves you, sister. We have the handicapped here all the time. No one's complaining, 'cause no one's perfect, only Jesus,' he said.

I was furious. Anita pulled me away. 'What's the matter with you?' she said. 'Calm down.'

We went back down the stairs. Dad had returned and was taking charge. He and a male volunteer each took one side of Mum's wheelchair, and a good-looking long-haired man in a black leather jacket took the back. 'One, two, three, up! Alleluia!' Dad said, and Mum and wheelchair were lifted into the air.

'Make way for a miracle!' Dad shouted to the people crowding the stairs. 'Miracle coming through!' The people parted, praising the Lord. Mum adjusted her skirt around her knees, held onto the armrests, cast her eyes down to her lap and did not look up until we reached the top. She should have been walking up those stairs, swaying this way and that, in her small-stepped, alluring way. The volunteer soon disappeared but the man with the long dark hair lingered to introduce himself and ask if there was anything else he could do. He had an attentive yet reserved manner that made me wonder what he was doing at the rally. Mum thanked him and he shook her hand and ours before moving on.

I took the wheelchair handles. I told Mum we should complain to management about the access, that it was ridiculous a faith rally should be held at a place where people who needed healing couldn't get in.

'Let us be humble, Natasha,' Dad interjected. 'Remember the crippled man in the bible who was dropped through a hole in the roof so he could reach Jesus?'

'Mum's not upset – why should you be?' Anita said. Taking the handles from me, she pushed Mum towards the auditorium.

Inside, our gaze rose to see thousands of people filling the aisles and seats over three levels. With joyful and expectant faces, they hugged and greeted each other. The hall buzzed with excited chatter, electric guitars tuning up and microphones being tested. We made our way to the front area below the stage, where the leaders of the movement congregated. Every few steps, someone would stop Mum to tell her she was healed, to rise up or to throw the wheelchair away.

At the front, Dad immediately joined the suited men, the leaders of the renewal. They clapped each other on the backs, spoke in loud voices and guffawed. I heard the garrulous Geoff Atkins before I saw him. The leaders' wives surrounded Mum, crouching down to speak with her, as though to a child.

I slunk away to the side and leant against the wall, where I feigned reading a pamphlet. I was free to watch.

Dad was talking to Terry Morris. Terry, his wife and four daughters led the most popular local prayer group in Melbourne, drawing several hundred each week. They were a fine-figured, good-looking family. When they were up the front leading and singing, they could have been on TV.

Staying close to Mum, Anita talked to a middle-aged couple. She could fit in anywhere. Patsy and Maria joined the gang of youth surrounding the Morris girls. The Morris girls were no longer in their teens but were still the centre of attention. Lara, the eldest, had been a heroin addict. Many times I had heard her testify about her five years on drugs, her 'living hell', and how one day, when she was lying in her own vomit, Jesus spoke directly to her. She had told her story hundreds of times, but the intensity with which she delivered it never flagged. Lara did not look like her younger sisters. Where her face was craggy and worn, theirs were cherubic. Where her power was in preaching, theirs was in singing. I smiled, remembering Bonnie's imitations of the Morris girls – all flounce and simper and singing like a bird when she was doing the younger sisters, then, spinning around, she would do Lara – hunched over, shooting up, smoking, gravelly voice saying 'my living hell'.

Towards the back of the auditorium, leaning against the wall, was the guy with the long hair who had carried Mum's wheelchair. He was alone, watching, like me.

The lights were lowered, there was a momentary hush, then a tinny sustained chord, a drum roll and we were off. Patsy, Maria and I ran to take the seats Anita had saved for us next to the aisle where Mum sat in her wheelchair. Lights strobed across the stage, the band revved up, rhythm and sound rose in key and volume, and the praise began. The fifty-strong choir taking centre stage sang, clapped, flung up their arms and kicked their legs in victory. The audience gave it back. We were a mosh pit of bounding bodies, raising our voices to a roar. Dad and Mum, faces rapturous, lifted their intertwined hands to Jesus. Patsy clapped and sang, and Anita and I watched Maria, who had left her seat and was dancing and jumping like crazy in the aisle.

Each song was more jubilant than the last. Closing my eyes, I tried to silence all the negative and critical voices in my head. I forced myself to clap, opened my mouth to sing. Gradually I let the music and the vast pulsating crowd take me. Higher, faster and louder, I jumped, clapped and sang until I felt an electricity course through me, the way it had felt when I was born again. I could not help smiling. God was the answer, people were good, everything would be all right!

Then the singing stopped. Lou Mercier, the leader of the Victorian chapter, came on stage. I knew the order of proceedings. First songs, then announcements and collection, then more songs, the guest preacher and finally the healing of the sick. Lou told us that the visiting American preachers wanted to know why they didn't see more Mercedes, BMWs or Volvos among us Aussie believers. '"Don't insult Jesus," they said. "He don't want no second-class followers!" Let us show the world that we are winners for Christ!' Lou exhorted.

'What's so insulting about Dad's old Holden?' I said under my breath, and had Patsy and Maria giggling just like old times.

While the collection-takers waited in the aisles, Lou spoke of God's promise that whatever you give, you will get back tenfold. He told people to ask Jesus to put on their heart what they should give. It did not have to be cash – cheques, gold watches, pearl necklaces would be accepted too. I saw Dad take out a fifty. That was more than enough from the whole family, I thought, trying to pass the collection cup on quickly down the row, but Maria threw in thirty dollars, which I knew would leave her broke for the week.

More songs, then Tom Bronson was introduced. He came running onto the stage, punching the air and swinging his microphone like a rock star. He was stocky and wore a white suit. 'Can I have the lights?' he boomed. 'I want to have a good look at my Australian brethren. Do us a favour – when the lights reach you, shout out "Amen!"'

As the lights circled the hall, the amens rolled out like a never-ending wave.

Now Tom closed his eyes. 'Thank you, Jesus, for showing us the light, for bringing us here today. I know there is a football game at the MCG just a mile from here. I heard you Australians like your football. There's 100,000 people at the MCG right now. Well, don't you love the Lord, creator of mankind better? Jesus, you will reclaim the people. Soon *we* will be at the MCG! Lord, we are hungry for your miracle. God is perfect. Are we made in his likeness? So aren't we perfect?' Tom asked, and to each of his questions the audience responded, 'Amen!'

'Sickness belongs to the devil. Tell me, who does sickness belong to?'

'The devil!' shouted the crowd.

'There are some who say we must carry our cross just like Jesus did. But Jesus don't want no martyrs. Satan says, that's your life, the mediocre life, the life of pain, the life of make-do. Jesus says, get thee behind me, Satan. We have been reserved the kingdom of heaven . . .'

His voice was deep and thrilling; at times he was almost singing, bringing us high and bringing us low, speaking in a whisper and building up to a crescendo. The content, however, was the same old stuff.

Gazing at the stage, I remembered the day my parents were born again, less than a year after arriving in Australia. It was here at Dallas Brooks Hall. The preacher had called out to members of the congregation to come forward and be baptised in the holy spirit. Before the preacher could finish his sentence, Dad had jumped out of his seat. It was as if he had been waiting all his life to be called. Taking Mum's hand, he pulled her with him up to the stage.

Mum and Dad looked like children next to the tall, blond preacher in his tight blue suit. I felt anxious at how small and Asian they appeared. The preacher crouched down. 'Where are you from? Do you speak English?' he asked.

To the preacher's surprise, Dad leant over and grabbed his microphone. 'I am fair dinkum Aussie! And I tell you, praise the Lord!' Dad's voice projected over the speakers loud and clear. The crowd loved it. When their cheers subsided, the preacher laid one hand on Dad's head and the other on Mum's. Immediately, Dad fell back as though he had been struck by lightning. Mum gently cascaded to her knees. Within a few seconds, Dad rose to his feet again and spoke in tongues. Volleys of gibberish shot from his mouth.

I had shivered uncontrollably. Hundreds of people were cheering and clapping for my parents. Something amazing had happened, and my parents were at the centre of it. Smiling and in awe, Mum stayed quietly kneeling. Dad sobbed in great guttural heaves. It stunned us, because it was the first time we had seen him cry. He often cried after that. I grew used to it and then later came not to trust it, even to be repulsed by it.

Now Tom Bronson's shouting drew my attention back. 'Over there in the back corner, I sense that there is a man with one leg shorter than the other – come on up!' He pointed to the back and beckoned. 'Someone who has been hearing voices. Only Jesus is the true voice – come on up!' He continued to point to people in different parts of the auditorium where Jesus put on his heart that a sickness lay. Finally he made the call for those with cancer. Dad had already taken Mum's wheelchair brakes off and was running with her towards the stage.

A line was forming in front of the stage. Leaders of the renewal took their places to assist with the laying on of hands. It looked like only about a dozen people would be prayed over by Tom himself. The rest would be prayed over by the leaders below the stage. Dad pushed Mum right past them and lined up. I counted the people in front of her: twelve. I could only see the backs of my parents but knew they were anxious.

The general call-up came. Tom stood with his arms open to the people. 'All the Lord's children! Ye who seek to be healed. Ye who rebuke Satan. Come forward!' he shouted.

They responded. The auditorium came alive with people standing up, clambering, filling the aisles and flowing to the front. The band started up.

'And Jesus said, come to the waters,' we sang, 'stand by my side, I know you are thirsty, you won't be denied.'

Patsy squeezed past us. I grabbed her arm, but she pulled away. *You don't need healing*, I wanted to say. *You don't need demons cast out. You're fine, you're okay.* She walked down the aisle and joined the yearning multitude.

'In the name of Jesus!' Tom shouted. He began to speak in urgent, rapid tongues. With both palms outstretched towards the people below, he walked across the front of the stage. As he passed, the people fell backwards, slain in the spirit. Some were caught by volunteers, and others, like Patsy, hit the carpeted ground without intervention. She pulled her skirt down as she fell. Bodies, some jerking and shaking uncontrollably, were strewn on the ground. Now there was a clear view of Mum and Dad. Mum sat with her eyes closed and a beseeching smile on her face. Dad knelt beside her, weeping and punching his hand upwards as though reminding Jesus, *I'm saved, we're saved!* Seeing them, I had to hold my own tears back. Next to me, Anita watched too. Her face looked sad. Maria, hands stretched out to the slain at the front, swayed and babbled in tongues.

The auditorium started to fill with the speaking and singing of tongues. In the unintelligible languages, I heard pleading, nourishing, anger and rejoicing. A thousand voices clashed and blended into a powerful, complete sound. I was tingling, wanting to open my mouth and join in as I had when I was twelve, but I wouldn't let myself. One by one the slain rose, and the laying on of hands began. In the background the music and singing continued, now soulful and worshipful.

A young woman was dragged up onto the stage by her parents. Swearing and spitting, her face twisted and ugly, she tried to pull away. Tom took one look at her and directed the band to stop playing. He conferred with Lou. The auditorium was hushed and apprehensive. Four suited Charismatic leaders strode onto the stage.

Tom turned his microphone back on. 'By the almighty power of Jesus, we will have victory over the devil which has inhabited her soul. Pray with me. But first, if anyone of you is a doubter, unclean or possessed of fear, you may leave the room. For when the devil is cast from her, he is going to be mad! And he will go looking for someone else to possess.'

I tried not to care what they thought. I stood up and walked out, looking at my feet, ruing the long walk of shame to the doors at the back. Maybe another thirty people left too, slinking, trying not to stand out. Volunteers directed us to sit in the foyer until we were called back in again. I ignored them and kept on walking, desperate to get out of the building.

I pushed the doors open, walked to the edge of the landing and stood there, looking out over Fitzroy Gardens. We had been in the hall for over three hours. The sun would be setting soon. A shimmering blue tint presided over everything.

Hearing the doors open behind me, I turned around to confront the volunteer I thought had followed me out. Instead it was the long-haired man who had helped carry Mum's chair up the stairs.

'Do you mind if I join you?' he said.

'What makes you think the devil won't find us here?' I said.

He grinned. 'You were scared that devil was going to jump into you? I just needed a smoke.' He leant against the stair rail and took out his tobacco and papers.

'Oh, please, can I have one?'

'Maybe,' he said, narrowing his eyes playfully at me. I watched his deft hands at work rolling the cigarettes. It was easy to flirt with him. As we smoked and talked, there was something familiar about him. He seemed casual but at the same time alert, his gaze continually shifting.

'The woman in the wheelchair with you. Is that your mother?'

I nodded.

'She's beautiful,' he said.

'Do you think so? She has cancer. She's supposed to die – the doctor gave her five months. That means she's supposed to have about two and a half months left.'

'I'm really sorry,' he said, and for a while he stopped gazing around and looked down. He seemed genuinely sad.

'It's okay, you don't even know us,' I said.

He laughed, then became serious again. 'I work as a carer for older people. I see so many of them die. Every time I hear of someone else dying, I think of all of them.'

'Well, my family doesn't see my mum as dying.'

He nodded. 'No, of course not. Sorry.'

'You don't sound very Charismatic, if you don't mind me saying so.'

'Praise the Lord!' His face creased into a smile. 'How's that?'

I smiled too. 'Nup.'

'You're right. I started coming to these meetings about a month ago.'

A volunteer stuck his head out the door to call us back in.

We butted out our cigarettes. He asked me my name as we walked back inside. His name was Eduardo. Ed for short, he said. I left him at his seat and walked down to mine.

Anita moved up one seat for me. 'Lucky you came back,' she said. 'Mum's going up next.'

'What happened to the possessed woman?' I asked.

'Which one?' Anita asked. Obviously things had moved on.

Mum's chair was being lifted up the side steps to the stage by Dad and two volunteers in their yellow T-shirts. At the top of the stage, they set her down. Dad took off her brakes and pushed her across the floor to Tom, who waited for them in the spotlight. Holding the microphone to Dad, Tom asked their names.

'We are Paul and Irene Chan, we are leaders of the Charismatic, and we love the Lord!' Dad said. Cheers and alleluias came from the audience.

Tom went down on one knee, facing Mum. She was very

nervous. 'Why are you in this chair, honey?' he said, his voice kind. He held the microphone to her.

'I have cancer,' she said softly.

He snatched the microphone away, jumped to his feet and shook his head. 'Why is she in this wheelchair?' he shouted. Now he pointed the microphone at Dad.

'That the victory of Jesus will be manifested!' Dad proclaimed.

Tom aimed his hands like pistols at Dad. 'Yes, sirree!' he shouted. 'Cancer. I hate that word. Doctors don't know how to cure it. But Jesus does. When we don't forgive, it grows in us like a tumour. Unforgiveness is spiritual poison. Sister, have you forgiven?'

'I must forgive ... Yes, Lord, I have forgiven!' Mum said with determination.

'Alleluia. Praise you, Jesus,' Tom said. He laid his hand on Mum's head and prayed in tongues. The whole auditorium joined in.

Bastard, leave her alone, I prayed with clenched teeth.

He removed his hand. 'You have been healed. Now, sister, go home. It will be manifested.' The band started, indicating that Dad and Mum were to leave the stage.

Dad asked if he could say a few words. Tom handed him the microphone and the band stopped.

'The Lord has spoken through you, Tom.' Dad turned to the audience. 'The Lord has commanded me to gather the people to my home to witness the manifestation of the miracle. You are all invited to the healing party at 7 p.m. on Sunday 19 September. On this night, in three weeks' time, you will see Irene throw away her wheelchair. Our phone number is 94871552. Our address is 17 Aquarius Court, Jackson —'

Tom pulled the microphone away from Dad. The leaders directed the band to start up. The volunteers who had helped carry Mum onto the stage came out of the wings to carry her down.

'That's so rude. He should have let Dad finish,' Anita said.

'Dad's too much, even for Tom!' I said.

The rally finished with more songs and speaking in tongues. Night had fallen by the time we were back in the car and driving home. Dad seemed all the more determined to hold the party, Mum was focused on forgiveness, and my sisters and I, tired and hungry, shared some irritable words with each other in the back.

*

At home, I locked my bedroom door and dragged out the cardboard box stashed under my bed. Jason had written to me. I hadn't expected him to, and if Dad had not finally remembered to give me the letter, I may never have known. He had handed it to me just as we were about to leave for the rally. I asked him when it had arrived, and he said one could not be sure, with the mountain of correspondence and Mum's medical bills demanding his attention, but maybe last week. I felt that familiar helplessness from the time I had lived here. Letters and phone messages passing through my parents' hands would be casually forgotten, disappeared or misplaced.

I pulled out the letter, sat on my bed and unfolded the single page. It looked as though it had been ripped from the pad that Jason kept by his bed. He would reach for that pad and fill it with the ideas that came into his mind on waking. His handwriting always surprised me. It was scrawled and flourishing, and so unlike the way he presented himself to the world.

The letter was dated three weeks ago. Would it really have mattered if this letter had been lost in the piles of paper in Dad's study, never to be seen again? I looked at the scramble of words and wondered how any message in them could possibly change the way things were.

When I had broken up with Jason, after the initial devastation I felt light-headed, almost exhilarated. I had caused an ending and created a new beginning. He had done nothing wrong, but I had been an actor, not a reactor, as my father would say. It would have gone on, and I would have become increasingly insecure, more like my mother – the smile that fell away when people were not looking, the anxious fluttering of her hand under her neck and the silent watchfulness.

Now I read his letter.

> I know things are hard for you down there. I can feel it. I can hear it in your voice. And can't you understand, I'd like more than anything to give you support and help, whatever you need, if you'd let me. You think I'm too selfish, that I'd only bring my own problems down there with me, but maybe you're wrong. I'd like to try, anyway. You should give me a chance. Maybe I'd surprise you. Sometimes I think it's that you won't let me help you, that you would prefer to think that I'm as self-centred as your father. You got me to open up, you're the only person who I've ever opened up to. It's like you can only bear to be with me when you're the strong one. At least I should be given a chance, not cut off just like that, in the middle of a sentence, while I was drinking and relaxed and when I least expected it. God, I can't even remember exactly what I was saying, the conversation.

It's true what you said about the new housemate. Yes, she is attractive. But I can say one thing to you, I would never do anything with her. Not while I'm with you. When everything seemed to be going well with you, yes, I could imagine myself with her, or talk to her or flirt with her, even. But then, the instant I realise you're moving away from me, I can't even think about sex with her, or anybody else. I doubt if I could even get it up. I just feel sick.

I know when I'm down, I feel like I'm wrong in some deep and horrible way, and I can't even say what it is or how to fix it. Maybe it's the lack of faith. I can't believe. Maybe I'd like to – I'm probably just the sort of person the evangelicals target, the lost soul – but I don't have that certainty you and your family seem to have. I'm uncertain even in my certainty, and you're certain even in your uncertainty, if that makes any sense.

You don't have to be the same as your family. You should be able to hold on to what you believe in without offending anyone. That's what I think, but whatever course you choose, I'm going to support you. Please don't shut me out. You have told me what your father thinks about me being an agnostic. That we're worse than atheists because we're lukewarm and God will spew us out of his mouth. But it's not that I don't care. I believe it's fair enough to say – this is something I don't know about, my puny human mind doesn't have the equipment to be able to work a thing like that out. All I know is, there are great mysteries in the universe.

Natasha, I love you. I went for a walk before. I walked along the foreshore, the same way we always used to walk together. I ended up at the jetty, and I saw that bloke you always used to stop

> and talk to, you know, the almost blind one, the one who's there every night. The sunset was beautiful, that purple magenta you get in the silver sky in the dry. I saw that bloke and I was thinking, why do you come to see the sunset, when you can't even see it? And then I thought, I'm just the same. I'm drawn to the sunset – instinctively drawn to beauty, seeking it out. I'm nearly blind as well.

Dropping the letter, I covered my mouth so my parents would not hear me cry from the next room. I knew I would not be contacting him.

I suddenly felt weak and tired. Fully clothed and unwashed, I clambered into bed. I had bought an electric blanket a few weeks earlier, and had left it switched on during the rally. The warmth was glorious and stupefying, like lying on sunbaked sand.

As I was about to sleep, I remembered how he had fucked me the night I found out that Mum had cancer. I had his penis in me and I was astride him, leaning my hands on his chest, my eyes closed, feeling sad and raw and taking him in deep. When I opened my eyes, I saw him looking up at me with such compassion that his eyes, usually a cool grey-blue, although not crying, looked to be dark and flowing. He turned us over, still inside me, and rocked me gently. He dipped his head down to mine, closed his eyes and pushed his tongue into my mouth. In and out, his tongue and penis pulsated in rhythm, kiss-feeding me.

IT WAS A COUPLE OF DAYS AFTER THE FAITH RALLY AT Dallas Brooks Hall. Maria was helping Mum shower. I ate toast by myself in the kitchen. Dad's urgent phone voice travelled down from the studio. Although the sun had barely risen, he was already making his calls, stirring people to join in with the preparations, and to serve, sing or dance at the healing party. He would not wait until 9 a.m. to ring, no matter how often we told him to. 'I guarantee that people want to rise, to be galvanised for important news,' he would say.

At yesterday's appointment with Doctor Richards, I seemed to be the only one listening. Mum had responded as well as could be expected in her situation after two cycles of chemotherapy, Doctor Richards advised. He then went into some detail about the risks involved in the third cycle. But this was scheduled in about five weeks, which was *after* the healing party, and Dad, Mum and Maria let the details skate over them, their vision filled by the imminent miracle.

Clearing the breakfast dishes, I studied the poster Dad had stuck to the kitchen wall. With an exuberant hand, he had sketched his plans for the party. There was artistry even in his planning notes. In the centre of the poster, he had drawn a cartoon of Mum rising from her wheelchair like an athlete springing from the blocks. Next to the drawing he listed the order of events at the party, starting with the food and song and finishing with the miracle. The poster had sections for contacts, to-do lists, room arrangements, and drawings of food. His menu planning was simple – more, more and more. Mum let the organising swirl around her. Anita argued with Dad about quantities, taking on Mum's usual role. My sisters and volunteers would need to be here every day in the lead-up to the party to prepare the wontons and curry puffs, which we would cram into the bulk freezer.

Dad came into the kitchen. 'You like my poster, don't you?' he said.

I agreed. His face was warm and lively, and he was giving me his full attention.

'You must come along to breakfast at McDonald's with Geoff and me this time,' he said, rubbing his hands together. 'The bacon and egg McMuffins are marvellous.'

Dad and Geoff had breakfast there several times a week, but this was the first time he had invited me. I told him I had to do meditation and massage with Mum when she came out of the shower, that I had eaten breakfast and didn't like McDonald's.

'We will be back in time. I need to talk to you over breakfast,' he said.

'Why don't we just talk here?'

'Geoff has something to share with you.'

'Could you just tell me what Geoff wants to say without me coming to breakfast?'

He was no longer smiling. He raised his voice. 'You have been called to have breakfast with us. Just do what you're asked. Now get to the car.'

I stared into the distance for a moment, then got up to get my shoes.

We arrived at our local McDonald's before Geoff. Even though it was not yet eight when we stepped inside, the air was warm and salty with the smell of frying, and the postbox-style bins were already overflowing with food wrappers and burger scraps. There was a queue at the counter, but most of the rows of small, square tables were vacant. Dad, beckoning me to follow, walked to a table next to the window overlooking shrubs and the car park. He moved the tray that had been left there with its used wrappers and half-drunk milkshake to another table, and went to the counter to order.

I could hear the boy behind the counter greet Dad by name and ask where Geoff was. Dad came back with a laden tray. He put my coffee in front of me.

'I got an extra apple pie,' he said, 'just in case you change your mind.' I ignored the pie. 'You know what I like about McDonald's?' he said, getting stuck into his McMuffin.

'It reminds you of the coffee shops in Hong Kong,' I said.

'Yes, you know those coffee shops. Nothing fancy – the tables and chairs are bolted to the floor like here. But you can just waltz in, choose a table and order drinks and food, and sit for as long as you like and no one will bother you. You know, Natasha,' he continued, all in the same breath, 'have I told you about the reign of terror in my childhood home?'

I nodded.

'I loved my parents and always wanted to please them, even

though they were, let's face it, imperfect. I was always looking for opportunities to make them proud of me. I could speak salutations in classical Chinese. My brothers never learnt them, only me. When my parents had guests, without being asked, I would come out and serve the oolong tea and impress them. I still remember the salutations I recited to them: 'May you prosper like the eastern sea and receive longevity as long as the southern hill,' and 'May your fortune come gratuitously and flow with profits.' Of course my parents gained face from having such a clever son.

'I was always fearful when my parents had a day at the races, and dreaded the moment they returned. If they returned with packets of *sao o fun* noodles, everyone could relax, down to the servants – it meant they had won. If they lost, everyone was scared. My parents would not be satisfied until they found someone to blame. They would ask who swept the floor, who dropped chopsticks? Sweeping and dropping chopsticks, like dropping your livelihood, are the worst offences when it comes to gambling. Inevitably one of my sisters or the servants would be beaten.'

I had heard most of this before, but still it touched me. I imagined that cute, smart, fearful boy and could feel my heart softening. I picked up the apple pie and took a bite.

'Mmm … it's good, Dad,' I said.

'Yeah, good stuff, eh?'

'Did your parents ever beat you?' I asked.

'Seldom, rarely, compared with my sisters. Once my schoolfriend and I were playing hide-and-seek in the house. I thought the boy was hiding in the bathroom, you know, the outdoor one by the drain. *Hiyah!* I kicked the door open, kung fu-style. How awful! I saw my mother sitting on the toilet! For that offence, my mother made my father cane me until I was striped all over. But you know what the terrible thing was? She didn't do it straightaway. She did it two days later – when I didn't expect it and thought she had forgiven me.'

It was a cruel, heart-rending story that he was telling me. But watching him performing the kick, the gasp at the sight of his mother, the swish of the cane, I became aware that it was the actor in him who was telling the story.

'Yes, forgiveness is paramount,' he continued. 'I have forgiven all my family. Even my brother Boon Meng, the sadist who beat my sisters. When I tried to protect them, he would have beaten me too if my mother had not intervened. I wanted to carve *Revenge* into my skin. I took out the blade, put it to the skin on my forearm.' He acted it out, digging into his arm with his finger and flinching. 'One prick – yow! It hurt too much and I stopped immediately.'

I laughed. He was being charming now.

Geoff walked in. 'Gidday!' He called out greetings to us. 'Great to see ya,' he said to the guys and girls working behind the counter.

'I've got your order,' Dad shouted to him.

'Praise Jesus!' Geoff shouted back. They acted like they owned the place.

He slid his pot belly under the table. 'There you are, princess,' he said. I said hi, but wouldn't look at him.

'I might be ugly as sin, but Jesus loves me,' he said, guffawing.

I took another sip of my coffee. Geoff started laughing and pointing at Dad and me.

'You've got a dirty brown coffee mo above your lip, Paul, just here,' he said, and pointed to Dad's face.

I saw the brown smudge above the left corner of Dad's mouth and laughed.

'And lookee here, don't you laugh, young lady – there's coffee in exactly the same spot on your face!' he said, pointing to my face now.

'We must have the same shape face,' Dad said.

'Yeah, round like a rissole,' Geoff said. 'Not like me, I'm like a dog walking backwards, that's what me mum always said. Ah well, we can't help our genes, can we? Nor our T-shirts either.' He laughed again. Dad and I rubbed at the same spot on our faces.

Geoff's face became serious. 'Let me tell ya, Jesus doesn't want us stuffing up. He loves you guys so much that He sent me another message last night. Jesus said to me, "Tell the Chan family that if so much as one of the Chan family doubts, it will hold your mother back and ruin everything."' Geoff stared at me. He went on, 'You are all at risk. The devil is jealous! If just one of you has resentment and doubts, that's him, in!'

'That's right,' Dad said. 'The Lord's protection has to cover us every moment. Especially now that the miracle is drawing near.'

I stood up. 'Are you doing this with my sisters too, Dad? Will they get a breakfast invitation?'

'Please, Natasha, sit down,' said Dad. 'For the love of Jesus and of your mum, let's pray together. This is what we do every time we come here, don't we, Geoff? You don't have to join in if you don't want to, but we're going to do what we always do.'

They bowed their heads, raised their open palms to the ceiling and prayed aloud. I sat back down, my head held high. A few people walking by looked startled by the sight, but the others on the nearby tables continued to eat, ignoring them.

'The spiritual battle is strong,' Geoff said. 'Strongest now. The devil roams like a restless tiger. By the mighty blood of Jesus, we will have the victory.'

*

Mum and I sat in front of the glass panels in her bedroom, looking out onto the backyard. A row of grey-green cacti, left to grow on their own until they were higher than humans, lined the wooden back fence. They were the only trees, if you could call those giant spiked stems trees. The ground was covered in thick waist-high weeds, except along the right fence where a path from the back door led to the Hills Hoist and the shed. Piles of cement rubble, old planks and debris leant against the left fence.

Normally the sight of the backyard would elicit bitter sighs and accusations from Mum for all the gardening that Dad had not done. But now she looked upon its unkempt and loveless state and didn't say a word.

Mum directed me to push the windows as far as they could go until they stood out at right angles. *Must let out the germs,* she always said. Cold air poured in, but so did the morning sun. I positioned Mum near the window so she could feel the fresh air but was out of the sun. I moved my chair into the shaft of golden light crossing the carpet.

'Get out of the sun, dear,' she said. 'You want wrinkles?'

'In a minute,' I murmured.

When we were both sitting comfortably, I talked us through the meditation as usual – *lightly in and lightly out, focus on the air passing through the nostrils, relax each part of the body starting from the crown of the head to the tips of the toes.* It was the part of the day I loved most, when everything, for a brief moment, seemed still and clear, and I felt some connection with Mum.

This morning, however, she kept clearing her throat and wriggling in her chair. She seemed impatient. 'No need for so much relax your neck, relax your arms, relax this and that. Anyone can relax. We need to forgive!' she said.

'Fine,' I said. 'I can change it if you want. Next time the meditation can be on forgiveness.' She looked at me, suspicious for a moment.

I turned her wheelchair and my chair so that we were facing each other. I reached forward to pick up her foot to massage it, but she said she would take her shoes off herself today. Her face was freshly made up, and she looked sweet in a purple floral skirt, matched with a pink cardigan and pink hair clips. Trousers were now too difficult to pull on, and tracksuit pants were *upchup* and sloppy, so Mum always wore loose dresses or skirts that Patsy had let out to fit over the lump on her stomach.

Mum lurched forward and took hold of one ankle with both hands. Jerking backwards, she hoisted her leg up. Sprawled against the back of the wheelchair, skirt fallen back, she lifted her foot towards her chest and yanked at her shoe. Her legs splayed, revealing pale knickers and bare thighs, still fleshy and not yet wasted.

I stood up to help her, at the same time averting my eyes – how coarse and clumsy she looked, but also sexy. An animality had appeared since her sickness that I had not noticed before. During all those years trussed in figure-hugging clothes, straight-backed and elegant, taking small steps and tugging her skirt down, she had been alluring but less alive than she was now. I wished Dad had caught a glimpse of what I had just seen in Mum. But perhaps he did see her like that behind closed doors. I hoped Mum had enjoyed sex, that somehow she was a different person in the dark, that she shed the constant self-discipline.

Dad had first noticed her, the prettiest and most elegant woman in Hong Kong, walking to and from church, surrounded by her suitors and friends. He had to work hard to attract her attention. He described her as 'exclusive'.

Dad had told me that while his seven brothers shared one small room and his sisters slept on the floor in the kitchen, he as the favoured son was allowed to sleep in his parents' bedroom until he was thirteen years old. A camp bed was kept at the foot of their four-poster bed for him. The first time Dad was woken up by their lovemaking, he called out, 'Get out! Get out!' He told me that in his half-sleep, he had thought someone was trying to saw a leg off the bed. 'Go back to sleep,' his father said. Dad imitated his father's gruff voice.

I never heard or saw my parents having sex. In my later teens, I realised how they had adapted to the thin walls between our bedrooms. First there was a click as the latch on their door came down, and then the rickety ceiling fan would be switched on to high, and soon all that could be heard was its thud, whirr and clank.

Up until our early teens, Mum would sometimes check on us in our rooms after we had gone to sleep. So quiet was she that often I did not wake until I felt her tugging at the bedsheet that was pulled up over my head. She feared I would suffocate, even though I told her that I always arranged the sheet so that there was a breathing-gap above my nose. Before leaving, she would sprinkle holy water on me and around the room. As soon as she closed the door, I covered my head with the sheet again.

On the occasions when Dad walked in, it was to wake us up because he had to share something that could not wait. One night he woke us at 2 a.m. to tell us he had seen the face of Jesus. He flung our bedroom doors open and spoke, walking up and down the corridor that joined the rooms, so all could hear. His voice was rich and full of wonder. 'It was not the gaunt face of Jesus at crucifixion as we see on the Turin Shroud,' he said. 'He appeared to me as he was in his element, preaching on the mount, walking on water, raising the dead! His face, how do I describe it? It was euphoric. Yes, boyish, brilliant and euphoric!'

Dad had woken us up before he became born again, too. Not long after we migrated to Australia, he got us out of bed to watch a late-night documentary on Hitler. 'One must know what this life is, and the infinite cruelty of man,' he said. I remembered how light my head felt, the same as when I was woken for Christmas midnight mass. I saw the image on the screen and thought how strange it looked and wondered why it was black and white when we had just bought a colour TV. A row of people were standing in front of a big pit. Maybe they were not human or they were in disguise, I thought, because their eyes were big and terrible, they had no clothes or hair, and they were as thin as skeletons. One by one, they fell into the pit after the pop from a soldier with a pointed gun. Mostly I remembered how Dad's eyes were intense and compassionate. Brow raised and head shaking, he looked at us and said, 'How could the world have let this happen?' He seemed heroic to me.

In that house on the hill in Hong Kong, before we came to Australia, my parents would wake us when they came home from parties. Sometimes Dad's voice was happy and excited, other times he and Mum were quarrelling. Anita had her own room, but Maria, Patsy and I shared a long room, like a dormitory. My bed was near the entrance, with Maria and Patsy at the other end, near the window. A few times after they quarrelled, Mum would enter our room and sit silently at the foot of my bed. Occasionally I heard a sigh. She seemed to stay there for a long while, a dark, still form.

I remembered one night when Dad came home raving and excited. He wasn't drunk – he hardly drank. He didn't need it, he said, he got drunk on life. The door was flung open and the light snapped on, hurting my eyes. His voice was sing-song and embracing: 'Wake up, girls. Taste the best durian cake in the world, the best! I said to the host of the party, "This is the best cake in the world, my daughters won't believe me," and she said, "Take, you must take some home for your pretty daughters, la."' My eyes were still straining under the light. He put his hand under my head. 'Come on, open your mouth.' His thick fingers shoved a chunk of sweet and sticky mush into my mouth. He stood in the middle of our room to tell us about the party.

'The most talented and handsome people in Hong Kong were there, and some Americans, you know how they speak, *Hiyaaaah youuallll.* This seven-foot-tall American in a gleaming white jacket is talking big in front of his sycophants. He pretends he knows all about modern art, and then I ask him in front of everyone, "So tell me, I'd be interested in your views on this, do you think the Dada movement can be said to be more of an art form or a philosophy?" "Uhh uhh uhhh" – this smart-alec man, as I guessed, had never even heard of the Dada movement. That silenced him. He should not be so vain!'

Maria, Patsy and I laughed, glad that Dad was happy and had shown up the American man.

'All right, sleep now, sweet dreams.' He switched off the light and was gone.

Suddenly the light came back on and it was Mum with a glass of water and a bowl in her hands. 'Here, gargle and spit. Do you want ants to eat all the sugar in your mouth?' This was the way Mum explained the effects of plaque. She went to Patsy first, making her sit up and sip the water. Patsy didn't know how to gargle, so Mum told her to drink it and then take another sip until there was no cake left in her mouth.

She came over to me, but I wouldn't sit up. 'What's the matter with you?' she said and pulled me up. 'Here, drink this water,' she said. I refused, and she forced the glass to my mouth, chinking the glass against my teeth. I spat the water out over the bed and started to cry, then to wail. I wouldn't stop. Mum went to get Dad and I stopped as soon as I heard him coming.

*

Mum was ready to talk now. She had taken her shoe off and smoothed her skirt down. I lifted her foot onto my lap and started to massage upwards, the way the physio had shown us, to move her circulation back up to her heart. Her foot, once sinewy and lined with veins, was now swollen and cold.

Usually I had my questions prepared. At the last session I had asked her about the period in Hong Kong after she married Dad. This time I was not sure what to talk about. I thought about Agnes, the servant and friend whom Maria, Patsy and I had liked most.

She had been getting too old for the orphanage where she'd grown up, so Mum had agreed to take her on as a servant to look after us kids. I could remember the first evening Agnes came to our house. She was dark-skinned, with rough hair and strong, thin limbs. All evening she hung her head low, answering yes or no when spoken to, but never looking up. It was only when Mum told her to help me make my bed and we were alone that she looked up and I saw she had pretty light-brown eyes, not dark-brown or black eyes like the rest of us.

'I will be your friend if you will be mine,' she said.

She was Anita's age but she was our friend, playing with us, even fighting with us when Mum wasn't looking.

But then one day I came home after school to a commotion at the foot of the stairs. Agnes was crouched over, clinging to the banister with both hands. Mum and Anita were wild and shouting, grabbing at her, tearing at her clothes, telling her to get out.

My next memory was of Agnes standing alone outside the driveway gate, crying. I asked her why she was crying. 'I'm not crying,' she said. 'I'm just sweating.'

I put Mum's foot down and picked up the other one. 'Remember Agnes, our servant from the orphanage?' I said. 'Did you know that after you fired her, she would come and meet us after school and bring us biscuits? I still don't know why you and Anita dragged her out of the house that time.'

'*Hmmmph.* Why do you always want to talk about bad things? So long ago. How can you even remember these things?' Mum said. 'You need to forgive and forget. Like Tom Bronson said. It will make you sick if you don't forgive.'

'Have you forgiven?' I asked.

Straightaway she said, 'Yes, I have.'

'Who did you have to forgive?'

'I have forgiven the Lord for taking Vincent from us.'

'What about Dad? Can you forgive him?' I tried to control my voice.

Her expression turned into a sneer. 'What for?' she said.

I rubbed my face. What did I want from her?

'It's you who must forgive your dad,' she said. 'He is a good man. He was very modern, but he is changed since he was born again. Many men are bad – they are like that. It's good he's not like his terrible brothers. Anyway we have Jesus now. We are saved.'

She pulled her foot off my lap. 'I'm tired,' she said. She pressed the lump on her stomach and screwed up her face.

'Sorry,' I said, but I don't think she heard.

'Why did you have to leave home like that? You didn't even finish school. Forgive!' she said.

I thought about the time when I was about thirteen years old, when I was so angry that I sat on a chair in the lounge room and would not talk or move. I couldn't remember now what had made me angry. Over three hours passed, and my sisters started to get scared. They pleaded with me, scolded me, poked, pushed and then hit me. Their blows hurt, but still I didn't move. As soon as I heard my parents arrive home, I got up and acted normal again.

If Mum could forgive, why couldn't I? Who was I to judge whether she had really forgiven him?

I could forgive. As Dad said, it was a decision, not an emotion. I could do it. I felt a weight lift off me.

THE LIGHT WAS ON AND THEY WERE BOTH IN THE room when I came to help Mum out of bed. It was Saturday morning, and the healing party was just two weeks away. She was sitting in her nightgown with the blanket pulled up to her chin. She smiled at me. Dad, freshly dressed and showered, was balanced on one side of the bed beside her. His eyes were serious and bright.

'Now, describe the dream again,' he said to Mum. 'Natasha will join me in bearing witness to it. Start from the beginning.'

'Okay ... I was sleeping,' she said slowly.

'Where?' said Dad.

'In my bed here, la.'

'Go on.'

'Then a man was standing right there with a big torch.' She pointed to where I stood at the foot of the bed. 'He was shining the torch at me.'

'How did he look?' asked Dad. 'Could you see his face?'

'No, he was in the dark.'

'That man, of course, is Jesus. Praise the Lord.' Dad clapped his hands, breaking the quiet of the room. 'Then what happened?'

'Suddenly I could walk. Then I was running. I ran into the backyard and over the fence.' She looked up to the ceiling, trying to remember more. 'That's all.'

'Right. What do you mean you ran over the fence? Which fence?' Dad said.

'This fence here.' She pointed to the window overlooking the backyard. I drew back the curtains. In the half-light of dawn, sky and fence formed two parallel strata. Beneath the layer of gleaming steel sky, the length of fence was black and impenetrable. 'I jumped over it,' she said.

'You *jumped* over the back fence? To the alley on the other side?' Dad asked.

'Yes.' Mum raised her shoulders, opened her eyes wide and gave a stricken, questioning smile.

'The Lord has sent us confirmation that you will be healed.' Dad clasped both of Mum's hands in his.

She closed her eyes and nodded. 'Isn't that good, Natasha?'

'Yes, that's a great dream, Mum,' I replied.

*

When I lifted Mum, it made a big difference if she could bear some of her own weight and move in sync with me. But this morning she was lost in her thoughts and it took twice as long to transfer her onto the shower bench. Emerging from the bathroom, I heard thuds coming from the backyard. I went to the window in Mum and Dad's room, and saw Dad standing outside with a spade in his hand. Clad in a stained terry-towelling hat, old brown skivvy, gardening gloves and socks pulled over his trousers, he looked like the peasant labourers I had seen in Hong Kong.

He stood on the paved path that stopped halfway down the right-hand side of the backyard. At the end of this paving was the Hills Hoist and a shed – the only reasons we ever ventured out there. Dad walked to the edge of the pavers and gazed across the sea of weeds and long grass to the other side of the yard. Then he raised the spade, shouted out '*horrr, worr, hiyah!*' and violently and repeatedly stabbed the ground in front of him. He then stepped off the pavers onto the ground he had attacked. He raised the spade again and repeated the whole process, making his way forward through the grass one step at a time.

I found Maria in the kitchen and asked her to listen out for Mum in the shower. Returning to Mum and Dad's room, I opened the door to the backyard and stepped outside. Dad was halfway towards the opposite fence now. The air was cold and the smell of the crushed weeds was over-sweet. A thin trail of flattened grass led to him.

'What are you doing?' I yelled to his back.

He turned his head. 'Natasha? Good, I need your help. Stay on the pavers. Don't come here until I have frightened away the snakes.'

'What snakes?' I called back.

'What did you say?' he said, continuing his grunting and *hiyah* and stabbing.

'Never mind.' I went inside and brought out a load of washing to hang while I waited.

When he arrived at the opposite fence, he turned and shouted, 'See, I have created a safe corridor.' He gestured grandly at the cut through the grass. 'Now you can walk across. When you walk, you must stomp hard to show the snakes you're coming. Show them who's boss. Come on!' He stamped his feet, putting his whole body into it, as if dancing a jig.

I followed his trail. 'Stomp!' he yelled. I stamped my feet hard, making swarms of little insects rise. He grinned.

When I reached him, I asked again, 'What are you doing?'

'You will know soon enough,' he chuckled. He picked through the old planks that leant against the fence, making a pile out of the useable pieces and throwing aside the rotten ones. Then he threw me a rag and I set about brushing the dirt off the planks he had selected.

'Now we must carry these planks of wood two at a time over to the pavers. You take one end. I will take the front. *Hoi!*' He lifted, hunching his shoulders with the load, waiting for me to pick up the tail end. 'Follow me!' he cried, and we lumbered and lifted and stamped back and forth in tandem until a dozen planks lay scattered on the pavers.

He placed the four longest planks side by side on the ground so that they formed a long rectangle. The shorter pieces he laid crossways at regular intervals on top of the long planks. Stepping back, he surveyed his work. 'You know, I have never done any carpentry before. But once you have an artist's eye, you can visualise anything, unlock its internal structure. Like Leonardo da Vinci!' He gave me a hammer and showed me where to drive nails into the cross pieces.

'Are you making a table?' I asked.

He chuckled.

'What about a raft?'

'Too many bible stories,' he said, and we both laughed.

'You know, you must make kung fu sounds when you exert yourself. It's not just for show or to scare the opponent; it is to release the force in you – *wor, hor, yu, hiyah!*' he shouted. 'Now, watch me cut the wood. You do not push and pull the saw like an ox. It must be like Chinese brush painting. You get a feel of the medium, the poetry of it, you find the right angle and it's like slicing through butter. You see, in everything I do, there is art.' The saw in his hand screeched, caught and buckled on the wood. He stopped to catch his breath and again we laughed. 'Of all my daughters, you alone have inherited an understanding of art from me.' His eyes met mine and I knew he was flattering me. He was turning on the charm. Not for his audience or for the girls he wanted to admire him. For me. I turned my face away so he could not see my pleasure.

We had used up nearly all the wood and nails. The structure was around three metres long and a metre wide. 'Now bring your mum to the window,' Dad said. 'Tell everyone to stop what they're doing and come now! Then I will tell you all what I'm doing!'

I went inside and summoned them. Mum, showered and dressed, was taking her breakfast and medicine in the kitchen with Patsy. Charles had arrived with a second freezer to hold the food we were preparing for the party. He and Maria pushed and pulled it into the kitchen while Anita held Will out of the way. But now everyone stopped what they were doing and went to Mum and Dad's room. I positioned Mum at the glass panel closest to the paved area. The rest of the family crowded around us.

'I can't believe it – Dad doing the gardening?' Anita said.

'No. Wait and see.' I opened the door and windows as wide as they could go and stuck my head out. 'We're all here!' I shouted.

Dad looked up and smiled. Using the saw like a walking stick, and putting on a Charlie Chaplin waddle, he approached the window. His voice projected loud and clear. 'Your mother had a dream of the miracle. No, not a dream, but a vision the Lord has sent to us . . . She will rise from the wheelchair and jump over that fence.' He pointed to her, then to the back fence.

'But is it humanly possible to jump over such a high fence?' he went on. 'The Lord put it on my heart to build you a ramp, Irene. A ramp to help you jump over the fence. So we shall meet Jesus halfway! See these arms, see this saw, see this ramp!' Lifting the saw high, he waved it at the wooden structure sitting on the pavers. 'The ramp to salvation!' he cried.

Mum pouted and giggled. '*Sweia*,' she said.

'Not silly,' he said, emitting a mock-angry *harrummph*. 'We are stepping out in faith!'

It was wonderful to see them like that.

*

My sisters, Charles, Will and I plonked ourselves onto couches in the family room, buzzing with the work we had done that morning and glad to rest. Mum looked happy. Dad sat next to her, holding her hand. On Saturdays my sisters had other engagements in the evenings, so on this day we gathered for family prayers before lunch. Gentle light filtered through the drawn curtains. 'Come to me/ All who labour and are heavy burdened/ And I shall give you rest,' we sang as one. Dad thanked Jesus for our family, this special, blessed family, and for the vision of Mum jumping over the fence. I shut my eyes and soaked up the feeling of our closeness and beauty.

Dad led us into tongues. I would usually speak in tongues only in private, not wanting them to know I still spoke this way. But now I opened my mouth and let the words flow. *Unay unay astinor, umbala meshala . . .*

They thought that I had rejected the gifts of the spirit, but it wasn't true. I often spoke in tongues when I was alone. At night when I was scared, or at times when I was stressed; when I heard Mum had cancer and when I couldn't sleep; when a sight was beautiful and my spirit rejoiced, I did it without thinking. It calmed me, made me feel lighter, in the same way that meditation did.

Maria, Patsy and I had learnt to speak in tongues soon after my twelfth birthday. At a prayer meeting in the Christian Life Centre in Ringwood, Dad led Maria, Patsy and me up to the front to receive the holy spirit. Anita was not there. The three of us stood side by side, while Dad and the preacher and his wife stood facing us. We needed only to open our mouths, to make any sounds we liked and the Lord would start to speak his heavenly language through us, the preacher said. They put their hands on our heads. I got the preacher's wife. I peeped over at Maria and Patsy. Their eyes were closed. Suddenly a babble of words was coming out of Maria's mouth, first softly, then louder and she flung her head back and *be be be be be ne ne ne ne* issued in a machine-gun rattle from her lips.

'Out of the mouth of babes! Praise be to Jesus,' said the preacher.

It was amazing the way Maria, whom we thought slow to pick up new things, took to tongues in an instant. The preacher's wife intensified her prayer over me, vibrating her hands on my head and bringing her face closer to mine. I could still remember that thin, glamorous face almost touching mine, the suffocating sweetness of her perfume, her warm breath and its slight staleness overladen with mint. Worried about taking too long, I started to make sounds similar to hers – *shemala, shemala*. She praised Jesus. At first I was just copying, but after more prayer meetings, I was confident enough to open my mouth and say whatever came into my head, even if it sounded foolish. Soon the words and sounds flowed without thought or effort.

Now, as I joined my tongues to theirs, Mum looked at me, raised her eyebrows and smiled. I could have sat there in the dim light and the warm, candle-scented air with my family all day long. I knew the tongues of each of them. Dad's were like no one else's: a performance of sound and passion that told a story, travelling high then low, going from smooth to staccato, loud to soft, resembling Japanese then Russian. The Charismatic community knew his tongues well. Often, while the group was in silent prayer, he would break into tongues, as though overcome by the spirit. I knew Mum's whispery tongues, *usha, usha, sha*, Patsy's monosyllables drawn out into high, unearthly notes, and Maria's fast flow of babble, *ne ne ne ne be be be be*.

After prayers, we warmed up the noodles and chicken curry, Dad's favourites, that Anita had cooked. When we were seated, Maria called Dad to the table. He said grace. With a passive sadness, Mum gazed at the dishes of oily, condiment-heavy noodles and the fragrant yellow curry. Her eyes did not move from the glistening dishes when Patsy put a plate of steamed liver and vegetables in front of her.

'Mum, take a day off the liver and have some noodles,' I said.

'No, no, I can't eat it. You all enjoy,' she said. She spooned a lump of the grey liver into her mouth, then checked what Patsy had served herself. Only a few pieces of raw carrot and steamed broccoli sat on Patsy's plate. 'You can't eat just vegetables! Take the chicken!' she said.

Anita put some chicken on Patsy's plate. Patsy put it on my plate. I returned it to Patsy's plate. Maria was on her feet, passing sauces around and serving drinks, and Charles was trying to stop Will from flinging noodles all over the table. Only Dad ate without interruption. He would not talk until he had finished his first serve, and relaxed with a second.

Today he had words of praise for everyone. 'The Lord has chosen our family to lead and inspire His people,' he said. He praised Mum's vision of jumping the fence, my ability as his assistant in ramp-making, Anita's leadership and cooking, Charles's ingenuity in finding a freezer, Maria's faith and her achievement of drawing twelve new guests to the party, and Patsy's sensitive hands (she had given him a shoulder massage after his work on the ramp). 'Can we, who have the privilege of being called by Jesus of the Holy Cross to serve Him and spread the Good News, give our all?'

Sitting back in his chair at the end of the meal, Dad said, 'Oh yes, Natasha, a young Charismatic man rang. You need to ring him back.'

'I don't know any young Charismatic men,' I said.

'He said you met at the faith rally. I wrote down his name and number.' Dad pulled out a scrap of paper from his trouser pocket and unfolded it. 'His name is Ed.'

I thought of the long-haired, dark-eyed man on the stairs. 'But I never gave him my number.'

'Remember when Dad was on stage and announced his phone number and address to everyone?' said Anita.

'Why would he ring Natasha?' Patsy demanded.

'We met when he carried Mum's wheelchair up the stairs and again when the preacher was casting out the devil from that woman and I went outside.'

'What were you talking about?' Patsy said.

'Nothing,' I said.

Anita looked amused. 'Maybe he wants to ask Natasha out.'

Patsy gasped. 'That man is not allowed to use the number to ask us out – Dad gave out the number for the healing party.'

Dad laughed. 'You should all thank me, girls, if you single ones get boyfriends out of this!'

'Natasha's not single,' said Maria.

I steeled myself to tell them. Now was as a good a time as any, in fact it was better – with Dad there, and the family together, the discussion would stay on the surface. 'I am, actually,' I said.

Maria's eyes became sympathetic. 'Did you break up with Jason?'

'It was time,' I said, starting to clear dishes from the table.

Anita gave me an appraising look. 'No job and no boyfriend. You can come back to Melbourne now.'

Mum lifted her shoulders and smiled at me. 'Maybe it is God's will.'

'Go and call Ed back now, Natasha,' said Dad.

'When did he ring?' I asked.

'It could have been a week ago,' Dad said.

'And you didn't pass on the message?' I said.

'It was lost among my papers, but today Jesus led me to see it,' Dad said. 'The Lord put it on my heart that this man is the one who is going to clear the back garden for us. You must ring him now!'

'Dad, Natasha can't just say hi, Ed, by the way, come and do our gardening,' said Anita.

'He can only say no,' said Dad. 'But something tells me he won't. He seemed a nice man on the phone and he said he was inspired by Mum and me on stage. Ring him. See if he can come right now. Ask if he has something to cut long tough grass, like a scythe, a powered scythe.'

'You mean a brush cutter? I know where to get one,' said Charles.

'No, you are needed to set up the freezer. Let this young man get it,' said Dad. 'Now go and ring him, Natasha. Do it for the Lord. So I can put out the ramp and Mum can run through the garden and fulfil the miracle! You've finished your lunch. Go on, ring now. Have faith!'

*

'Is Ed there?' I asked, though I already knew it was him from his hello.

'Natasha, how are you?' he said. His voice sounded slow and nonchalant over the phone, uncannily like Jason's. 'Easygoing' was how people who didn't know Jason well described him, but they had no idea of the energy it took to maintain that drawl over his nervousness.

'Sorry I didn't ring back earlier. I only just got your message,' I said.

'I thought I might have offended you.'

'Why?'

'You know, using the number your father gave out for the healing party to ring you instead.'

'No, I would have rung you back. My father's rotten at passing on messages.'

'There's a Life in the Spirit seminar on at the Christian Ministry Centre. I thought you might be interested in going, or we could have coffee?'

'Coffee would be good.'

'Cool, when?'

'Actually, were you thinking about coming to the healing party?'

'Yes, I was, but I didn't want it to be, like ... I'll explain later.'

'Would you be interested in helping us prepare the backyard for the party – do some gardening? Some pretty heavy gardening, actually. It's a jungle. My father suggested it. You can say no. He just wanted me to ask ...'

'Sure. When?'

'Are you free this afternoon? You've probably got something else on —'

'I can leave in about an hour.'

'Also ...' Now to ask for the brush cutter.

'Yep?'

'Do you need our address?' I couldn't. I would get the brush cutter from Charles's friend instead.

*

It didn't take me long to pick up the cutter. I carried it to the backyard and laid it on top of the ramp. CTJ, singing ministry members and others were starting to arrive for practice. I made tea and coffee for the visitors and looked out for Ed. When he arrived at the front door, Dad, who was in the lounge room with his drama group, got there first. He was shaking Ed's hand and patting him on the shoulder when I reached them.

'Hi,' I said, giving him a small wave. Urbane and good-looking, he smiled at me, and I suddenly felt nervous.

Dad led Ed into the lounge room, where Maria introduced herself with a big, welcoming smile and a hug. Watching her clenched hands, I thought how open she would appear to be to anyone who didn't know that she couldn't tolerate touch unless it was her hugging you or giving you a massage. She could give, but not receive.

'Say hello to Ed, our wonderful new volunteer,' said Dad, presenting him to the members of the drama group. Dad directed the actors to do scene two again, starting with Maria's part. 'Just watch for a few minutes,' he said to Ed. 'I am very proud of this group. They are performing a play I wrote specially for the healing party.'

The lounge furniture had been moved aside to create a stage area by the front window. The actors took their places. On Dad's instruction, the actors in the background started shaking their heads and wagging their fingers at each other. Maria stepped forward with a cushion under her shirt. She fell on her knees and spoke to her padded tummy. 'I can feel you; you are real, you are alive! But if I keep you, I will lose my husband ... What can I do?'

Now the attractive young actor, Dad's favourite, came out. She spread out her hands to the audience. 'They tell me I have cancer, that I will never dance again ... What can I do?'

The other actors filled the stage, all singing, 'Choose life, give it a go, choose life ...'

Ed watched with a polite half-smile on his face. Dad clapped his hands and shouted, 'Marvellous! Carry on!' to the cast, then opened the glass doors that led into the family room, guiding Ed through. I followed. Patsy on keyboard, a teenage boy on drums and two middle-aged women on guitar sang in rock-opera style. 'Dare to believe. Dare to be filled. Dare to rise up ...' Patsy's voice soared above the others. Her face, usually introverted and stiff, became flushed and even pretty when she sang.

When they finished, Dad applauded, and Ed and I joined in. 'Splendid,' Dad said, turning to Ed. 'Like it? Lyrics by me. The song will make its debut at the healing party! Tune by Patsy, my youngest daughter. She has real talent. Patsy, this is Ed.' Patsy gave a shy smile and shook Ed's hand. 'Carry on singing,' he said, and led us towards the kitchen.

Dad walked slowly, looking with intent at his pictures lining the walls. He stopped in front of a recent favourite: a face of Jesus about three metres high in thick black outline. Inside the giant face of Jesus, myriad small faces were depicted, some prayerful, others evil and lascivious. Blood, represented by a writhing mass of red paint, spouted from Jesus's head where a crown of thorns pierced it.

'Is this too much, I asked, when I finished it – is this too ... too ... phenomenal for the Australian public to take? Tell me honestly, Ed, what do you think?'

'I don't know much about art, but this picture and the others – are they all yours? – seem very powerful to me,' said Ed.

'Yes, powerful. All my art is made to serve the Lord. Even the ones I do on commission, I will place the cross of Jesus in it somewhere so whether or not the buyer realises, it will witness to them!'

We entered the kitchen. The wives of the Missionaries for Christ community were here to help. Their busy hands chopped, washed up, stirred steaming pots. One husband crouched on the floor with Charles, setting up the wiring for the extra freezers and ovens. Anita walked around, directing operations. Her voice was clear and confident: 'Chop up twelve more onions, please ... put the oven there to make more room ... time to turn off the pan ...'

'We shall feed the masses at the healing party,' Dad called out. 'Not just food of the spirit, but also food for the stomach!' He guffawed at his joke and ushered Ed over to Anita. 'Meet our outstanding chef and master of ceremonies, my firstborn, Anita. She was recently made a manager, you know, at an international property development company!' He started to introduce Charles, but was called to the other room by a drama group member.

Anita managed to make conversation with Ed while keeping an eye on everything in the kitchen and instructing the volunteers. In just a few minutes, she found out that he worked as an attendant in an old folks home, lived by himself in a rented flat in Collingwood and had finished a psychology degree about five years ago.

With the living areas overrun, Mum was confined to her room. I brought Ed in to say hello. Mum was propped up against pillows, talking and praying with Maureen and Liz from her cell group. She wore her day clothes and dainty slippers, with the bible open on her lap. Maureen and Liz sat on chairs pulled up to the bed. Maureen read from her bible: '"Cast all your anxiety on him because he cares for you. Be alert and of sober mind. Your enemy the devil prowls around like a roaring lion looking for someone to devour."'

'That's a great passage,' Ed offered. He walked over, manly and well mannered, took each of their hands in turn and introduced himself. He asked after Mum's health with warmth and concern, and reminded her that they had met at the faith rally.

'You carried my wheelchair up the stairs, didn't you? That was so nice of you,' she said. She lifted her shoulders and smiled in that girly way she had. I felt proud that I had brought him home to the family.

In the backyard next to the Hills Hoist, Dad spoke to Ed like a prophet running out of time. He bounced on his feet, his eyes flashing, and spittle flying from his mobile mouth. He told the story of the dream, pointing to the ramp, the earth and the sky, and exhorted Ed to civilise the garden. Not only would the weeds need to be cleared, he said, the cactus would also need to be cut back to make way for the ramp. 'Watch out for snakes and use the corridor I created through the grass.' He grasped Ed's shoulder. 'We thank the Lord for sending you to us so we can bear witness to the world of His power and mercy.' Dad rushed back inside, leaving us in silence.

'Well, there you have it,' I said. I searched Ed's face for a reaction.

Turning away from me, Ed pulled off his leather jacket. He had a faded black T-shirt on underneath, and his long, thin, muscled back showed through. I had sensed a connection between us. Maybe I was wrong.

'Ready to get started,' he said, swinging his jacket over the Hills Hoist. Then he turned around and winked. It was one of those casual Aussie winks that involved cocking the face to one side. I didn't know what it meant, but it felt conspiratorial and I liked it.

For the next three hours, we cleared away wood and debris, cut down the grass and weeds, and raked. I appreciated the way he made sure we took turns pulling on the cord of the brush cutter to get it started, although it was obvious that he had the longer arm and the stronger pull. When it blared into action in his hands, he invited me to go first. Initially I held it almost horizontal, scared of the rapacious blade. After a few minutes I found the right angle to carry and control it without it being too high or too close, and how to adjust the strap so that most of the weight was taken across the shoulders, not in the arms. At the blade's touch, foliage flew in all directions. I held the cutter until my arms trembled, then Ed took over. He worked fast and fervently.

When the last bushy corner was mown, we turned off the cutter. The racket stopped and the white spinning slowed until the blades could be seen. We surveyed our work. The back garden looked flat and open and somehow smaller, emptied of its dangers and mysteries, like a pool with the water drained. All that remained were the ten cacti lining the back fence. Dad had planted them about thirteen years ago, at two-metre intervals. They were pot-plant size back then. Now they were taller than the three-metre-high fence and so wide that their stems tangled with each other.

'We should finish up now,' I said, but Ed was determined to keep going. Covered in sweat and smeared with dirt and grass, he picked up the saw and strode towards the first of the four cacti that Dad had marked for removal. I left him there while I went to have a shower and take the brush cutter back to its owner. We planned to go out for dinner after I got back.

*

When I returned to the backyard an hour later, only a few cactus stems were shorn off and tossed on the ground, and Maria stood next to Ed at the back fence. She was doing all the talking. She spoke with half-closed, dreamy eyes. A smile played gently upon her lips. I caught a few words before they noticed me coming: '… the unconditional love and truth of Jesus … break the chains of anger … spiritual healing …' Her voice was rich and self-possessed.

Maria saw me, and the dreamy look left her. 'Oh, I'd better let you get on with it,' she said. 'Thanks for talking.' She gave Ed a radiant smile and walked inside.

Time had flown while they were talking, Ed said. He wanted to finish removing the stems from one cactus before it got dark. I left him to it and walked back inside to look for Maria. She, Mum and Patsy were at Mum's window, watching Ed work.

I went straight over to Maria. 'What were you talking about with Ed?'

'He was interested in joining my Agape group. He's searching for spiritual healing of his past.'

'You mean you were poking and prying. Trying to find out

people's problems as usual. So you can preach,' I said.

'Tsk-tsk-tsk, don't be like that, Natasha,' said Mum.

'He wanted to talk. Can't we just talk?' said Maria.

'Sure,' I said. 'As soon as you see someone you think might be vulnerable, you just home in!'

'Maria talks with people so she can help them,' Patsy said, her voice trembling. 'What about you? What were you doing with him at the faith rally?'

'What are you going on about?' I said.

'Why did he ask you out? Were you at the rally to flirt?' said Patsy.

'What's the matter with you, Patsy?' I said. I could have said, *Are you jealous?* but that would have been too mean; we all knew she had never had a boyfriend or even a male friend. Instead I gave a patronising shake of my head. She stood there in her pinafore, prim, prudish and furious.

'Tsk-tsk,' Mum scolded again. 'Anyway, he's a very polite, Christian man. Very good in the garden too.'

We all watched him in silence for a while. He was stretched up on his toes, reaching for the higher cactus stems with the saw.

'Where are you going tonight? Don't let him take advantage of you, okay?' Mum said.

'Mum, did you really have to say that?' I said.

'Pity Jason wasn't a Christian. He seemed like a good man,' Mum said. 'Why didn't you get engaged? So long you have been together. Must never have sex before marriage. Why marry if they can get what they want?

'Jason was nice,' said Maria.

'I know,' said Mum. 'Anyway, now you will go out with a Christian man. Don't be a srut, okay?'

'Mum!' Patsy, Maria and I said.

*

Ed showered at our home and put on a good shirt that he had brought with him. I had on a collared shirt under a black wool jumper. At the last moment I took off the collared shirt and put the black jumper back on so there was nothing under it but my bra, and my cleavage showed at the V. I covered up with a jacket before leaving my room. Ed suggested he book an Italian restaurant on Lygon Street, but I didn't want it to seem as though he was taking me out on a date. I insisted it was my shout after all his work in the garden, and told him I preferred something tasty and quick, like Vietnamese in Richmond.

It was dark by the time we got to Victoria Street. I was immediately excited by the smells, the food and the bustle. Everywhere were Vietnamese restaurants with menus written on tiled walls and plastic chairs and tables, filling up with hungry diners. Walking along the footpath, we skirted around people and the wares and crates of produce spilling out of the shops. Anglo Australians towered over the Vietnamese. A couple of older Vietnamese walked around in pyjamas, as they did in Hong Kong. Ed walked close to me, so that occasionally we bumped shoulders.

'Crowded around here. I'd better not lose you,' he said.

'Can't tell us Asians apart?' I said, and he laughed and seemed to be more at ease.

Ed liked the look of a restaurant that was only half full, but I persuaded him that a crowd was a sign of good food. I was enjoying myself, and feeling confident enough to say what I liked. I remembered the easy excitement at the start of a new relationship – how effortless it was to be thrilled at each other, the pleasure of feeling immersed. Before Jason, all my relationships had lasted a few months at most. They started with a bang and petered out as more and more self-doubt crept in. I became pathetic, constantly trying to second-guess what was expected of me.

But right now I felt I could do no wrong. I pulled Ed into a crowded restaurant. We squeezed into the only available table, ordered, then went outside for a smoke.

'Your father and mother on stage at the rally – they really moved me with their faith,' said Ed. 'I wanted to come to the healing party. And I wanted to see you, too. I didn't want to use the party as an excuse to see you, or to confuse the two things. That's why I decided to ring and ask you out. I thought that if you said no, then I wouldn't make you feel uncomfortable by turning up to the healing party.'

I didn't feel flattered or wonder what he had seen in me. I knew that sometimes guys liked you for reasons that had nothing to do with you.

When Ed was not talking or engaged, his gaze kept shifting around. I took the opportunity to look at him while he rolled a cigarette. He had a sharp, cultivated face and dark liquid eyes half hidden under heavy, long-lashed lids. I liked his eyes, his long hair and his nose too, which had a bulbous drooping tip and saved him from handsomeness. Bending his mouth to the cigarette, he licked the length of the glue-lined paper and looked up at me through his lashes.

An old man came up and asked Ed for a cigarette. A minute later a youth who looked like he had been sleeping rough asked Ed if he could spare some change. With each of them, Ed obliged with a warm courtesy and found something to talk about before they went their way.

Through the restaurant's glass front, we saw the food arrive at our table. We stubbed out our cigarettes and went back inside. I ordered a beer but Ed, looking down at the table, said he would stay with the tea. The waiters zipped around, unerring with their hot, heavily laden trays. I thought he was being over-polite, stopping them to ask how their day was and to thank them. I liked the way he ate. He divided stuff up, pushed portions over to my side and said to me, 'Eat.' Some men, like my father, ate with an eagerness that bordered on desperation. Others, like many Anglo men, ate with a disdain for the food, but Ed ate well and with ease.

'Your family are really funny and nice,' he said.

'Funny and nice. I'm glad you said that and not "inspiring", which makes me want to throw up.'

'They are, though. Something about the way your father talks makes you feel there are exciting possibilities in this world and you can be part of them. And your mother is beautiful. And your sisters are very interesting. And your cacti are out of this world and *inspiring* ... I can't believe I'm slaving away for that ramp your father made. Worst piece of woodwork I've ever seen.'

We laughed, but his eyes were moist and I thought, *Oh no, he has fallen for my family.*

'What would you normally do on a Saturday night?' I said.

'There's a meeting at the Christian Life Centre in North Fitzroy.

Tonight there's a preacher from South Africa. Would you like to go to that? We could catch the end of it after dinner.'

I shook my head. 'You must have the wrong idea about me. I was only at the faith rally for my mum.'

'Were you ever into it?'

'For about two years when I was twelve years old and my parents became born again,' I said, then changed the subject. The last thing I wanted was to swap conversion stories.

After dinner, I wanted to go to the Tote for a drink. It was only a few blocks away, I remembered. I had not been there since Bonnie and I would sneak in when we were seventeen. Ed was not keen, but in my assertive mood, I persuaded him to go.

He drove the couple of blocks, past a bluestone school, boarded-up warehouses and rows of toy-like wooden cottages, and we saw the tired old pub on the corner.

We felt the thumps before we entered the narrow door. It was half dark, crowded, fuggy and smoky; a punk band screamed from the low stage.

'What would you like to drink?' Ed shouted in my ear.

'A vodka and soda. I'll be over there.' I pointed to the gyrating throng in front of the band. Ed made his way to the bar. I squeezed closer to the stage and soon I was jumping in rhythm with the group next to me. Some minutes later, I turned around to a tap on my shoulder. Ed handed me my drink and gestured that he would be on the other side of the room. He looked too serious. I emptied the glass, closed my eyes and bounced around some more to the beat. Then I left my space near the stage and went looking for him.

He sat with his back against the wall in a corner near the door. His jaw was held at a weird angle and his eyes, surveying the room, looked agonised.

'Why aren't you drinking?' I shouted at him, almost angry.

'I'm an alcoholic,' he shouted back.

Of course I knew. The realisation had been growing since I'd met him – the way he seemed so lost and vulnerable, his eyes that were always on the alert, his careful courtesy to others, his reluctance to drink or go to the pub.

Without talking, we walked outside and found the car. In the car he pulled me to him, pushed his lips against mine so fast and hard that our teeth clashed. He poked his tongue deep into my mouth. With one hand gripping my neck and the other my back, he clasped me to him, his heartbeat frantic at my breast. I kissed him back, caressed his hair, his back, stroked down towards his hips, his groin.

He pushed me away. His breath was ragged. 'I'm sorry. I want to respect you,' he said.

'You are respecting me,' I said, and moved back towards him. He yanked open the car door and stepped out. With quick steps he walked to the corner and back, then got in and started the car.

He smoked one cigarette after another as he drove. On the freeway he asked me, 'Do you believe in God?'

'Yes, I do,' I said. 'An abstract one.'

'I knew you did,' he said.

'What about you?'

'Yes.'

'Did you before becoming Charismatic?' I asked.

'Yes, in an abstract way, too. I think it was beauty I was looking for, rather than God. But adoration of beauty causes pain. I remember looking at the sky as a child, seeing its blueness and crying because I couldn't hold it in my hands.' He glanced at me and shrugged his shoulders.

'And now?' I said.

'Now I find Jesus is tangible,' he said. 'Have you ever experienced Jesus in a real way?'

I put on my mock American preacher voice. 'Sister, have you experienced Jesus in your life?' I looked at his face and immediately regretted my gibe. 'I'm sorry, I know it was a genuine question,' I said. He picked up my hand from my lap and squeezed it. I stared out the window at the road and concentrated on answering his question. 'Earlier this year, in Darwin, everything seemed to be going wrong and I kept trying to get on top of it, find solutions, change, but it just made me more and more anxious. Finally, one night I was having a kind of panic attack. I felt like my head would implode. Then I just let everything go. I gave up control and suddenly felt God or some kind of peace or infinite power fill the space.'

'I know what you mean,' he said.

Blondie's 'Atomic' came on the radio. 'I love this song,' I said, and turned it up. My heart thumped with the urgency of the rhythm as it lifted off, the synth, her moans and the lyrics: *Uh-huh, Make it magnificent! Tonight*... I thought about the healing party a fortnight away, and of the magnificent efforts of my mother, my father and my sisters, and I felt so proud and desperate that I could have sobbed.

Ed dropped me back home and I saw him every day until the healing party. Each day, after he finished the early shift at the old folks home, he would arrive at my parents' house and do battle with the monstrous multi-limbed cacti. He would take to the thick, tough stems with an assortment of saws, axes and spades, starting with the outer layer and working towards the centre. He learnt to wear goggles after a thorn stabbed him near the eye, and he discovered that the white slimy cactus juice would infect the cuts that multiplied on his arms and legs. When the stems lay hacked and weeping on the ground and there was only stump left, Ed would dig, ram and saw into the ground to remove the cactus's massive root ball, buried deep and knotted in the earth.

THE COVER OF CLOUD HUNG AROUND ALL DAY, neither brewing into rain nor dispersing. Silver-grey and implacable, it filmed over our heads, too high, it seemed, to give the clear sign my family asked of God that all would be fine for tonight's healing party.

On the left side of our house, a cladded-steel gate blocked the driveway that gave access to the backyard. It had rusted shut, but we wanted to open it for the party, so people could enter without going through the house. Ed and I put our shoulders to the gate, rocking and pushing until the hinges screeched and it cracked free. We then moved behind the gate and pulled it open until we were sandwiched between it and the side of the house. Hidden behind the gate, we kissed.

How happy Ed seemed, working in our backyard. He had removed several years' worth of junk and wild growth. He'd tamed the lawn, vanquished the cacti and set up the ramp, even decorating it with fairy lights, all with an inordinate amount of pleasure and purpose. Not for the first time, I felt a twinge of sadness for him. What emptiness possessed his heart that he was so content to serve someone else's dream?

The guests were arriving at about six o'clock, just over an hour away. The drama group, musicians, friends and church people had been coming and going all afternoon, laden with crates, props, instruments, ice, eskys and trays of food.

Dad was sleeping in his studio to build up his energy. 'Wake me at five o'clock, or if there is an important call,' he had said. Mum was lying down in her room. The dozen or so members of the drama group were still rehearsing, directed by Troy, a priestly young man Dad had made his second in command. Patsy and the music ministry had set down their instruments and were bringing out the plates and glasses. Anita, in full director mode, could be heard snapping out orders in the kitchen and all through the house. She was clear and good-humoured with the ten or so mainly middle-aged ladies volunteering in the kitchen, the same ladies you saw preparing the refreshments at all the Charismatic gatherings. Out of their earshot, however, she would be terse, giving tongue-lashings to Charles and her sisters. Maria was well out of the way. She had been given the job of doorknocking the neighbours to remind them our street would be full of cars and visitors tonight. We had letter-boxed invitations a couple of weeks earlier and hoped their sympathy for Mum would lead them to be tolerant.

'Get off from there, you might fall,' I told Will and his friend, a neighbour's five-year-old daughter. They were crawling up the ramp, which took centre stage against the back fence, flanked by the six remaining cacti. Ed had put in hours of cutting, sanding and reinforcing to improve the ramp. Still, it remained what it was – a few pieces of timber knocked together by Dad, a rough and ready makeshift gangplank leaning against the fence at an odd angle.

The ramp was attached about three-quarters of the way up the fence, low enough so that it wasn't too steep to climb, and high enough so that Mum, in fulfilment of the dream, could jump over the fence. But who would do that unless they wanted to break their neck in the deep fall to the alley on the other side? All the same, there was something precarious and grand about it. You could imagine the ramp as a platform to raise you into the sky, maybe.

Neither Will nor his friend got off the ramp as they were told, so I strode over to them. Will sat halfway up the ramp with his legs out in front of him as though he were on a slide. The little girl, giggling, crawled up the ramp, past Will, then raised herself to a standing position and looked down her nose at me. 'Is Mrs Chan going to get up out of her wheelchair and run up here? That's what Will said!'

'Did not!' said Will. 'I only said she *might*!'

'Well?' they both demanded.

I realised I was exhausted. 'We can only hope,' I said.

They scrambled down and ran off, no longer interested, and I went back inside. The double doors between the lounge and family room had been pinned back to create a large open area. Furniture and effects had been removed and jammed wherever there was space in the other rooms. The floor had been cleared, but Dad's pictures stayed on the walls, taking on an even greater prominence. The house had the look and feel of a public gallery waiting to be filled.

I went to see if Mum was ready to get up. This was, of course, a different kind of party, but we couldn't help but compare it with the many Dad and Mum had hosted in the past. Mum should have been out there, taking charge of the kitchen and house, whipping up her dishes, counting the guests, calculating how much food and drink was needed, sorting out the serving, getting stressed and curbing Dad's excesses. A few times she had ventured out of her room to join in the preparations but had been distant and abstracted, and hardly able to string sentences together.

In the bedroom, Patsy was pulling a dress over Mum's head. 'Soon you'll be doing this yourself,' she said. 'You won't need me!'

'Praise the Lord,' mumbled Mum.

I helped her lean to one side while Patsy pulled the dress under her bottom and arranged it around her legs. It was the ankle-length blue silk cheongsam that Dad always said made her look like the glamorous Hong Kong star Nancy Kwan. Dad had insisted that the family wear Chinese garb for the healing party. 'Our guests will think it very cute and Asian,' he had said.

Patsy struggled with the zip of the dress. Mum's eyes slid away from the image of herself in the mirror. The dress had always cinched, slinked and slid in all the right places, but now it strained over her bloated belly and sagged everywhere else. Patsy draped a shawl over Mum and knotted it at the front.

'It's going to be difficult using the toilet with that long dress,' I said.

'That's all right. Mum's going to be healed,' Patsy said, lifting her voice at 'healed' and smiling. Patsy had her ascetic look on, which was usually reserved for singing. Mum nodded and forced a smile. I started to arrange her shawl as an excuse to stroke her shoulders.

She pulled away. 'You haven't dressed yet?' Mum said to me. 'Go on. Wear something nice. And wake up Dad now.'

Dad was already showered and dressed in a bright Confucian-style shirt. He was gleaming with freshness and the Brylcreem in his hair. Geoff had arrived and was in the studio with him. They were in deep conversation about some further messages God had given Geoff about the healing party. Geoff craned his thick neck forward, droning on. Dad nodded at everything he said. 'I rang Father Lachlan,' Geoff was saying. 'He said he's gonna be late tonight. Of all the bloody nights. He's doubting. Satan is on the prowl. We'd better pray.'

'While we pray, Natasha will go and get us an early dinner,' said Dad. 'I always eat before a party so I can focus on being the host. Natasha, bring up a plate of food for Geoff, with the lot. And one for me too.'

After they had eaten, there was the blessing. Dad, Geoff and Mum proceeded through the house. Maria followed, carrying a bowl of holy water and sprinkling it to her left and right. Ed and the volunteers outside switched on the fairy lights and laid down canvas sheets for guests to sit on. In the kitchen, Anita, Charles and the helpful ladies administered the final touches. Patsy and her group started to sing the beautiful 'Come to the Water' song: 'I know you are thirsty/ You won't be denied . . .' The drama group, who had finished rehearsing, were the first to join in, and then came the busy people in the kitchen. Soon everyone inside and outside the house was singing. Over the weeks, I had come to know some of the Charismatics who helped us prepare for the party. We had never connected before; it had always seemed to me that they didn't really see who you were or who they themselves were, and that they only did things because they thought God told them to, or to resist the devil. But now I felt gratitude, warmth and the bond of shared effort.

What a beautiful ending to our weeks of toil and preparation, I thought as I sang. From the back window, I saw Mum, Dad, Geoff and Maria continuing the tour, making their way to the ramp. Dad pointed out to Geoff his handiwork in constructing the ramp. Maria positioned Mum at the base of the ramp and put the brakes on. She then stepped around Mum and ascended the ramp. At the top, she held the bowl of holy water high, turned it over and let the last drops fall. Mum sat there facing the ramp, as though she were about to roll up it. Suddenly the reality of the party hit me. Tonight, Mum was supposed to rise up out of that chair and walk up that ramp. Is that what we all believed? Her chair would be pushed back, she would stand tall, her dress rippling, her body erect, her head and shoulders held high, and she would walk, placing one foot after the other, up that ramp. Panic swept through me.

Then I closed my eyes and sang with the others. I screwed my eyes shut tighter and shouted the words of the song. *All will turn out well*, I told myself. There was nothing else I needed to know. A warm, vague feeling returned. That's all hope was.

*

Right on six o'clock, the first guests arrived – neighbours who warned us they could only stay for a few minutes, because they had a prior engagement. Next through the door were the Charismatic families, with their van-loads of children. Then Maria came back with three men and one woman she had picked up from a Catholic hostel for the homeless. At first the guests came in dribs and drabs and we had time to offer them a drink and somewhere to sit, but soon the door was left open as more and more people spilled through.

Formally dressed churchgoers, young dating couples, Chinese and Italian Catholics, a family of shy, recently arrived Burmese refugees, brassy Pentecostals, the euphoric recently born-agains, hippies, goths, conservatives, the destitute, the glamorous or crazy-looking – all came through our door. Mum was seated in a corner of the lounge room next to an armchair. People waited to greet her, each sitting on the armchair in turn. She never stopped smiling and nodding, though her eyes often wandered.

Every time I came back out of the kitchen with another tray of drinks, the house looked fuller and the noise was a notch louder. Of their own accord, people were flowing deeper into the house, the kitchen and the backyard, finding a space and helping themselves to food and drink from the tables set up here and there. The spring rolls, wontons and curry puffs were going fast. It was dark outside. When had that happened? The air was alive with chatter, laughter, enthusiastic greetings, high spirits and hilarity. 'No alcohol needed,' they boasted – 'we have the holy spirit!'

The tempo picked up again – Lara Morris and her boyfriend, both recovered heroin addicts, walked in the door with their followers. A further frisson ran through the crowd when the imposing Terry Morris and the rest of his family arrived, and, fifteen minutes later, Lou Mercier and his family. The two celebrity families of the Charismatic movement, in our house at the same time! It was a success: the leaders were here, and the young ex-heroin addicts too. People turned their heads, called out, greeted them and parted the way.

Anita and Charles barely stepped out of the kitchen. Maria whirled around the house, seeming to know and love everyone. Patsy and her group played their guitars and sang their hearts out, but you could scarcely hear them above the throng. Dad joined the other Charismatic leaders, working the room like a politician – kissing the ladies, clapping the men on their backs, laughing uproariously. The people kept on coming. Dad led Terry Morris and Lou Mercier up to his studio. At the top of the staircase, the three of them turned around, and gazed down at the party. With a satisfied smile. Dad threw out his hand and grandly swept it across the scene spread out below him.

For a while I sat with Mum in her corner, making sure she had something to eat and drink. She refused to leave her spot while people were waiting to talk to her. I tried to answer for Mum so that she would have a chance to chew or sip. 'How are you, Irene,' they said, kissing her cheek, holding her hand or squeezing her shoulders. 'How lovely you look, what an inspiration to all of us, what a wonderful party, the Lord will bless you and your family, He will heal you tonight – yes, tonight!' Mum nodded with a haggard smile. 'Praise the Lord,' she said, over and over again.

Patsy and her music ministry moved outside, where it was less noisy and crowded and they could be heard. Ten or so single girls danced, waving their hands in the air. Couples held each other tight and swayed. Lara sat on the ramp at the back fence and held court before a large group including Ed and Maria. In the middle of the backyard, on the canvas sheets, about twenty young men and women stood in a circle, holding hands. Geoff Atkins, standing in the middle of the circle, the only old man among the young, stretched his hand heavenwards. 'Jesus!' he shouted, and babbled in tongues. He placed his hand on a woman's head. She fell backwards. He touched the next person – he fell. One by one, Geoff felled them where they stood, so that in the end their bodies radiated from the inner circle like petals on a flower.

Later, while I was trapped in the lounge room talking to Kevin, an awkward middle-aged man who turned up at every prayer meeting and whom most people avoided, I noticed Dad on the other side of the room beckon to Ed and pull him aside. From the look on Dad's face and his gesticulations, he had something urgent to say. At the end of his conversation with Dad, Ed signalled to me that he was going out. I guessed he was checking on the parking.

When Ed had been gone for almost an hour, I went out to investigate. Our guests' cars clogged the end of the court and spilled out onto the oval. I walked down the street and around the oval, but could not see Ed. The darkness and silence of the field drew me in deeper. It was colder the further I got from the warmth around our house. From the middle of the oval, the party's noise was deadened to an even thrum. I gazed back at the house, which glowed and vibrated with light and verve, and looked like a magical living thing.

Car lights turned into the court and stopped at the house. I ran back. It was Ed's car. He double-parked and opened the door. 'Anyone for chicken?' he said, grinning. The spicy aroma hit me before I saw the red and white stripes. Buckets of KFC filled the car. His happy laughter grated on me.

'Did my father tell you to do this?'

'He *asked* me to,' said Ed. His face tightened. 'What's wrong?'

'We've slaved over the cooking for weeks, and then he sends you out to get a carload of chicken! Stay away from Anita. I'll go and talk to her before you start bringing it in.'

I ran inside and called Anita out of the kitchen. 'That's it!' she cried. 'No more! Unbelievable! Dad didn't even have the decency to tell me!' Her nostrils flared. She paced up and down, threw off her apron and gloves. 'We might as well start chucking out the rest of the food we cooked, because it won't get eaten now.'

The guests, oblivious to what was happening in the kitchen, went for the KFC buckets as soon as they were laid out on the tables. Even the leaders dipped their hands into the buckets and could not wait to sink their teeth into the oily, battered pieces of chicken.

Mum still sat in her corner next to the sofa. Her face was grey, her eyes bloodshot. By now her smile was so strained that it looked like a grimace. I tried to pull her away to rest, but she asked me to get her another codeine. 'Must trust in Jesus,' she said.

Father Lachlan arrived. The crowd spontaneously broke into applause. He was loved for his rich, laughing voice, his melodious tongues and shining face. With a natural, understated charisma, he bent down gently and smiled and greeted people. Dad and Geoff immediately led him up the stairs to the studio.

We gave up our plan of having the performances in the living area, as the 250 or more guests could not squeeze in there. Instead, the volunteers shepherded them outside. People crammed into the yard and driveway. 'Sit down on the ground,' they were told. The guests folded to the ground in a lovely synchronous moment. A pool of faces glowed in the dark.

Maria and the drama group assembled against the back fence in front of the ramp. It was the perfect spot. The remaining cacti made for a monolithic backdrop, and the ramp, lined with fairy lights, looked like a runway to the night sky.

Dad hopped up onto the ramp and welcomed the people. He had his stage face on – glittering, darting eyes, too-big mouth and too-loud laugh. 'You were chosen to be here tonight, from the lowliest of you, like myself' – he bowed and waited for the laughter to stop – 'to our esteemed leaders' – he pointed to Lara and the leaders, whom he had insisted should sit at the front. Then he paused dramatically. 'The Lord has put it on my heart that I must share with you this song, "I Believe", a song of profound wisdom and faith.' Each verse began with the words 'I believe'. The first declarations were of belief in nature and the life force. As the notes rose and the tempo quickened, the declarations turned to belief in goodness and a God who will show the way even in the darkest night. Each profession of belief became bolder than the next, until the climax, when a state of belief was all that mattered. The song finished with just the two words 'I believe!' Though I had heard Dad sing the song at least twenty times, I was still astounded by the emotion he poured into it. Starting in a throaty whisper, he built up the volume with each verse. His mouth opened wider, his head started to vibrate ... then he was in the throes of passion, belting out the lyrics, throwing up his arms. With the final 'I believe', his voice broke and he was left gasping.

An actress from CTJ came forward to hug him. When he had composed himself, he introduced the drama group with exuberant and emotional praise. They took their places. In Act 1, the characters stumbled in confusion, in Act 2 they howled with pain, and in the final act they danced and sang with joy. Their over-acting was strangely apt and moving in the night air.

Dad called Geoff, Father Lachlan and Mum to the stage. How Mum kept the smile on her face, I could not say. Though wrapped in a coat and a blanket, she was pale and cold. She could not move, wriggle and rouse up warmth like the rest of us. Not a shimmer of her blue cheongsam could be seen under the woollen layers. No trace remained, except for her over-bright smile, of the glamorous hostess who had stood next to Dad at earlier parties. She should not have been out in this cold night, below an uncaring sky, next to thoughtless men, in front of a waiting audience. I yearned to get up from where I sat, just three metres from her, take off the wheelchair brakes and whizz her away from there, into bed, and help her get warm.

'This night was prophesied,' Dad shouted. 'Two months ago, Father Lachlan, Geoff and I gathered in His name to pray for a young lady with child – that she would choose life and not abortion. The young lady did not show up. For a reason. The Lord Jesus wanted to send us a message. Suddenly Geoff prophesied: it is Irene who must choose life. Everyone is given the choice of life over death. Not just to choose life for a baby, but to choose your own life. Irene has chosen life. Irene will be healed, so that we can proclaim this message.'

And the guests cried out, 'Alleluia, praise the Lord!'

'Now if that wasn't enough, the bountiful Lord sent Irene a dream to confirm the miracle. In the dream, a light shone upon her, causing her to rise up and walk, run out into this very backyard and jump over this fence. To meet Jesus halfway, I made this ramp, to see Irene across! We call it the ramp to salvation. Not bad carpentry, eh!'

'Alleluia,' they said, and laughed and clapped.

'Tonight the might of Jesus will be on show. Irene will get up and walk, healed of cancer!'

The crowd broke into tongues. Geoff jumped up and down on the spot, shouting out his tongues. Father Lachlan looked down and frowned. It was the first time I had seen him so serious.

Dad called on him to lead the healing prayer. Father Lachlan walked over to Mum, turning his back to the audience to face her. Quietly, he asked if she was fine and wanted to be prayed for out here. I couldn't hear Mum's answer. Dad took hold of Father Lachlan's arm and guided him to stand behind Mum. He and Geoff stood on either side of the priest so that the three of them faced the audience. Father Lachlan laid one hand upon Mum's head and raised the other heavenwards.

'God, the Father, Son and Holy Spirit,' the priest said, his voice trembling. 'Look upon your child, Irene. You are the alpha and the omega. You are the mover of mountains. Your ways are higher than our ways. You can bring good out of any situation. All diseases come at your call, and go at your bidding. Heal Irene, if it be Thy will.'

Geoff, standing next to Father Lachlan, stared out at the audience and shook his head vehemently. 'Give us a minute,' he said, drawing Father Lachlan and Dad to one side. Terry Morris joined them, and the four men talked in a huddle. Tense mutterings rose from the audience. Dad got Patsy to start up a song. Then Father

Lachlan shook hands with the other men, bid Mum farewell and was seen out by Dad.

'Unfortunately Father Lachlan had to leave us for another commitment,' Dad announced when the singing stopped.

Geoff stretched out his hands towards the guests. 'Blood of Jesus, cover and protect your people. Satan get behind us. We choose life! Do you choose life?'

'Yes! Amen!' they shouted back.

'Righty-o, let's get down to business,' said Geoff. He stood in front of Irene. 'Irene, do you choose life?'

'Yes,' she said, in as loud a voice as she could muster.

'Diseases don't come from God, and don't let anybody tell you that. Diseases come from the devil. The Lord is perfect,' said Geoff. He led the crowd into tongues, told them to go louder and higher. Dad, Geoff and the leaders encircled Mum and laid their hands upon her head and shoulders. I could no longer see her.

Suddenly Geoff pushed the others aside and stood in front of Mum. He took her hands and tried to pull her up. Mum's eyes darted from side to side in alarm. Looking uncertain, Dad crossed his arms but didn't intervene. 'Stand up and walk!' Geoff shouted. 'In the name of Jesus, stand up and walk!' He yanked at her again.

Anita got to Mum before I did. 'Irene needs to go inside now,' she said, in a loud, clear voice to the audience. 'A small group of you can go inside to pray with her, and the rest of you keep on praying outside.' Before Anita could finish speaking, I grabbed the wheelchair handles and pushed Mum towards the house.

Mum wanted to go to the toilet. I pulled off the coat and blanket. Her skin was freezing cold. She was so stiff that I couldn't lift her properly and had to set her back down on the wheelchair. Maria knocked on the door. I let her in and we lifted Mum together. Afterwards we quickly got her into the bedroom. I rubbed her numb feet and Maria brought her a hot cup of tea. Mum asked us to redo her make-up. We did not talk. It was as though we were between acts and getting ready to go back on.

Anita moved between rooms and outside, managing things. Lara Morris could be heard from the backyard, leading the guests in prayer, and Patsy kept the music going.

Geoff, Dad, Ed, Terry and a handful of others were waiting for Mum in the family room. Dad positioned Mum in the centre of the family room. Again, they circled her, laid their hands on her head and prayed. Then Dad and Geoff, taking Mum under each arm, pulled her to her feet. She floundered.

'Come on, Irene, step out in faith. Try to take a few steps and God will do the rest,' Dad said. Mum jerked one leg forward, but as soon as Dad and Geoff tried to release her weight, she began to fall. They sat her down. They prayed some more, denounced the devil, called upon the Holy Spirit, and shouted out their tongues.

'Yes, we will claim the miracle!' Geoff shouted, dragging her up again. Four or five more times they pulled her up and exhorted her to walk. Each time we would see the spastic flailing of her legs as she tried. Her face was dull, expressionless, closed down, all her energy spent on persevering.

It was almost midnight and people were leaving. Some left by the side door without saying goodbye. Others came through to the family room to take their leave of Mum and Dad. By now the leaders had left and no more singing and praying came from the backyard. The departing guests trooped past, their faces greasy with KFC.

Geoff knelt down in a corner of the family room and seemed to pray silently. After a minute, he bounced up and announced that the Lord had told him to slay Irene in the spirit. He told Ed to take one side of Mum while Dad held her other side. Ed tried to catch my eye, but I would not look at him. Geoff pulled the wheelchair away to one side. He stood in front of Mum and laid both his hands on her head. He spoke in tongues, then shouted, 'In the name of Jesus, you are healed!' He pushed Mum's head back, and Dad and Ed lowered her to the floor.

'Now Irene is on God's operation table. Leave her there, and let the Lord do his work,' Geoff said. She lay on the carpet, pitiful and twisted. Dad arranged her legs, straightened her back and put a cushion under her head. Ed took off his leather jacket and placed it over her. Now she looked better, but I couldn't bear for her to sleep with all of us looking at her.

I went out to the backyard. It was abandoned, except for Patsy and her music ministry packing up in the back corner. Paper plates, glasses, chicken bones and a shawl were strewn across the lawn. The night sky was still cloudy and the light it reflected back was dirty.

Back inside, Anita, Charles, Maria and a few volunteers trawled through the rooms with big plastic garbage bags. They picked through the tables, which were piled high with crushed KFC cardboard, empty bottles, trays half full of cold curry puffs and wontons piled on top of each other, used plates and cups and stinking bones.

'Just throw it all away!' Anita said. 'What a waste.'

Dad called us all into the family room. 'It's time to wake Irene up,' he said. He knelt on the carpet beside her and shook her shoulder. 'Irene, Irene, wake up, praise the Lord. You are healed.' Her eyes opened and for a moment, between waking and consciousness, before her mask of endurance could reassemble, I thought I saw something there. For a split second, her eyes were soft and lit with hope.

Tears came to my eyes. I tried to force them away and to control my breathing, but that caused me to gulp.

'Who's crying?' Mum said, looking around until she found me. 'No need to cry,' she said, in that scolding, maternal way of hers.

'Sorry,' I said, and rushed out of the room into my bedroom.

Anita followed me. Her face was trembling and her mouth curled in a horrible snarl. 'You spoilt brat! You're always so selfish!' she spat. 'You think it's all about you, don't you?' She stormed out, slamming the door.

I knew I had to go back there. I steadied my breathing and walked back into the family room. The family, Ed and the remaining volunteers were saying their final prayer. They held hands in a circle. Mum was back in her wheelchair and part of the circle. Dad, undeniably tired, declared, 'It is done. Irene is healed, and we proclaim its manifestation.'

Geoff suddenly did a ludicrous jump into the middle of the circle. He kicked his legs in the air. 'Hooray! She's healed. Irene is healed. Thank you, Jesus! Alleluia!'

Expressionless, Mum repeated, 'Thank you, Jesus.'

Then we all sang, 'Rejoice in the Lord/ I see the miracle.'

IT TOOK ONLY A COUPLE OF DAYS TO RE-ESTABLISH A routine. As usual, I rose before the sun was up and headed out to the oval. My fear of the dark had gone, pushed out by nasty, seething thoughts. They kept me on edge, even in my sleep, burning my belly, waking me with dreams of violence.

There were no trees or birds here. I laughed, breaking the silence on the oval. It was a hard, bitter laugh, more like a strangled cough. I was thinking of the way I could pull up past incidents at will and get angry and feed on them as though they happened only yesterday. Resentments that I had struggled to keep at bay since coming home were rushing back, one after another.

My thoughts returned to the house on the hill in Hong Kong and the moment Agnes had been expelled. I could see it all as I had when I was nine – Agnes in the simple cotton shift that she wore to mop the floors; a young Mum and teenage Anita shouting at her to leave, pushing her down the stairs; Agnes resisting, clinging to the banister; Mum and Anita tearing at Agnes, ripping her dress open at the back, exposing her bra, peeling her arms off the banister, pushing her cringing, howling form out the door. 'Stop it! Why, why?' Maria, Patsy and I had wailed.

Dad, Mum and Anita would never speak about it. And where was Dad on that day? I flicked through the images in my mind – he definitely wasn't there during the commotion. But his presence pervaded this memory.

How many laps of the oval had I done? I had no idea – I had not even felt my legs moving. I kept on walking.

My mind drifted to another time, when I was about twelve years old, after we had become Charismatic. I had gone shopping with my parents. The shopping centre was a steel and glass barn rising out of a vast black-tarmac car park. It was a hot, crowded day, just before Christmas. The air vent in our car blew hard and noisy, but its wind was tepid. Row after row of parking spaces were taken. We had joined the line of cars circling, desperate for a spot. A shopper pushed her trolley towards a car. The car in front of us stopped to wait for her to load her bags into the boot and vacate the spot. We were stuck. 'Praise the Lord!' Dad said, in the way that you might say shit or damn. From the back seat, I saw Dad's brown forearm sizzling in the sun and his hand tapping on the steering wheel. I felt anxious for him.

Suddenly Dad pointed at a car reversing in the next parking lane on our left. 'See the car leaving that spot?' he said to Mum. 'Go and stand there and reserve it until I can move from here.'

'No, la, Boon Chin, we can't do that,' she said.

'All you have to do is explain it's reserved. Go on,' he commanded. 'Now! Before it's too late!'

Again she resisted. 'Not right, cannot, la.'

I remembered thinking, *Why can't Mum just do what Dad says, why does she have to be so incompetent?* 'I'll do it!' I said, and got out of the car.

'Good girl,' Dad said. Mum told me to get back in the car. When I refused, she followed me out.

Seconds after we reached the vacant spot, a black four-wheel drive with a gleaming steel bull bar pulled up. The driver blared his horn. Mum pushed me back and stepped forward herself. She gave a shy wave and tried to smile at the man behind the windscreen. Through the tinted glass, we could only make out his silhouette. 'Sorry,' she called out, 'it's reserved.'

The man stuck his head out the window. He was square faced and fair haired, with black Raybans and a mean-looking mouth. 'Move, you fuckin' Chink, or I'll run you over,' he shouted. He jerked the car forward, halting inches from her.

Mum's legs trembled on her high heels. She didn't move. I heard the gear change and he let the car go. The bull bar hit her thighs with a thud. Mum fell backwards.

Scrambling to her feet, she limped away, dazed, pulling me with her. Dad wasn't in the lane where he had left us. Mum crouched between two parked cars and put her face in her hands. Then she lifted her skirt. An angry red swelling appeared above her knees. I couldn't bear to see it. I started looking for Dad's car. There he was, pulling into a vacant spot in a lane closer to the shops. Mum pulled herself up again and limped towards Dad. 'Wait till he sees what happened,' she hissed.

'It's not Dad's fault. You could have moved before he ran you over!' I said. She flung out her hand and struck me across the cheek and ear.

I fed on that slap for months afterwards. I would relive the shock of it, the humiliation, the injustice. Alone, I gloated with such intensity that tears of resentment towards my mother would fill my eyes. Later, my focus shifted, but not to the ugly, aggressive man who had struck Mum with his car. His evil was of a kind beyond my range. My thoughts turned against Dad. I replayed his command to Mum, his urging voice, his 'Go on. Now!' It was the first time I had realised he made us do things, careless things.

On and on my poisonous thoughts would go. The one who most deserved to be hated was myself. I was a stupid, mean child who did not appreciate my mother. I always took Dad's side and did his bidding. I wished it had been me who had stood in front of the bull bar. I never stuck up for her, never had the courage to say anything to Dad.

*

A thin figure walked towards me from the half dark of the oval. I stopped dead in my tracks. The big hair, the long thin legs. She reminded me of Bonnie. Or perhaps I'd already been thinking about Bonnie before she turned up. The figure came closer. It was a middle-aged woman whose tired features bore scant resemblance to Bonnie's alert eyes and vivacious mouth. Walking past, the woman nodded at me. Tears fell down my face.

Obsessed with the idea that she was getting fat, Bonnie had run laps around this oval every morning when she stayed with us. Bonnie and I had met at a youth Jesus camp when we were both twelve. She was there because a boy she had a crush on was going. I was there because at that time, just a few months after becoming born again, I was a believer. Instantly we bonded. I loved the way she always found something to laugh at. 'Come deep inside me, Jesus,' some earnest girl would pray out loud, and Bonnie would be off. Her hand would clap over her mouth, her shoulders would shake; she would bend over double, then explode in fits of laughter. She was lithe, long-limbed and funny to my short, stiff and serious.

After the camp, we became close friends. Bonnie thought my family warm and exotic, if a bit weird. She lived with her mother in a commission flat a bus ride away from our place. She would meet me at the Chu after my shift. She didn't like me to visit her flat. 'It's a dive,' she said.

Bonnie said her mother had her when she was already an old bag. Her father, who she said was funny and handsome, and spoilt her rotten, had left home for work one day when she was nine years old and had never been seen again. She kept his photo in her wallet. Bonnie got her pixie nose and bushy hair from him. 'I don't blame him for taking off,' she said. 'I'd do the same if I had to get into bed with that old hag.' Then she'd crack up laughing. A school-friend of Bonnie's told me that her father had been forced to leave by the police for abusing Bonnie and her mother. But Bonnie denied it.

By the age of fifteen I hated going to prayer meetings. Dad would say to me, 'The spirit of ungratefulness and selfishness is in you. Whether you like it or not now, you will thank me one day that we have claimed you for Jesus Christ.' He forced me to keep attending. None of my friends, not even Bonnie, understood why I couldn't just refuse to go. But Dad's hold on us was absolute. I knew I had to get away from home. I intended to leave as soon as school was over, with the money I had saved up from working at the Chu.

While I did Year 11, Bonnie dropped out of school and got a job as a sales girl at a newsagency. We dreamt about moving to Darwin and sharing a flat after I finished Year 12. We had seen pictures of sandstone pillars rising out of the dust at the Lost City, in Litchfield National Park, and something in its desolate beauty captured our imagination. Then she started going out with Tyrone, a skinhead mechanic with wealthy parents, and we saw less and less of each other.

For about four months we lost touch. But one evening after I had started Year 12, I received a call. 'Nat, oh Nat, it's so good to hear your voice. I'm sorry I haven't contacted you, I've been so fucked up,' she said, and started to sob. It frightened me. I had never heard her sound like this before.

We met at the oval that night. As she walked towards me, she looked like a model, tall and skinny in high heels and miniskirt, with a big head of hair and her face all made up. But when she drew close, I saw that she was too thin. She clasped me in her bony arms. 'Sorry, I'm sorry,' she wept. 'I'm so ashamed to have you see me like this.' Bonnie's eyes were enormous in her skeletal face. She told me that she was bulimic; she was cracking up and had to get away from her insane mother.

I told her I would ask my parents if she could stay with us until she found somewhere else to live.

Mum didn't want Bonnie to stay, but Dad overruled her, saying it was our Christian duty. Bonnie shared my room. Each morning she left for work at 8.15 and returned at 5.45. She held it together for work, but couldn't stop weeping when she came home. Mum did not show Bonnie affection but fed her at mealtimes as though she were one of her own. Dad made up for Mum's lack of affection with his warm attention. He lent Bonnie a camera and praised and instructed her on photography, and encouraged her spiritual growth. It was decided she would stay with us for three months until a place came up in the Christian single women's household.

It was a condition of staying with us that Bonnie came to prayer meetings. At one of these meetings Bonnie was born again in the spirit. Like most of my friends, Bonnie had always admired Dad. Now she thought he was amazing.

But then, seven weeks after she moved in, Bonnie left without a word to anyone. 'So ungrateful,' Mum said. 'She didn't even say thank you or goodbye.'

'Has she fucked off?' screeched her mother, when I rang. I had more luck with the owner of the newsagency, Shirley. Over the year that Bonnie worked there, Shirley had taken a maternal interest in her. She told me that Bonnie had come into work distressed, saying she needed to leave urgently and that she was going to stay with her old boyfriend, who had moved to Mildura. Bonnie left no contact details.

Three months later, Shirley called to say there was a letter. I went to pick it up. Bonnie's writing had been round and flowing, but now it was jagged, and in places the pen had been pushed down so hard that it ripped the paper. The letter was six pages long. She ranted against self-serving governments, violent and abusive husbands and fathers, religious hypocrites, the rich bullies of the world and their plan to round up the weak and poor in ghettos and high-rise commission flats so that they self-destructed. I focused on the few details she gave of her current life. She was working at a pub for an aggressive prick, she needed to give up smoking, she had passed out on the floor while writing the letter and couldn't keep writing now because it was time to leave for work. She was living with a guy who was no good, but not as bad as some. She said about the two of us, 'Can you see the string connecting us, curling around our necks?' But she left no address.

There was no contact again for another two months, until Shirley informed me she had received a call from Bonnie that seemed to be local.

I decided to visit her mother. At the commission flats the lift enclosed me in its grimy steel walls and took me up to the fifteenth floor. I looked for the numbers on the identical doors along the corridor. Halfway down the corridor, a poster of Bono's latest album was stuck to a door. I ran there, my heart racing. Bonnie had to be home. 'Bon?' I called out, and knocked. I heard the footsteps, and then the door was flung open and there she was. We laughed with joy to see each other again. She had put on weight, and looked normal. She held me close and buried her face in my hair. I knew her smell. 'I'm sorry, I'm sorry,' she whispered.

From the front door, I could see Bonnie's mother wearing a large floral dress and sitting on a threadbare armchair. I went inside to greet her. The place smelt of cats. Bonnie's mother levered herself up. 'Nobody told me you were coming. Want a cup of tea?' she said, snorting.

Bonnie took my hand and pulled me towards the door. 'No, we're going out.'

We took the lift down and sat on a plastic bench bolted to the ground in the foyer. Bonnie talked, pulling frequently on her cigarette. She had moved back home a week ago but only until she found another job; she and Tyrone were no good together, took too many drugs; Mildura was okay if you liked hicks …

I interrupted her. 'Why did you leave my parents' home without saying anything to me or anyone?'

She started breathing fast and hard. 'I didn't want to tell you,' she said. 'That's why I kept away.' She was suddenly angry. 'I went up to your father's studio to bring him his coffee. He cracked onto me. I thought he was giving me a hug, but he grabbed my tits and tried to kiss me. I had to push him away.' Her face contorted. 'It was fucking disgusting. Why do things like this happen to me?'

I knew I should comfort her, but I felt numb. I said nothing.

'It's not your fault, Nat,' she said. 'You can't help having a prick of a father. I felt so sorry for your mum. She was just downstairs.'

I started to cry, and then it was Bonnie who comforted me. At last I said I was sorry. 'What do you want me to do?' I asked.

'Nothing,' she said. 'Just tell the evil bastard never to come near me again.'

After prayers that night, Dad went to the studio and I followed him up. I was shaking with fear. 'Dad, there's something I need to talk with you about,' I heard myself say. My voice sounded unnatural. I had never been the one to raise anything with him. It was always he who did the talking. And now what I had to say was unthinkable. I thought he hadn't heard me. But he put down the photo he was studying and slowly turned around.

'What is it?' he said.

'I saw Bonnie today. Did you kiss Bonnie in a sexual way on the day she left?'

He strode to the door and shut it, then faced me with panic in his eyes. 'Have you said anything to your mother? I don't want to hear you speaking like that. Do not say a word to your mother. There'll be no end to this if you say a word to her. She must not hear a word. Do you understand?' Spittle flew from his mouth.

'Bonnie said you grabbed her breasts and kissed her.'

'No, I didn't. I don't want to hear a word of this ever again. That's the end of it. Do you hear? You have really upset me. How dare you! Now leave.' He opened the door.

A day later I tried to speak to Anita while we were hanging out the washing. 'So what?' she said. 'Things like that happen all the time!' She flung her hands up in the air to demonstrate it was no big deal, though her eyes watered and her mouth quivered as she did this.

'You shouldn't have invited her to stay,' she went on. 'I should have said something. I knew it would be no good.'

'Didn't he do the same with your friends?'

'That was before he was a Christian. He was a different person then. He has changed. You need to understand,' she said, picking up and hanging the clothes with rough, jerky movements, 'many men are like that. Artists have stronger sexual urges. Yet he tries. Give him credit for that. Don't over-react. It's no big deal. So what, a little kiss? We're not made of cottonwool, are we? You haven't said anything to Mum, have you?'

'No,' I said.

'Don't. Not to her, and not to Maria and Patsy either. There's no use upsetting them for no reason. Promise me.'

I nodded.

She stood still, rubbing her arms with her hands and trying to compose herself. Her professional voice came on. 'Anyway, Dad told you he didn't do it. Bonnie is not exactly stable, is she? Her mother is mental, and didn't her father have to leave because he was abusing them? Why would you believe her and not your own dad? Look at all the good things he did for her. Taking her into our home, teaching her photography. She is very unstable. Maybe you told her some things that made her imagine it.'

Bonnie went back to Tyrone in Mildura. She said it would only be until I finished Year 12 and we moved to Darwin together. I couldn't study. The endless rounds of prayer meetings became more difficult and sometimes I couldn't bear being near Dad. I felt I was going to burst. I decided I couldn't stay in Melbourne or even wait for my exams. I left two months before they were to begin. Bonnie said she would join me in Darwin as soon as she could.

Dad insisted on driving me to the airport for my flight to Darwin. His eyes were tired and disappointed and for the whole trip he didn't lecture me as he usually did, but instead sang one hymn after another. The hymns he chose were solemn and reverential. There were moments when I wanted to say to him, *Please forgive me, I'm so sorry. I believe you. I should never have doubted you.*

Three months after I moved to Darwin, Shirley phoned. She told me that Bonnie was dead. She had jumped from the Flinders Street railway platform into the path of an oncoming train.

Obeying Dad's command, I never spoke to him again about Bonnie's accusation. Over the years, I alternated between knowing he had done it and lied to me, and feeling like a treacherous daughter eager to believe the worst. Sometimes I told myself that it was *her* father who had been abusive. Dad had had a hard childhood – look how damaged his siblings were, whereas he had risen above it. I reminded myself that Dad was a reformed man. He tried so hard. I shouldn't have asked her to stay. But still, in all that time, until news came of Mum's cancer, I couldn't bring myself to go home.

*

The morning sun shone into my eyes. The tears had dried on my face. It was light on the oval – bright enough to see from one end to the other and beyond to the quilt-work of houses and their square fences. I had not noticed the sunrise. How many laps had I done? I had no idea. Mum would be waiting for me to get her up. I ran all the way home.

'I'm sorry I'm late,' I said, bursting into her room. Mum and Dad were both laughing at some story Dad was telling.

'Natasha, don't over-exert,' Mum said. 'Aiya, your face is all red.' She was already out of bed and sitting in the wheelchair. Dad was standing behind her, giving her a shoulder rub.

'I had the opportunity to get Mum up myself!' Dad said, with a lilt in his voice. He continued to tell her the funny story. He was trying to make Mum happy.

SINCE THE PARTY A WEEK AGO, ALTHOUGH OUR routine had stayed much the same, there were some definite changes. I was aware of these while I massaged Mum's feet after breakfast. You could see the pain was bad this morning from the way she held her belly and her neck twisted to one side. But she never admitted to it anymore. Instead, she would start looking for things to blame: the food she ate, bad thoughts, not enough prayer. If I offered Mum any food other than Patsy's diet of vegetable juices, salmon, rice, ginger and lemon, she would look at it as if it were poison. For some weeks I had been frying Mum's liver in bay leaves, garlic and a teaspoon of olive oil. Cooked this way, the liver was browned and shiny on the outside and juicy on the inside, and much more palatable than the grey tasteless lumps that resulted from steaming. Though you could see that she preferred fried, she had told me to go back to steaming the liver.

She seemed to distrust anything that gave her enjoyment. Yesterday, we had taken her to St Kilda beach. Ever since we came to Australia, the St Kilda foreshore had been a regular haunt for Mum and Dad. Dad especially liked the bluestone wall separating the sand from the raised walking path, and the green lawn rolling down to the sea. He said it reminded him of Stanley Beach in Hong Kong, the part built up by the British, where he had taken Mum when they were courting.

So once a week after Sunday mass, if she was well enough, we'd been taking Mum on a drive to the beach. If it was a fine day, we would take out the wheelchair and push Mum up and down the jetty. If it was too cold or windy, we stayed in the car, parked where she had a good view of the waves. She would practise her deep breathing, sucking in mouthfuls of the fresh air and coughing out the bad.

Yesterday at the beach, the weather had been brilliant. The tide was so high that the waves rode up the sand, all the way to the wall. Blue shimmering in the sky and sea, white boats, seaside restaurants, cyclists floating past – everything was sparkling and weightless. Mum didn't practise her deep breathing that day. With slow-moving, moist eyes, she took in the view. She seemed so wistful when it was time to go that we kept putting off the walk back to the car.

'No need to go to St Kilda again,' she said, after we had helped her back into the front seat. The announcement took us by surprise. Maria asked if there was another beach she wanted to visit. 'No, no need. I've seen so many beaches. So many years I've been coming here. What for need to see it again?'

My hands moved from Mum's feet to her calves. 'Am I hurting you, Mum?'

'No,' she said, 'do harder.' She held her stomach.

'Is the pain in your tummy very bad, Mum?' I asked.

'No, I am healed,' she said.

The muscles in her calves had lost all suppleness and felt like bone. As I rubbed, I thought about what to ask her. She had become even more reluctant to answer my questions about her life. Still, I was not prepared to let it go. The desperation to know rose up in me again.

'What food do you like?' I asked.

'You already asked me,' she said.

'I know, but you didn't answer.'

'I like everything.'

'But there must be a food that you don't like?'

Mum thought for a while. 'When I was a child, my mother always scolded me for not eating my liver. I used to spit it out.'

'Don't you like liver?' I said.

'No.'

'You never told us that. You've eaten liver every day for almost three months and it's the one food you hate?'

'So what? It's good for me.'

Something snapped. 'Have you been happy in life, Mum?'

'What a silly question. Of course I'm happy. We have Jesus, a good family, a good home.'

'Has anything ever made you unhappy?'

'Of course everyone has some sufferings. But we give them to Jesus.'

I stopped rubbing her leg and leant forward. 'But have you ever been unhappy?'

'When my baby boy died. If only I had not been so stressed at the time I was carrying him.'

'Were you stressed because you found out about Dad's affairs?' I asked.

She screwed up her face. 'Your stupid questions,' she said, and her neck twisted further. I saw the incomprehension and disgust in her eyes.

*

The rest of the day we got ready for the third cycle of chemotherapy that Mum would have the next morning. No one questioned whether we were to go ahead with it, even though Dad continued to assert that Mum had been healed on the night of the party. He said the deed had been done. She just had to claim it, and it would be manifested.

When I heard Anita coming through the front door, I rushed to the kitchen to make sure that I had not left any food out. Anita swept in every evening after work like a supervisor. She checked on Mum and Dad, the state of the house, whether dinner had been cooked, appointments kept and medicine taken. She was tense and prickly, especially with me. *Don't get out of line*, her narrowed eyes would say while she questioned me on Mum's day and issued instructions.

She sat down with Mum in the lounge room. I went back into the laundry room, where I was sorting some clothes. Soon I heard Anita striding down the corridor, calling out for me. 'I'm here,' I said.

She barged in, halting two steps away from me. 'What did you say to Mum today? She's very upset.'

I was too startled to answer.

Her mouth was clenched and her nostrils flared. 'She said you were bringing things up about the past. About Dad.'

'I just asked one question.'

'What did you ask?'

'I asked whether his affairs had affected her.'

'Why? Why?'

I didn't know what to say.

She had the same look of disgust on her face that Mum had had. 'What's wrong with you? Do you deliberately want to hurt her? That was a long time ago, before they became Charismatic.'

'I'm sorry,' I said.

'You were too young to even know what was happening. Now Mum thinks I told you.' She was shaking, her face crumbling. 'It was me who went through all that. Not you. What do you think gives you the right?'

'I'm really sorry,' I said. Her shoulders slumped. I wanted to put my hand on her. I took a step closer.

She stiffened. 'No, you're not. I can't believe you would do such a thing. Just shut up.' She stormed out.

*

We were running late. There was a review appointment with the oncologist, Doctor Richards, scheduled before the chemotherapy. Dad dropped Mum, Maria and me at the hospital entry, and drove off to park. We rushed up to the clinic, only to find a queue at the reception desk. Three people were ahead of us, clutching their medical forms and staring silently ahead. In a loud, patronising voice the receptionist was explaining to the elderly man at the front of the queue that she could not schedule an appointment more than six months in advance. Her layered red hair flapped around her face as she talked.

Dad arrived. 'No, oh no, praise the Lord. Still in the queue? That isn't possible!' he said. He grabbed the handles of Mum's wheelchair and pushed her past the queue and up to the desk.

'*Mo cho*, Boon Chin,' Mum said to Dad. 'Don't fuss.' Her head barely reached the desk.

'Excuse me,' he said. The receptionist stood up. 'It is most important that my wife does not miss her urgent 10 a.m. appointment.' He clipped his words in the British manner he had learnt from Hong Kong's expats. 'Kindly inform Doctor Richards that Mrs Chan is now ready.'

Unmoved, the receptionist told him to wait in line to be seen. He looked so short next to her and the others in the queue. I was not used to seeing Dad put in his place.

Twenty minutes later, the queue had disappeared. Everyone was sitting down and waiting, but few were being called. On the other side of the room, Maria had struck up a conversation with a shy young woman who covered her head with a soft hat of the kind that cancer patients wore. As the woman described her condition, Maria listened with her eyebrows knotted together, mouth downturned and eyes dripping with compassion. I reminded myself that even if it looked fake, Maria was trying to help. She handed a pamphlet to the young woman and started to evangelise to her about the power of prayer.

'Isn't Maria wonderful? She doesn't miss an opportunity,' said Dad, who was sitting next to me. On his other side Mum was silent, tired out by the journey and worried about the chemotherapy.

Dad told me to go up and ask the receptionist how much longer we would have to wait. I answered that Maria had already asked her fifteen minutes ago and she had explained that it depended on how long the person before us took.

'Don't be so afraid of what people might think of you. It's a simple question to which there is a simple answer. Ask and you shall receive! Go on, now!' he said, annoyed.

I rose and walked towards the reception desk. Halfway there, I stopped. It occurred to me that I would not obey him. Heart thumping, I changed direction and headed for the water dispenser.

Though Dad was upbeat most of the time, there had been an edge to him since the healing party. If we weren't all sitting around the table, waiting for him when he came down for dinner, he would storm back up the stairs to his studio. When a packet of biscuits wouldn't open the first try, he threw it in the bin. I knew that anger, I rippled to it. He no longer met Geoff every morning at McDonald's. Geoff, he said, had fallen victim to spiritual pride. That's all he said about it, but Geoff hadn't set foot in our house since that night.

Dad stood up. He was angry, I could see.

Fortunately, just then Doctor Richards entered the room, fair, well-groomed and considerable in his suit. The nurses at reception stopped what they were doing and immediately gave him their attention. He had the same benevolent and authoritative manner as a priest. His speech was unrushed, delivered in full confidence that he was being listened to.

He looked up from his file at the waiting patients. 'Mrs Chan,' he called, nodding to us. We followed him into his office. Shaking our hands in turn, he invited us to sit down before he sat in the armchair behind his polished desk. A narrow, tinted window overlooked a park. The furniture was dignified, the wall hangings sombre and the colours muted. I wondered about the lives that had been devastated or restored with a few words in this room.

He directed his benign, almost sleepy gaze at Mum. 'Irene, I am pleased to say that the test results show you are doing as well as can be expected after two cycles of chemotherapy. The spread of the cancer has stabilised in the bones, and the growth occurs at a lesser rate in the liver and large intestine.'

Mum smiled and nodded, her eyes still tense.

Dad sat forward on his chair. 'Let me tell you the truth, Doctor,' he said. 'You know we are born-again Christians. We are not therefore surprised at the positive results. The Lord has promised to heal Irene and we believe this with all our heart!'

The doctor was fully awake now. 'I cannot comment on your beliefs, Mr Chan. I can only tell you what the medical and oncological position is. The goal of the chemotherapy is to provide Irene with the best quality of life for as long as we can in the circumstances. The results show that the two cycles of chemotherapy have been effective in slowing down the metastases. As we have discussed, the third cycle in this kind of case is usually the unknown. There is no guarantee that we will see further gains.'

Doctor Richards consulted his file notes. 'I understand you've made an appointment to start the third infusion today.' He looked up again. 'Irene, do you still wish to go ahead with the third and final cycle of chemotherapy?'

Mum nodded. 'Yes.'

Sighing, Dad shook his head at the doctor. 'You really know so little about the treatment you have recommended?'

'This is the nature of chemotherapy,' said Doctor Richards. 'It is the most effective treatment we currently have, but it is not as exact as we would like it to be. I always say to my patients, "It's like throwing a bucket of paint against a wall. Some of the paint will hit its target, the rest will wash off."'

Dad scraped his chair back and stood up. 'If you will excuse me, I must move the car. The rest of you carry on. Before I go, let me share something with you, Doctor. You may think you are helping people with your smart paint metaphor.' Dad's face contorted when he said *smart*. 'Let me tell you the truth – and you don't need to be a Christian to know this. People need to be inspired. Question yourself, whether you need to be inspired. And you know what the best inspiration is? Jesus.' Dad walked out.

*

That evening, after the chemo, Dad came up with the idea of holding a prayer vigil at our home until the healing was manifested. 'The Lord put it on my heart,' Dad said. 'Satan is on the prowl, desperate to rob us of the victory of Mum's healing. We must call on the Lord's protection at every moment.'

He instructed Maria to create a roster, to keep a candle lit all day and all night at the family altar, and to make sure that at every moment between 9 a.m. and 10 p.m. someone was rostered to pray there. He had wanted the vigil to be non-stop for twenty-four hours, but Anita dissuaded him. 'If you want it to go all night, you organise it, not Maria!' she said.

The vigil began the next day. Maria spread a fresh lace tablecloth on our small altar table and rearranged the standing crucifix and the Turin Shroud portrait of Jesus, the rosary beads and vase, to make room for two special pillar candles that would slow-burn for up to 240 hours. Organising the vigil roster was stressful and consuming for Maria. She was constantly on the phone, trying to find volunteers for the one-hour slots of the roster, or kneeling at the altar herself, filling in for people who didn't turn up. Mum, my sisters and I wanted the altar moved from the family room to the spare bedroom so that we would have some privacy from the volunteers, but Dad said no, the altar must be in the heart of our home. At nearly every waking moment, there were visitors in front of the altar in our family room.

For the first few days after the chemo, Mum was unwell and seldom came out of her room. This time, she was also coping with hair loss. Mum's much-admired hair, which she had oiled, massaged, coiffured and prettily arranged around her face over a lifetime, began to abandon her. No artful combing and pinning could hide the baldness. Chunks of her hair were left behind on the pillow when I lifted her out of bed in the morning, and they clogged the drain after her shower. It was a slow torture. She averted her eyes from all mirrors except for the pocket compact she used when applying her make-up. The remaining sorry tails of hair sticking out of her head and the patches of bald skin gave her a derelict appearance.

*

About a week after Mum's chemotherapy, Anita surprised us by leaving work early and coming over after lunch. Carrying two bulging plastic bags, she headed for Mum's room. 'I've been shopping,' she said. Anita often brought catalogues, magazines and newly bought items to show Mum. Shopping was their thing. Before the cancer, they would spend hours together on weekends, walking the malls, hunting down bargains and trying on clothes. Anita was the big spender, always finding more things that she needed, while Mum browsed. Mum often complained about her spending too much.

I followed Anita into the bedroom. She pulled a chair up next to Mum, who sat at the window overlooking the backyard. 'This is such a fantastic buy,' Anita said, pulling a blue button-up shirt with a 400-dollar price tag out of the Myer bag. 'A designer brand, reduced by 50 per cent. People were fighting for it. It fits me perfectly.' I remembered the advice Anita had once given me – act with confidence, and no one will disagree.

'Now, guess what I have in the other bag,' Anita said. 'Your wig. It arrived this morning. It came nicely wrapped in tissue, but I opened it.'

'You have such a nice-shaped head,' I said to Mum. 'Now that you have a wig, you could shave all your hair off, like some other women who have had chemo.'

'No!' Mum said with sudden vehemence. 'I am not a man!'

Anita glared at me. She pulled the wig over Mum's head. It was a jet-black shoulder-length bob, similar to a hairstyle she'd had in the sixties. Anita tried several different arrangements, combing the hair behind Mum's ears, sweeping it to the side. When she found the right style for Mum, Anita put Mum in front of the dressing table. Mum raised dull eyes to her image.

'There, young again,' said Anita. The glossy thick wig looked impressive until you noticed how its vigour accentuated the pallor and sag of Mum's skin. 'You wear the wig in the daytime and at night you wear this hat,' said Anita. She showed Mum a soft black knit in the shape of a turban. Grabbing the wheelchair handles, Anita pulled Mum away from the mirror so she would not have to look at herself when she took off the wig to try on the hat.

A few minutes later, Patsy arrived, carrying a jar in outstretched hands like a chalice. She walked straight over to Mum without seeming to notice the wig on her head. 'This oil has been anointed by the bishop,' she said, with a proud tilt of her chin.

Maria was having a short break from vigil coordination. I went to the family room to check whether the next person on the roster had arrived. They hadn't, and Rob and Vishka, an elderly couple from the Friday night prayer group, had finished their hour and needed to leave. Kneeling down, I took their place but instead of praying, I tidied up the altar, which had become cluttered with flowers, cards, scapulars and other prayer aids. Worried that I would have to fill the hour myself, I looked for the roster. Janice was scheduled on next. She was the eighteen-year-old daughter of one of Mum's cell group members and had been coming over nearly every day of the past week. Plain as she was, there was a light shining from Janice's face. When she was silent, a smile played upon her lips as if she were hearing a heavenly song. When she talked, she did so with utter conviction. People called her the young Joan of Arc. Mum always joined her at the altar when she came. She disturbed me, but I tried to focus on the fact that Mum took comfort from her presence.

I heard the front door open. People coming for the vigil had been told to let themselves in and out. It was Janice. I went to get Mum.

While Janice and Mum set themselves up in the family room, Patsy and I lingered in the kitchen. Patsy put on the kettle. I put away some dishes. We pretended to be busy, but were mostly hanging around the kitchen table, from where we could see and hear Mum and Janice.

Janice pulled their chairs close together in front of the altar. She held Mum's hands in hers and looked deep into her eyes. 'Jesus loves you,' Janice said. 'I see Him right now, looking down on you, putting His arms around you.' Her voice was compelling. 'He is saying to you, "You are perfect. You, Irene, are my precious child. I love you. I will never abandon you. I will never fail you. Give all your sufferings to me …"'

My heart rose to my throat. I put down the dishes, unable to concentrate on anything but Janice's words. *You are perfect. I love you. I will never fail you.* Yes, this was exactly what Mum needed to hear.

Leaning in closer, Janice cupped Mum's head in her hands and described a vision of Mum rising out of the wheelchair, laughing and rejoicing, witnessing to and bringing many people to Christ. Her lips were a few centimetres away from Mum's face. Mum must have been inhaling Janice's breath.

It amazed and embarrassed me to watch them. In my family we never got that close, pressed against each other, eyes locked, breath on each other's faces. To pick Mum up from bed, I had to wrap my arms around her and squeeze her to my breast. I enjoyed holding her – it was the only chance I had to be close to her – but I couldn't bear it if we were too close. I always turned my head away so that I would not smell her. I was shy of that deeper smell that was hers only, made up of her inherent chemistry, that not even the strong drugs Mum was taking or the cancer could alter.

I looked at Patsy. She stood transfixed, listening and watching. Her shoulders were slumped and her face crestfallen. I could feel her hurt. When we were children, people had called Patsy and me the twins. We had been able to take one look at each other and know what the other was thinking. After Mum and Dad were born again, I rebelled, while she became more obedient. Slowly we had moved apart, but still I yearned for that former alliance.

'She doesn't even know Mum,' I whispered to Patsy.

Patsy frowned. 'What did you say?'

'She doesn't even know Mum,' I said, louder.

'I don't know what you're talking about,' Patsy said.

*

I took a walk up to the corner shop. When I came back, it was quiet in the house. Anita was rinsing vegetables at the kitchen sink, Carmel from the drama group was at the altar, praying, and Mum was lying on the couch in the lounge room.

I went into the kitchen and started to peel the onions. Anita, ignoring me, looked to be fuming about something. *What now?* I thought. Maria came downstairs from the studio, informed Carmel her hour was up, chatted with her for a few minutes and saw her out.

Maria had the next hour. Before she took her position at the altar, she beckoned me over to her in the family room and warned in a low voice, 'Your book about dying – Mum and Dad are really upset.' My stomach turned. Entering the lounge room, I saw it sitting on the coffee table next to Mum's reading glasses and bible. The title, *On Death and Dying*, stood out, stark black in capital letters against the tomb-grey cover.

Mum was pale. Without looking at me, she pointed to the book with a jerk of her chin. I flipped the book over so the cover couldn't be seen and sat down next to her.

'I'm sorry, Mum. I didn't mean for you to see it,' I said.

'You tell your dad,' she said.

Dad strode down the stairs into the room. I realised he had been waiting for Carmel to leave.

He stood in front of me, face terrible, arms tense at his side, fists clenched. 'We are a family of believers!' he said, his voice thick. 'We have claimed the miracle! We reject the evil of Satan!' Jutting his head forward like a bulldog's, he jabbed his finger at me. 'Now take that book away!' he shouted.

I picked up the book and went to my room. Maria followed me. 'Are you all right?' she said. I pushed past her.

'I'm going out. I'll be back after dinner,' I said, then grabbed my handbag and rushed out.

*

It was strange how alive I felt as I walked away from the house. Dad's anger still tore through me. It had been no more than I deserved.

I fought the urge to ring Jason, to hear his slow, hesitating voice, to feel that we belonged together, to tell him how Mum was getting sicker and more silent, how all of us had to say she was healed, and that I now felt angry or guilty nearly every moment I spent with my family. But I couldn't ring him. Maybe he had moved on. Besides,

I knew what he would think about the book incident – he would be on my side. That wasn't what I needed. My family might be right.

I caught the bus to Ed's place. Since the healing party, he had continued to come over to help Dad with his projects and to take part in the vigil, but I had avoided being alone with him. I felt he had more in common with my family than with me.

It was the first time I had been to his house in daylight. If he wasn't home, I decided, I would just wander around the city for a couple of hours. I turned down streets lined with tiny weatherboard cottages. Most of them were unrenovated, with peeling paint and overflowing bins in the concrete rectangles standing in for their front yards. They were student houses now, most of them, with Tibetan prayer flags in their grimy windows and wet, sagging sofas sitting abandoned by the rusty letterboxes. Ed's front door came up nearly to the footpath, with just a thin strip of well-tended garden in between. For five years he had rented this place, he told me. Even through his worst bouts of drinking, he had never missed a single payment. There was the sound of a vacuum cleaner running inside. I rang the bell. The vacuuming sound stopped and I heard footsteps.

'Hi.' He stood in the narrow corridor, looking confused. It hit me that I shouldn't have come. He had driven us here twice when we had first started going out. Each time, it had been for one purpose only. Rushing to get into the house, fumbling with keys in the dark, we had not talked. He had not even turned on the lights. He had pulled me into the black corridor, then into his bedroom, semi-lit by streetlights shining through the window.

'I'm sorry for barging in like this. If you're busy, I can go,' I said.

'Come in,' he said, and stepped back to let me walk ahead of him down the corridor. I glimpsed his bedroom through the half-open door on the left as we passed. The low futon bed was neatly made, the beige cover pulled over the pillows. Last time I was here the sheets had been tangled and fouled up and the futon pushed halfway off the frame with our thrashing. I had been surprised by his violence.

The corridor led to a light-filled, open room. In one corner was an old, brightly painted wooden kitchen cabinet, in the other corner a sofa, and in the middle of the room a small round table with two chairs. The house was clean and orderly, simple but stylish. Except for a newspaper on the table, nothing was out of place. He picked up the newspaper and slotted it into the magazine rack with the same fastidiousness I had seen him display when we prepared for the party. He would be a careful and considerate carer for the old folks, I thought.

He pulled out a chair at the table for me. 'Have a seat,' he said. He made a pot of coffee and sat down across the table from me. 'What's up?'

'It's all this stuff about Mum being healed. I feel like some kind of ... of ... curse upon my family. I've been so angry. I've been unfair to you too – I'm sorry,' I said.

'Forget it,' he said. 'But that's not what you're here for, is it?'

I took a sharp breath. Since when had he become so suspicious of me? 'I thought you'd be good to talk with because you know my family,' I said. 'You've been through the healing party with us, you're a Charismatic, but I can still relate to you. And you're sensitive.'

'What about your sisters?' he said.

'They're the thought police.'

He smiled, poured the coffee, lit a cigarette and waited for me to begin.

'You know the book on death and dying?' I said. 'That one by Elisabeth Kübler-Ross?'

He nodded, blew smoke away from me.

'I've been reading it and some other books on terminal illness. I knew Mum and Dad wouldn't like it, so I kept them in my room. But this morning I read *On Death and Dying* out in the lounge room. Then I accidentally left it lying around. They found it. Mum looked at me like I had sentenced her to death. Dad was shouting, as though I was a traitor to the family. I should have explained to them why I was reading it. Instead, I said I didn't mean for them to see it. I'm such a coward. The thing is, I must have known what I was doing when I started reading it in the lounge room. I must have wanted them to see.'

'Of course you did.' He winked at me. 'Stirring things up a bit in the Chan household again.' He put his hand on my shoulder and squeezed. I liked the way he did that.

'But it upset them so much,' I said.

He smiled at me with his warm eyes. 'They'll be fine, darl. Their faith is rock-solid.'

'You mean their denial of reality is.'

'The five stages of grieving in the *Death and Dying* book,' he said, 'we used them in Alcoholics Anonymous. But what's the big deal, knowing what stage you're going through? Say I get through the denial and the anger, and learn to accept that I'm an alcoholic. Then what? Self-awareness is over-rated. It doesn't change anything.'

I sat forward. 'But if we could stop pretending the cancer

wasn't there,' I said, 'or if we could at least talk about it, maybe we could cope with it better. But then, I guess, if we're coping with it, we're not rising above it ... No, that's not what I mean.'

'Take your time,' he said. 'Have your coffee.' He slid my cup, which I had not touched, closer to me.

'Maybe we can't rise above sickness without first accepting it ...' I took a sip of my coffee. 'Sorry, I don't know what I'm saying.'

'People need to be transformed,' he said. He fixed his eyes on me. I had never seen him so strong and serious.

'How were you transformed?' I asked.

Ed stubbed out his cigarette, moved his chair closer, grazed my legs with his. 'I'll only say that I was delivered. I didn't have a hope in hell. I could do fuck-all myself. No amount of self-awareness or therapy or medication could stop me from drinking myself to death. It was only spiritual intervention, Jesus, that changed everything.' Ed's eyes, rimmed in dark lashes, glowing with fervour, held mine.

He spread his arms out on the table, his hands only inches from mine. 'I recognised something in your father the day I saw him onstage at Dallas Brooks Hall,' Ed continued. 'He has this powerful, childlike faith. I knew it must have been from what he had experienced. He told me his story, that before he was saved he had a Yaoguai in him – or however he pronounced it. He explained it was a demon that had abducted and was consuming his soul. That is exactly how I was before being saved. Salvation, to him, was a miracle. That's how I feel too. I hope to have his childlike faith one day.' Sensing his excitement, I suddenly felt sad.

'You're nothing like my father. I mean that in a good way,' I said.

'Explain?'

'He wants everyone to think he's a new man – a saint, in fact. But he's not.'

'Well, no one's perfect. Give the man credit for trying.'

I bit my tongue.

'And your mum is sweet and at the same time so strong,' he said.

'Underneath she's full of fear.'

'That makes her even stronger,' he said.

I didn't feel that this was all true, but it was good to hear, and he was kind. I felt immense gratitude. I put my hand on his. He pulled his hand away, picked up the coffee pot and walked to the sink. 'You should probably go home now,' he said. 'I'll walk you to the station.' I followed him to the sink. 'You should go,' he said, without turning around.

'I don't want to,' I said. He turned around and we started to kiss. I could feel his heart thumping against my breast.

'Not like the other times. Gentle,' I said, leading him to the sofa and guiding him down beside me. 'Slowly,' I said, trying to hold his hands back. He was sweating, his breath wild, his mouth and hands desperate and groping. I tried to slow him down, but caught his fever. He put me on my back, slammed into me. I gripped him to me.

As soon as we had both come, he pulled away. He sat on the edge of the couch and lit a smoke. His body turned away from me.

I waited for my jagged breath and nerves to settle. I sat up, gathered my fallen clothes and held them in a bundle to my breast. 'Are you okay?' I said.

'I am trying to live as a Christian. You are not helping me.' He still wouldn't look at me.

'I didn't know how seriously you took the "no sex before marriage" rule. Many Charismatics don't worry about it, or if they do, they just ask God for forgiveness afterwards.'

'Don't mock.'

'I'm sorry. I just can't see how this can be wrong. You're just being true to yourself,' I said, feeling pathetic.

'If I was being true to myself, I'd scull a bottle of Scotch right now. I'd fuck anything in sight,' he said.

He finally turned to face me. 'I don't like being used,' he said. He looked so distant and cold that it frightened me.

I pulled on my clothes, getting more and more angry. 'I was wrong about you,' I said. 'You're just as fucked up as the other Charismatics. You're not changed. You've just replaced alcohol with Jesus. And you want to know who's really using you? Paul Chan. That's right, my father is using you. He shared his touching testimony with you, right? He said you're special, creative, so deeply spiritual? He's always looking for someone vulnerable. Someone who will admire him and do his bidding. Just be grateful you're not a girl, because —' I stopped myself before I could say any more, and ran out of his house.

*

I let myself be swallowed up in the rush-hour crowd flowing up and down the city pavements. These people, going about with such busyness – what thought did they have for the saved and the damned, faith and disbelief, who is with us and who against us?

When it got dark, I took a train and then a bus home. On entering the front door, I could hear praying from the family room.

I tried to make it to my room without being noticed, but Patsy came to my door. 'Dad wants you to join us,' she said. She took a look at my face. 'It's okay, he's not angry at you anymore.'

I followed Patsy out. The whole family was there, as well as Troy, Dad's assistant director, and Bridie, his favourite actress from the drama group. They sat in a close circle around the coffee table laden with burning candles, their faces gentle in the light. A radiance came from the corner where the altar stood with its pillar candles still glimmering.

'Oh good, Natasha's here. You have come just in time,' Dad said, standing up. I sat down on the carpet behind Maria, but she moved over for me to join the circle.

'The Lord has asked me to share something with all of you,' Dad said. 'We need to be able to see for this.' He bounded over to the switch and harsh, yellowish light saturated the room. 'Now, how shall I present this?' Rubbing his hands together, he positioned himself in front of the TV where everyone could see him. 'I know, in a quiz. A quiz. A test for your intelligence and imagination. Each of you will have a turn to answer. This is the question.' He paused and raised his hand. 'What is the worst sin? We start with you, Anita, and we'll go round this way.' He gestured clockwise. 'What is the worst sin?'

'Okay. It is a mortal sin to reject Jesus when he has shown you his grace,' Anita said.

'Good answer, but not correct.'

'Really? That's what I learnt in catechism,' Anita countered.

'Then we must update your learning.' Dad said.

Anita pulled a cheeky face. 'Oh, really!'

I ran through some answers in my head, preparing for my turn, starting to feel nervous.

Troy was next. 'Isn't there something in the bible about using God's name in vain?'

'So there is. But this, the worst of sins, you will know it straightaway when I say it,' said Dad. 'Now Patsy next.'

Patsy held herself rigid. 'Thou shalt not have other gods before me – the first commandment,' she said. Her eyes darted up, eager for approval.

'Very true, but not quite,' Dad said. 'Irene, your turn.'

'No, la,' Mum said. 'Ask someone else. I like to listen.'

'Pride is the worst sin,' Charles said.

'Uh-huh! Now we're getting somewhere. Natasha, your turn.'

'The worst sin is killing unborn innocent babies in the womb,' I said, choosing the words Dad commonly used but injecting them with sarcasm.

'Well, I hoped for more imagination from one of my daughters,' Dad said. 'I will give you all a hint. What does Satan represent?'

'Evil?' Maria said.

'Try again,' Dad said, bouncing on his feet.

'Deceiver?' Patsy said.

Dad clapped his hands. 'Got it. Satan is a liar. God is truth. The worst sin is lying. All the worst evil is caused by lies.' I knew this was meant for me. His theatrical gaze embraced everyone in the room, but excluded me.

IT WAS 3 P.M., TIME FOR MEDITATION. I HEADED TO Mum's room to see if she was awake.

Our meditation sessions were the one thing I felt I could offer her. I continued to modify the Vipassana technique I had learnt so that she would accept it as Christian meditation and not 'worship of the Self-God', as Dad called it. It seemed to me that it helped still our minds, and gave respite, at least for a few minutes, from all that hoping and anxiety.

When I walked into her room, Mum was sitting up in bed, waiting.

'I don't want any more meditation. It's no good,' she said.

She might as well have slapped me. 'But I thought you liked it.'

'Do not open yourself to other gods,' she said.

'The focus is on Jesus,' I lied.

'No!' she said.

'It's good for you, it helps you to relax, it's —'

'No more!' She jerked her head away from me and scrunched up her eyes.

I flinched. Was there some evil in me that she needed to shut out? She must have guessed I had been lying to her about the meditation being Christian-based.

'Read the bible to me,' she said. 'Just open any page.'

I set the book on its spine and let it fall open, the way the Charismatics did when they asked Jesus for His message to them. Trying to muffle the hurt in my voice, I read from the top of the right page. The bible had opened on the Book of Ezra, Chapter Eight. A list of names of the descendants from Babylon ensued. The passages were insignificant. It didn't matter, I thought. Anything to shut me up. Who had I been trying to fool? She had no doubt suspected me from the start but was probably trying to please me, in the way she tried to please so many people.

I closed the bible. 'Mum, I need to go back to Darwin. I've been jobless for nearly three months. I was thinking of buying a ticket for next week,' I said. I started to shake. I had been considering leaving for a few days now, but the suddenness of my decision surprised even me.

Her head drooped. She said nothing.

'Mum, did you hear me?' I said, feeling cruel.

'Oh, yes,' she said, 'your job is important. You have already stayed so long.'

'I will come back to Melbourne in a couple of months' time, around Christmas.'

She was silent again. When she lifted her head back up, she had put on a stiff smile. 'Maybe I will visit you in Darwin before then, when I am healed,' she said.

At dinner, I told the rest of the family. No one had much to say. 'That's life. When work calls, we must answer,' Dad said. Anita shrugged, as though she was thinking, *Do what you like, that's what you always do anyway.* Patsy also said nothing, but I saw her lip curl in disapproval. Only Maria expressed regret. 'We'll miss you and all your help,' she said.

That night, I booked and paid for my ticket. I would leave in seven days' time. I felt guilty, but also in a mood to celebrate. I thought ahead to the rush of freedom I would feel when the plane's wheels left the ground.

*

By the next morning, I felt loathsome. I tried to tell myself not to feel guilty. I had come wanting to make things better for Mum, but had seemed only to make them worse. Let them get on with it – who did I think I was, trying to change things? They didn't need or even want me here. Mum was responding well to the chemo, and Maria and Patsy could take on her morning care. Besides, I had been living off my savings for the last three months and needed to work. And there was Jason – I had to face the shameful way I had broken up with him.

I hid in my room. At least here the walls were bare, free of Dad's montages of bare-breasted women, leaping tigers and faces of Jesus dripping red. Shouts and song and Dad's urging voice came from a drama rehearsal in the lounge room. In the family room, a vigil group chanted the rosary. All day long, people streamed in and out to keep the vigil going, letting in the cold, soiling the carpet with their shoes, making a public space of our house. I wondered what I was doing here, and why I had stayed so long.

The sound of Maria's and Patsy's laughter came from Mum's room. Maria had a date that night with the nephew of an elderly couple who belonged to the Missionaries for Christ community. So far I had gleaned that his name was John, he was Catholic and had a public service job. It was Maria's first date in about five years. There had been a string of boyfriends until she was about twenty-two, but then they stopped. At family prayers, Mum often prayed out loud that Maria would find a good boyfriend. Mum believed a girl should be married and starting a family by the age of twenty-seven.

It was hard to believe, but I had never seen Maria nude, or even in her underwear. She changed in the bathroom or toilet, where the doors had locks, never in her bedroom. If she had to go swimming, she would enter the water with trousers and a T-shirt over her bathers, and get dressed in a toilet cubicle rather than an open change area. I remembered the time I soaked her with a hose in the garden of the house on the hill. Mum told us to take our wet clothes off before coming inside. It was before we were old enough to have boobs, but still Maria refused. Mum grabbed her and started pulling off her T-shirt. I remember how desperate and wild Maria looked, like the stray cats that we chased and caught by the tail. She bit Mum's hand and ran away. It was the only time I saw Maria disobey either Mum or Dad.

Maria's early boyfriends were mainly clean, good-looking Christian boys who came to our prayer meetings and eventually found themselves working on one of Dad's projects. Maria was always evasive with them. The poor guy would almost never get her to himself, and she never as much as held hands with him, at least not in front of us. Whether at a prayer meeting or party or disco, she made sure there was no opportunity for intimacy. She would invite other friends to join them or abandon the boyfriend for the night and flit from one person to another, witnessing to them about Jesus.

She did behave differently with one man – brash and handsome Walter, with the silver car. It was he who did the socialising and evangelising, while she followed him around, timid and mute. When she stood by his side, he had a habit of standing with his foot pressed over hers. I remembered thinking, the first time I saw it, how sexually thrilling that simple act of dominion was. But the more we saw of him, the more everyone except Maria disliked Walter. After I moved to Darwin, I heard he had dropped Maria and taken up with a new member of Missionaries for Christ. Gradually, Maria stopped dressing up and started to live in baggy tracksuits, except when she had to dress for prayer meetings. As far as I knew, she didn't go on any more dates – not unless you counted the down-and-outs and needy guys who'd think she was asking them out, when actually she was trying to convert them, like some kind of hooker for Christ.

Maria came to my door. 'Hi, what are you up to?' she asked, in her caring voice.

'Reading,' I said, without lifting my eyes from the newspaper in my hands.

'Are you all right?' she asked, stepping inside.

'Why shouldn't I be all right?'

'Mum wants me to choose one of her dresses to wear tonight. Come and help us.'

'It's okay,' I said, looking up for a moment and seeing the sympathy in Maria's eyes. 'I've got things I have to do.'

Patsy came to the door. 'Natasha, did you remember to use the holy oil when you massaged Mum's feet, like I said?'

I didn't look up from the paper or answer her.

'Come on, help us choose a dress. We need your good taste,' said Maria. 'I need you to do my make-up too.'

Maria had always been kind. When I was too young to go out, she had let me do her make-up before her dates so that I could share in the fun. But right now, her kindness enraged me. 'Why are you even going out with him?' I said.

'Leave Maria alone,' said Patsy. 'We never asked you why you went out with Ed, did we?'

I put down the newspaper. 'We were attracted to each other, that's why Ed and I went out. Maria's not attracted to John.'

'Pity it didn't work out between you and Ed. There's more to relationships than attraction,' Patsy said.

'And you would know?' I said, and immediately regretted my cheap jab. Patsy looked away, pretending she hadn't heard me, but I knew she was hurt.

Maria leant against my bed. 'I admit I don't find John good-looking, but he seems all right.'

'Crap. You're doing it for Mum. Which is not a good reason to go out with someone,' I said.

'The Lord put it on Dad's heart that I should give him a go,' Maria said.

'How about making your own decisions?' I said.

Patsy snorted. 'It would be so much easier if Maria and I did what we wanted rather than what God wanted. It's easy to make your own decisions when you're selfish.'

I glared at Patsy. 'So you're saying I'm selfish.'

'I'm not saying anything,' said Patsy. 'I'm just stating a fact. It's easy to make a decision when you think only of yourself.'

Maria looked at Patsy and me, and made a funny chomping motion with her mouth. 'Come on, you kids!'

We heard Mum calling. Patsy went to help. When Mum came out of the toilet, she called for me to join them and that settled it. I got up and walked into her bedroom.

Mum kept what we called her 'glamour' clothes in a grand old cedar wardrobe that covered part of one wall. Next to it was a smaller, modest pine wardrobe in which she kept her everyday wear. Since the cancer, the pine wardrobe was opened and shut several times a day as we selected clothes for Mum to wear. The cedar wardrobe, however, had only been opened the one time we picked out the silk cheongsam that Mum wore for the healing party.

Maria, Patsy and I flung open the three doors of the grand old wardrobe and the cool cedar-and-mothball air flared out. At first it was dark in there, but then an overhead fluorescent light flickered on and myriad colours appeared. Hanging from a two-metre-long railing, pressed tightly against each other, were clothes of every imaginable colour, material and texture. Together they represented the forty years of Mum's adult life.

Get three new sets of clothing at Chinese New Year and throw three old ones out, Mum had told us. But she seldom threw anything out. Until the cancer made her stomach bloat, she could still fit into clothes that she had worn when she was twenty-five. My favourites were her tailor-made cheongsams and, from the sixties, the slinky jacket and trouser suits in metallic fabrics.

Whether it was she who selected the clothing or Dad (he said he chose the fabrics), to me they were Mum's artistry. As a child, unseen, I would crawl inside and squeeze through the tangle of clothes. I remembered falling asleep curled up at the bottom of the wardrobe, enfolded and caressed by their soft weight.

'Take them all out,' Mum said to Maria, 'choose something young. Try whatever you like.'

Maria flicked through the garments, but they were all tight-fitting, whereas she liked baggy clothes. 'Help me choose,' she said.

I knew what I was looking for. It was a dress Mum had worn for the parties at the house on the hill. I pushed and pulled at the hangers, but the clothes were so densely hung, they wouldn't move. Grabbing with both hands, I prised them apart. The sight of the dresses brought up photo-like scenes – where Mum had worn them, the look on her face, the impression she'd made. I felt an urge to hug the dresses to me, run my face and hands over their textures and smell their dank perfume.

I crouched to pick up some dresses that had fallen from their hangers, and my hand knocked against something hard and cold. It was the old tin that Mum kept in the back corner of the wardrobe. The tin had been there for as long as I could remember. Mum had always pestered Dad for extra shopping money, and every week she would secretly put some of this aside. None of us was supposed to know, but we all did. I wondered how much was in the tin now. It felt heavy.

I caught a glimmer of hot pink and pulled the dress out. Purple and red embroidery swirled over the pink metallic fabric. It was a halter-neck dress with a Mandarin collar and a deep V cut out at the cleavage. Fitted at the top, the dress flowed into a maxi skirt.

'Trust Natasha to go for the sexy *humsup* dress,' said Patsy.

Mum gazed at it. 'Oh yes, this dress,' she said. 'When I wore it when I was your age, the men always look.' She opened her eyes wide with a curious mixture of coyness and disbelief. 'They cannot control themselves.'

We all laughed.

'Choose something else, it's not me,' said Maria.

'Yes! Just right,' Mum said. 'Maria needs to be more sexy.'

Maria groaned, and took the dress into the bathroom. Just then Anita entered, back from work. She asked Mum for the day's news, then went to have a look in the wardrobe herself. She went straight to Mum's more sophisticated outfits, pulling them out, trying on a jacket.

Maria stomped out of the bathroom wearing the dress, red in the face. She hadn't taken off her socks and sneakers, or her T-shirt, which poked out the arm-holes of the dress. None of the dress sat right – the bodice was pulled up so high that material bunched above her breasts, and the skirt was twisted almost back to front.

Mum's head wobbled – her face crumpled, tears welled in the corners of her eyes and her shoulders shook silently. Then *Ug . . . Ug . . . Ug . . .* gasps like sobs erupted from her.

'Mum, are you all right?' said Patsy.

Mum covered her face, her body still shaking, took another look at Maria and was off again: *Ug . . . Ug . . . Ug.* We stared, unable to tell if she was laughing or crying. Anita was the first to make up her mind and she began to snicker along with her. Then the rest of us joined in.

'Stand still,' Anita said, grabbing Maria's shoulders. Anita pushed and pulled on the dress, straightened the halter, twisted the seams till the V sat over her cleavage, and tugged the bodice down to the waist. Anita stepped out of her high heels and told Maria to put them on. Maria took off her sneakers, stepped into the heels, and stood in front of Mum.

'Shoulders back, bust out,' Mum said, and Maria uncurled herself and stuck her chin up. Suddenly she looked erect and elegant. Even with the T-shirt underneath, the cut and the shimmery material brought to life every curve and hollow and made Maria glow. Mum gazed at Maria for a long time, stunned at first, and then wistful.

'I'll do the sexy walk Mum taught me,' Maria said. She lurched forward, swinging her hips in a ridiculous fashion. We began to giggle. 'Make room! Open the door!' she said, heading towards the backyard. Patsy opened the door for her and cold air blew in. Maria stepped out, heels sinking into the grass. Careening all over the place, she walked towards the ramp that Dad had built. She stepped onto the ramp like it was her catwalk. She gyrated her hips, she sashayed and boogied. By now we were all crying with laughter. Twirling around at the top of the ramp, she shouted, 'I'm healed, on behalf of Mum, I'm healed!'

Mum was no longer laughing. She seemed to be unbuttoning her shirt.

'What are you doing, Mum?' I said.

She had a big smile on her face. I could see her teeth. She never usually showed her teeth when she smiled. 'Time to change,' she said. 'I need to shower.'

'But you've had a shower,' I said.

'Are you all right, Mum?' Patsy said.

'Where's my lipstick?' Mum said. 'I need to shower!' She pulled her shirt off and started tugging at her bra.

'Are you all right?' Patsy repeated.

I held Mum's shoulders and made her look at me. 'What year is it, Mum?' I asked.

Mum opened her mouth as though about to answer, then nodded and smiled again. 'Where's my lipstick?' she said loudly.

'Shit, something's wrong. She's delirious,' Anita said. 'I'm calling the hospital.' She rushed to the phone on the bedside table.

Mum pushed at the waist on her skirt, trying to lower it over her hips. I knelt in front of her and took her hands in mine. Mum pulled her hands away and pushed back on her armrests, trying to stand up. She fell back. Maria came running in. She took one of Mum's arms while I took the other. We sat her upright and tried to stop her lunging off the wheelchair. While this was happening, Patsy stood there, watching, eyes big with shock, praying in tongues.

'Go and get Dad,' I told her.

Soon Patsy came back with Dad. 'Irene, Irene,' he said, and we moved aside. He saw her sitting there in her bra with the big simple smile on her face, laid his trembling hands on her head and prayed, 'Jesus, Jesus.' Love and fear were in his eyes.

Anita got off the phone. 'The doctor says we need to take her to the hospital straightaway.'

'Get to the car!' Dad shouted. 'Where are the keys?'

Anita found the keys. She ran through the house, telling the vigil group and the drama group to leave. Maria and I got Mum's shirt back on her and put her in the car. She didn't resist our handling. All the time she kept smiling.

I opened the back door to get in the car. Anita wouldn't move up for me.

'You stay back to lock up after the drama group leaves,' she said.

I refused. 'Wait for me, I'll fix it up,' I said. 'Don't go without me!'

I ran inside, found Troy from the drama group, threw him my keys and barked out instructions. Before he had time to answer, I ran out the door and towards the car. Dad had reversed out of the driveway onto the road and was starting to move forward. Desperate, I banged the car window with my open palm. The car stopped.

'What are you bashing so hard for?' Anita scolded. They let me in.

All the way to the hospital, we sang hymns in loud, brave voices. Dad drove fast. Mum asked for her lipstick. Anita gave it to her. Mum asked for her lipstick again.

'It's in your hand, Mum,' Anita said.

'Oh!' Mum said. She would pause a while, then ask for her lipstick again, and Anita would remind her where it was.

At one point Mum twisted her head around to look at us in the back seat. 'Oh, you are all here, my daughters,' she said. She looked at us as though we were the most beautiful things in the world. As though we were the sunrise. My sisters felt it too, I could tell, because while she was looking, we sat still, shoulder to shoulder, barely breathing, smiling back.

When we arrived, everything moved so quickly. They pushed her in through the double doors to the emergency department. Only Dad was allowed to accompany her.

MUM WAS ADMITTED TO EMERGENCY immediately, as was a man who arrived with raw burns to his hands and face. The six or so other patients, who had to wait, sat alone or accompanied on the rows of plastic bucket seats in the windowless waiting room, looking ill and lost in their own predicaments. My sisters and I took the seats that converged in the corner. In a quiet voice, Maria led us in the rosary, while Anita, Patsy and I whispered the responses.

We raised our eyes every time the automatic double door to the emergency clinic swung open. Flashes of activity could be glimpsed – a trolley rolling past, medical staff calling out, someone running, a curtain pulled back to reveal a patient on a drip. Then the doors would close again.

Our group grew. First Charles and Will arrived, then John to take Maria out for dinner. Though Maria wanted to cancel, Anita had insisted she go ahead with the date. Charles handed around takeaway containers of noodles. Maria played matchbox cars with Will and mostly ignored John, who was seated next to her. Anita tried to fill the gap, asking John about his work as a finance officer at the transport department.

At last the doors swung open and Dad walked through. 'Praise the Lord,' he said, with twinkling eyes and his arms raised like a celebrity host. 'All is well.'

Anita bent down and hugged Will to herself. 'Thank you, Jesus,' I heard Maria and Patsy say. I breathed out.

'Now I must eat something,' Dad said, sitting down. Charles handed him a noodle box. Through mouthfuls he told us that Mum was asleep, she would stay the night in hospital, and he would explain everything when he had finished eating.

Anita started organising. 'Right, one of us needs to stay with Mum. Maria is going out with John, I have to go home for Will, and Dad needs to rest.'

Patsy and I both offered to stay. I knew, as I spoke, that Anita wouldn't pick me.

'Patsy will stay,' Anita said. 'She can pray with Mum when she wakes up.'

Dad was ready to talk. Noticing John for the first time, Dad greeted him. He then stood up so that he could see everyone.

'Thank Jesus for His great love for Irene and for all of us,' he said. 'We saw it, didn't we – that beatific smile on her face? I felt very palpably His love for each of us, shining through Irene.' As he talked, he made eye contact with each of us in turn, working his way slowly from right to left and also connecting with the people on the other benches in the waiting room.

'But why the medical emergency, Dad?' asked Anita.

'Of course the doctors put it down to chemotherapy drugs, which upset the blood chemistry and cause a delusional state. This is the one-dimensional view, man's truth. And then there is God's truth.' Dad's voice was rich and melodious. 'We know it is His way of showing us that the important thing is to be open like the gentle flowers around us to the sunshine of God's love, trusting that good will come out from everything. You know what the wonderful thing is —'

'What's happening? Is she going to get better? What did they do to her?' I blurted out.

'You know what the wonderful thing is?' Dad continued. 'It is Jesus's way of saying she needs a rest, that we all need a rest. Let them care for her. She must stay in hospital for at least two weeks. I told the doctor that, and he listened.' Dad paused. We were quiet, waiting for his next words.

'They inserted a tube, a drip – poor Irene, she suffers from those needles.' Dad shook his head sorrowfully. 'They gave her a blood transfusion and sedatives. Suddenly the smile fell from her face, her eyes closed, her mouth sagged open, her hand in mine became lifeless. A man once died in my arms, you know. But the Lord reminded me she was resting in His love. And then – and this is the Lord's miracle to us – I smelt the oranges. The perfume suffused my senses just like the time Jesus first told us she would be healed ...' He gasped for air, his voice cracked. 'Thank you, Jesus, for reminding me to hold on to the miracle, to not lose faith, to never lose faith. Let's sing one song right here in the waiting room before we go our separate ways tonight.'

Together we sang all four verses of 'I Believe'. After the first verse, he encouraged the other patients in the waiting room to sing with us. A few of them joined in. Tears rolled down his cheeks. My heart felt full. I was moved despite myself.

That was the first of many songs we would sing in hospital over the remaining six days I had in Melbourne. Later that first night, Mum was moved from Emergency into a room in the oncology clinic. She shared the room with another patient, a bony middle-aged woman with a bandaged head who we learnt had brain cancer.

On waking the next morning, Mum couldn't remember what had happened to put her in hospital and was unnerved to find a catheter sticking out of a vein in her chest. Once she got her bearings, however, she claimed she was glad to be in hospital. Staying there would make it easier for everyone, she said.

In many ways, it did make it easier. At home, there had been the constant fear that we were giving her too many painkillers or too few, or the wrong food, or overtiring her, or exposing her to bugs and not taking enough precautions. Mum's reluctance to tell us how she was feeling or what she wanted made it even more difficult to guess if we were doing the right thing. It was a relief now to submit to the authority of the hospital.

Once a day Doctor Richards or the duty oncologist would do the rounds of the ward, spending five minutes with each patient. In the past, Dad would have demanded answers, challenged the doctor and preached to him, but now he stood up when the doctor entered, nodded and listened, and watched him leave without trying to detain him.

Every hour or so, with comforting regularity, a nurse entered Mum's room. How grateful we were for these efficient women. They would greet and chat, check the notes on the clipboard at the foot of her bed, shine a torch in Mum's eyes, stick a thermometer in her ear, dispense medication, and check oxygen levels and blood pressure. Each day they would also draw blood to check her chemical balance. Mum was grateful that the blood could be drawn from the catheter so she was spared the needle's daily forays into the fine veins of her arms. Through the catheter they also administered miniscule amounts of morphine, in the form of a pale-yellow liquid, several times a day.

Food was delivered at set times on clean plastic trays. Grilled or baked meat, chicken or fish, steamed or boiled vegetables, potatoes and gravy. The hospital diet seemed decadent compared with the regimen Patsy had put Mum on at home. It even included sweet milky shakes to boost her protein levels. For the first time in months, Mum seemed to take pleasure in eating, and, best of all, there was no more liver. My sisters and I stopped quarrelling about what she ate. Except for replacing the white bread the hospital supplied with wholemeal, we accepted what came.

After two nights in the shared room, Mum was moved into her own room with a tall window and just enough space between the bed and the wall for her wheelchair. At least one family member was always around. We took turns staying overnight on a brown vinyl armchair that reclined into a narrow bed.

Come morning, the nurses would hoist Mum up and wheel her into the bathroom. She would be returned to her room an hour later, toileted and showered and clothed in a freshly laundered hospital gown smelling of chlorine. At this point, Mum would take control of her attire. She instructed my sisters and me to wrap her purple silk robe over the hospital gown, arrange a pink cashmere shawl around her shoulders, and place embroidered slippers upon her feet. She made up her face – foundation and blush to hide her skin's pallor, brown pencil to outline her eyes, and pink lipstick to embolden. Finally, she put on the wig. When Dad came into the room, she would be sitting by the window waiting, a charming wooden doll.

A romance grew between Mum and Dad during those days in hospital. Living apart for the first time in decades, they seemed to see each other with fresh eyes. I discovered them sharing shy smiles and private jokes, and singing old love songs together. I imagined I saw them the way they were when they first met. He raved on about his ideas, passions and ambitions, while she listened and smiled. One afternoon, I watched Dad sitting cross-legged at the foot of her bed, his face shining across at her as he talked. 'I will send my script to all the most prominent producers and let them fight for it,' he said, 'and only the producer who promises to keep true to the message of salvation in my work, and to tour it around the world – not just Paris, New York and the big cities of the world, but also the small forgotten villages and hamlets – will win the contract.' She didn't answer, 'Don't be absurd, *eeh eeh eeh*,' or 'Stop dreaming,' or 'If you have so much money, why don't you get the roof fixed?' as she usually did. She listened to his words and smiled and admired, and didn't criticise.

Dad's way was to give compliments in the third person. He praised Mum to whomever was in the room. 'You know,' he would say, 'your mother was the pearl of the Orient, the most stunning but also humble woman Hong Kong had ever seen. She was elite. At first I hung around at the edge of her pack of admirers, trying to win her attention. I even wore a shiny golden shirt . . . Look at her, she is still beautiful!'

Her room, though no larger than a cell, was crowded with family and visitors for most of the day. Dad had cancelled the vigil at home and called on friends to pray at the hospital.

When we took Mum to hospital, I had thought I would have to cancel my ticket to Darwin. But there was no better time to go. She seemed happier than she had been for some time, and to have less need of me than ever.

A couple of days before I left, I bumped into Ed in the corridor outside Mum's clinic. He said hello and was about to keep walking, but I stopped him. I wanted to thank him for visiting Mum and for helping Dad with errands and the drama group. I glanced at his face and thought again how deep his eyes were, though now there was no warmth in them for me.

'I'm going back to Darwin, and just wanted to thank you, and say I'm sorry for everything,' I said.

'Patsy told me you're going,' he said, and hesitated.

'I'm glad you're looking well and still seeing my family. They're much better than me,' I said.

'God bless,' he said, and walked on.

*

In the evening after dinner, the family and a few extras would cram into Mum's room for prayers. Sometimes there were so many that the IV stand and medicine trolley had to be pushed into the corridor, and people would be spilling out the doorway. Maria approached patients in the clinic on the slightest pretext and invited them to join us. The woman with brain cancer and the Italian patient down the corridor hadn't missed an evening prayer session yet. Patsy would strum the guitar, and Dad would lead us in song. The sound would billow down the corridor, into the other rooms and reception area. No one told us to pipe down.

I overheard one nurse call it the Chan invasion. But some of the other nurses seemed to welcome it. They smiled fondly at us. *Oh, the singing Chan family. They are so close and inspiring.* Whether the nurses and patients were believers or not, I could see that my family brought significance, colour and warmth to the sterile confines of the hospital. Against the desperation that you could almost smell in the cancer ward, little Will, laughing or playing hide-and-seek behind the curtains, was life itself. Every moment of life or joy was heightened a thousand times over.

Everything, Dad said, was God's plan – Mum and the family had been sent to the hospital to inspire those facing their own mortality to choose Jesus, choose life! Mum had an African nurse's aide called Faith and a nurse called Joy. Jesus is faith and joy. Surely that was a sign. We looked around for a Hope.

During this time, I was relieved that Mum looked happier, but she was further away from me than ever. I no longer had time alone with her. Even if a break came in the flow of visitors, you could be sure that Patsy would be there, often just praying silently in the corner, but always there. Anita, too, commented that Patsy had become more possessive of Mum. I counted the days until I left and tried not to put a foot wrong.

*

The house felt desolate without her. My sisters no longer came over, and the pillar candles on the altar had gone out, petrified into pitted and blackened shapes. Only when the drama group came over for rehearsals did life and noise return for a few hours, but even these were more subdued than usual.

In these days before leaving Melbourne, there was little for me to do except cook Dad's lunches of fried noodles, keep the house clean and make sure there was food and drink for the drama group. Dad would work in his studio from seven in the morning, have an early lunch and leave for the hospital at about one. He returned home at about eight, except when it was his turn to stay overnight. Dad and I barely saw each other. Most of the time, it was just his sounds that let me know he was there. In the morning I listened for his 6 a.m. alarm, his footsteps in the corridor, his gargling and spitting in the bathroom, his plates clinking in the kitchen. As soon as I heard him walk up to the studio, I would go to the kitchen, cook, clean up and leave to catch a bus to the hospital. After I left for Darwin, it would be Maria's job to come to the house each day to cook and clean for Dad. I told her I felt guilty, but she said it would be okay, it was only until Mum got better.

A couple of nights before I left, Dad returned from the hospital half an hour after I did. Hearing his footsteps stop outside my room, I made no sound, hoping not to attract his attention. He knocked on my door.

'Natasha, were you at prayers?' he said, when I opened the door. 'Oh yes, you were, wasn't it wonderful? Did you see how many patients and nurses we are bringing to the Lord? Praise Jesus.' He paused, clearing his throat. 'There is a tin of money in the bottom of your mother's wardrobe. It is money she has been hiding away, but she has been healed of her attachment to it. We need it to help pay the medical bills, and to support CTJ to put on its next show. Go and find the tin and bring it to me now.'

'It's Mum's money. Have you spoken to her?' I said.

He frowned with a righteous anger. 'What do you mean, have I spoken to her?'

I couldn't respond.

'You may not intend it, Natasha, but I sense a spirit of criticism in you. Do not entertain it. Of course Irene and I discussed the money. She asked my forgiveness for not trusting me enough. I forgave her. Immediately, and with all my heart. You see, God not only forgives the sinner but forgets the sin, and so must we. Even if you have not requested it, know that I forgive you, Natasha.'

He sighed. 'Now take the money out and put it on the kitchen table.' He turned his back on me and walked down the corridor towards the family room.

I imagined striding after him, yelling, *Mum needs* your *forgiveness? Get the money yourself!* I took a few steps after him, then froze. I could not disrespect him. It would be beneath his dignity to get down on his hands and knees and scrape around the bottom of Mum's wardrobe. The very idea was inconceivable.

I tried to subdue my anger. In a few days I would be gone. I went to Mum's wardrobe and got the tin.

*

On the night before I left for Darwin, Anita had scheduled me to stay the night with Mum. At the end of evening prayers, packed shoulder to shoulder in her room, the group sang 'Rejoice in the Lord Always' at the top of their voices. Afterwards, the family streamed out, taking their body heat, colour and verve with them, leaving Mum and me alone. A spell had been broken and all that remained was a harsh white cubicle. I could smell the bleach and formaldehyde again, see the things I didn't want to see: the red emergency button, the screen monitors, the wires sticking out of steel plates in the walls, breathing tubes, fluid tubes and catheters.

How silent it was without all of them there. I felt my own inadequacy, my inability to bring cheer. I asked whether she wanted me to put some music on, or the TV. Or did she want a massage? No, she just wanted a glass of water and for me to sit with her. Trying to think of things to say, I told her what I had cooked Dad for lunch and what he had eaten in the hospital cafeteria for dinner, and about the new patient I had seen wheeled in on a trolley to the room at the end of the corridor. We went quiet again. I reminded Mum I was leaving the next day. Since she had not mentioned it, I wondered if she had forgotten. She murmured something. No, she had not forgotten.

A young Filipino nurse, April, came in to take Mum to the bathroom. She was cheerful and very attractive, and I was glad for Mum's sake that Dad had gone home. While Mum and the nurse were in the bathroom, I extended the recliner and made it up with sheets I had brought from home. They returned twenty minutes later, Mum in a hospital gown with crease lines across the front where the fabric had been folded. April hoisted Mum into bed and performed the standard medical checks on her.

Mum pulled the neck of her gown down to reveal the catheter sticking out of her flesh like a carbuncle. April took hold of the catheter in one hand, and with the other injected it with a flushing fluid. She attached the morphine solution to the IV stand and pulled it closer to Mum.

'Why do I need this morphine now when I don't feel any pain! Can't you wait?' said Mum.

'Ma'am, remember what Doctor Richards told you?' said April. 'We can't wait for breakthrough pain. It makes it more difficult to manage. Then you will need a stronger dose. So sorry.' She fed the tube from the morphine solution into the catheter in Mum's chest, turned on the pump and left the room.

At home, Mum had liked to wait until the pain got bad before she took her next dose. I could understand how she felt. How would you know if the pain had gone if you just kept topping up the painkiller? This treatment didn't allow for the possibility that a person might get better.

Mum frowned at the bead of pale-yellow liquid descending the tube. I sat on the side of the bed. Looking at the worry on her face, I wanted to touch her but felt nervous. I put my hand out slowly and rested it on her head.

'Shall I massage your forehead, Mum?' I said.

'No, la, you need to rest. Aren't you tired? You've been here all day.'

'I'm not tired.' I moved my fingers over her forehead and face and felt her bones, fine like a cat's, under thin, loose skin.

Her eyelids fluttered a few times, then closed, her mouth softening. Her breath came out in puffs from her lips. I watched another liquid bead form at the top of the IV tube, then falter and break, dribbling down the tube into the vein in Mum's chest.

She suddenly shook herself awake. 'Enough massage,' she said.

'Very nice, thank you. Now let's read the bible.' She said it with such resolve that I knew she was up to something. 'Open it where I put the paper,' she said. 'Read where I've marked it. There.' She pointed to a paper serviette wedged between two pages of her bible.

I felt my heart quicken. She had thought of me – she knew I was staying the night and she had prepared for me.

It was the parable of the unmerciful servant in the Book of Matthew. A servant is forgiven a debt by his master, but refuses to forgive a debt owed him by another servant. When the master finds out, he beats and punishes the unmerciful servant. Mum had underlined the part where Jesus tells the servant to forgive his brother not just seven times 'but seventy times seven'. As I read the words aloud, I kept thinking, *Yes, my mother knows me. I am the one with sores, the resentful one.*

I closed the bible. 'I might get a cup of tea, Mum. Do you want one?'

'Wait,' she said. 'What do you think of the bible reading?'

'Well, shouldn't the master have forgiven his servant for being unforgiving?'

'Don't always question things,' she said, sighing. 'Natasha, you need to forgive! Let go of bad thoughts.'

'Okay, Mum, I forgive. If to say I do is enough, then I forgive.'

She frowned at me. 'No, you don't.'

'No one needs my forgiveness,' I said.

She rubbed at her throat. 'What about your dad?'

'He needs it least of all.'

'Natasha, you must forgive your dad.'

'What would I be forgiving him for, Mum?'

'Aiya, don't be a bad child. None of us are perfect.'

'What would I be forgiving him for? See, you can't say it. No one can say it. Do we all need to play along that he's a saint?' I stood up. 'Don't get me wrong, I do feel for him. I know his childhood was hard. But that doesn't mean he can just —'

'Do it for yourself and for God!' Mum cried, raising her voice and pointing her finger at me. 'I used to have bad thoughts. Then the Holy Spirit filled me, and I gave it all to Jesus.' She waved her arms and tried to lift up her head. 'If you don't forgive, it will make you sick!'

'Mum, rest, please! Lie back.'

'Why can't you listen?'

'I'll try,' I said.

She sighed again. 'Now, take my prayer book and read it out. Where I marked it.' Another paper serviette was wedged into this book. In that crumpled serviette, which she had saved from her dinner tray and folded into a book so that she could deliver me a message, I felt her love for me.

'"O Lord, Jesus Christ, Redeemer and Saviour,"' I read. '"Dispel with your love my resentment and bitterness. Allowed to fester, these sins will destroy and kill. I ask that You forgive my sins and give me the grace to forgive others. You forgive us seventy times seven. You forgive so that you do not even remember our wickedness."'

I stole a look at Mum. She smiled and nodded. 'Keep on reading,' she said.

'"Baptise me with the Holy Spirit, help me to cleanse my memory, so I can also forgive and be forgiven."'

I read the prayer in a monotone, not wanting to show any emotion, but each word pierced me. *You are pretending*, I screamed to Mum in my head. *You go into this fog so you don't have to feel the rage. You can't even look at another woman without thinking,* Is she his type? My mother, my sisters and I, we all knew what to look out for – she would be a natural beauty; she would have something of the pleasing little girl about her. He would be so kind to her. He wouldn't even know what he was doing.

I looked at Mum again. She was smiling nervously at me, grateful that I had recited the prayer. Forgive and forget? I wouldn't know where to start.

*

The morphine ensured that Mum slept. I moved in and out of consciousness. Flashing buttons, lit displays, beeps, muffled footsteps and voices reminded me where I was. We kept the door slightly ajar, but it was not enough to stop the sickly-smelling gas that came from Mum's intestines building up in the small room.

A nurse with a pen torch came in to check on her. She walked out. I must have fallen asleep because the next thing I knew the nurse was there again with the dimmer lights on and a trolley. I sprang up from the recliner. 'What's wrong?' I said.

'Nothing to worry about, dear. She's had a little accident. It's very common with the medication she's on. I'll just clean her up.'

The nurse pulled at the sheets. I saw the wet patches on them and on Mum's gown, and smelt the warm tang of it. 'She did this last night when I was on duty as well,' the nurse said. 'I'll just clean her up and she'll be none the wiser. She's got enough on her plate as it is.'

She pushed Mum onto her side while she pulled the sheet from under her. Mum was completely out of it. I tried to help.

'It's all right, love. You need to sleep. I'll do it. That's what I'm here for,' she said. We had not met before. She was one of the older nurses, with large strong hands and a tired, kind face. I lay back down, but did not sleep. I watched the nurse's deft movements and her gentleness with Mum. In a low, calm voice, she explained to Mum every time she was about to move her, although Mum was lost to the world. 'That's right, love, I'm going to put you on your left side now so I can put the nice fresh sheet under you.'

She looked after her like a mother would. 'There, I'll just wipe you so you won't smell it in the morning,' she said, brushing Mum with a warm towel and putting a fresh gown on her. When the nurse left, I got up and pulled Mum's sheet down. The nurse's care had touched and amazed me. There was no reward for her other than the wellbeing of her patient. Mum lay there, asleep, warm, dry and clean, in tenderly smoothed-out sheets and gown. I bent down and hugged her, laying my head softly in the crook of her neck and feeling her breath on the top of my head.

*

The next morning, Mum was agitated – her eyes were clouded and her hands could not keep still. We could find nothing to talk about. It was time to say goodbye and there was nothing else in my mind. Patsy had arrived early. A young couple whom I had never met before, who knew Mum and Patsy from a prayer group, arrived after breakfast. I ignored them.

Patsy was on the guitar, and the man and woman were singing and laughing. It was time to go. Mum sat in her wheelchair by the grey-tinted window, its glass so thick that everything outside, though the sun gleamed and the wind swayed the branches of trees, looked not quite real. She smiled at the couple and sang quietly. My backpack was ready and packed, sitting outside the door.

Abruptly, while they were singing, I stood up, squeezed Patsy's shoulder and turned to Mum. 'Bye, Mum,' I said. 'I'll see you at Christmas.' I bent down to hug her and let go quickly so that she did not have the chance to lift her arms to me. I walked out of the room, frightened that I would break down. Outside, I grabbed my backpack and turned to wave. Patsy kept on with her strumming and the couple with their singing. Mum had turned her wheelchair towards the window. She did not even pretend to sing anymore. She gazed out the window with haunted eyes, already departed from me.

AT DARWIN AIRPORT, I JUMPED INTO A TAXI. 'Could you let me off here?' I said to the driver on impulse as we drove by the foreshore, still a couple of blocks from home. He let me out at the pub opposite the beach.

My watch, still on Melbourne time, said it was 4.30 p.m. Around now, Mum sometimes visited the small hospital chapel on the ground floor for a last prayer before it was locked for the day. Here it was 3 p.m. Through the wire mesh that formed the walls of the pub, I could see a man hosing down the concrete floor, removing last night's beer swill and preparing for the next onslaught of drinkers. It would be standing room only inside the cage by sunset, and I would be able to hear them from where I lived.

I crossed the road to the parkland of the foreshore and walked down to where sandstone rocks jutted out, broad enough to lie on, and casuarina trees cast some meagre shade. There wasn't a soul in sight. Leaning my backpack against a rock, I took out the letter I had written to Jason on the flight. In the past few weeks, I had started this letter many times, but it still felt wrong. A voice in my head would say, *You don't deserve to be forgiven by him*, or else, *You were right not to trust him – he's sure to have moved on and a letter now will just make him feel awkward.*

God, I'd almost forgotten how hot it was this time of year. Holding the letter still folded in my hand, I walked down to the water. From there I could see a recess further along the foreshore where a handful of Aboriginal men and women camped. I loved this stretch of sea, knew it glistening and full, and so depleted that it seemed you could walk halfway to Asia on the flat sand.

The heat was overpowering. It pressed in on me, making my skin burn and my insides melt. I unfolded the letter and read it.

Hi Jason,

I hope you're well and you've completed your drawings for the show and they're exactly how you wanted them to be. I'm not sure you want to hear from me after our last conversation and the way I didn't reply to your letter.

Thank you for that letter – it was beautiful and undeserved. My father didn't give it to me until three weeks after it arrived (he said he forgot) and then it seemed like it was too late to reply. I did try to write a few times but everything sounded wrong.

I'm in the aeroplane on the way back to Darwin. Mum went into hospital last week. Her blood chemistry was upset by the chemo, but now she's stable and is expected to return home in the next few days. I remember saying to you before I left how I wanted to be closer to her before she died. I think I had a very naive idea of what getting closer to her would look like. I think maybe I wanted her to open up to me, tell me her life story, and I'd be able to tell her things back. Well, we've never communicated like that in my family, so I shouldn't have hoped that we were about to start. I'm always trying to change myself and the people around me. I wish I could just be an accepting type of person, who sees and brings out the best in people.

After I broke up with you, I met a born-again Christian guy recovering from alcoholism and got involved with him. It only lasted about three weeks. He was a nice person, but he wasn't what I was looking for, not that I was looking for anybody. I wasn't what he needed either. I think he was actually besotted with my family, not me.

I haven't said I'm sorry for everything yet, because I don't know where to start. I've shown you how mean and destructive I can be. But you could be thinking, it's a good thing she showed her true colours. What a relief I got away from her.

You're a very good and true person. I'm going to drop this letter in your postbox as soon as I get to Darwin, so I don't take you by surprise if we bump into each other at Rite Price or around the traps.

Love

Natasha

I walked back to the rocks and took a pen out of my bag. I couldn't think in this heat, but knew there was more to say. At the bottom of the page I scrawled,

Jase, I'm sorry, I'm so sorry for hurting you. Sorry for being destructive, for not handling my own fears, for pretending you had the problem when it was really me. You gave me love and I threw it back in your face.

You might be with someone else, or you might not want to see me at all. Still, you should know that your love has been precious to me. Thank you.

I had to deliver it before he got home from work. I put the letter in the envelope, picked up my stuff, ran all the way to his place and dropped it into his postbox. I didn't dare look at his house, at the window where his bedroom was, even though I was sure he wasn't there.

To get from his place to mine, I walked through the small park and zigzagged through the backstreets that curved around the foreshore. The glare of the sea, the hot sky and verdant gardens seared me. My step was light, though my backpack weighed heavily on me and sweat ran down my face and body. 'I'm home!' I said with a joyful heart when the house I rented with Shelley, Ian and Pip, elevated in the treetops, came into view.

Music, voices, Shelley's deep laugh and the smell of incense travelled down through the cracks in the floorboards. I climbed the metal steps and saw Shelley and two women sitting on the verandah.

'Hey, look who's here! I told you to ring me to pick you up from the airport!' Shelley said, springing up.

'I took a taxi,' I said.

'Is that sweat dripping off you?'

'I stopped for a walk at the beach.'

'Walking around the beach in the middle of the day during the build-up! What are ya, a bloody tourist?' she said, laughing.

'Yep, I've been away too long,' I said.

'Welcome home.' She stood at the top of the stairs, sarong wrapped around her, with open arms.

'Don't touch me, I stink,' I said, then realised that sounded a bit uptight. Not right for here. She took me against her loose breasts and hugged me close.

*

At dinner that night, on the verandah with housemates and friends, Shelley raised her glass of pinot. 'To Natasha's beautiful mother, Irene,' she said. Leaning into the candlelit table, we clinked our glasses. I thanked them for their concern and told them it was good to be home. I was nervous to be the centre of attention – they seemed so effortlessly intelligent, witty and stylish. Dad would probably call them politically correct, self-serving humanists. Shelley, who held the lease, had handpicked her housemates. They were all social activist and creative types. I felt grateful to have been included. Even after three years in this household, I still wondered why she had picked me. I gulped down my chilled wine.

A distant flash of lightning showed on the horizon, and the air was hot and damp and scented with frangipanis. For a while we caught up on each other's personal news. I hoped Jason would come up in the conversation, but no one mentioned him, even though he had been a regular here. As with so many of our dinner parties, the conversation soon turned to social justice issues. Ian had been scratching his shirtless chest and rocking on the back legs of his chair, unstimulated by the catching up. With the change in topic, he sat forward.

Pip was writing an article about reforming laws that discriminated against same-sex couples. A discussion ensued that had the whole table going. They were so clever, fluent and strategic in the comments they made, while I went mute.

After a few wines and a joint, everything seemed to glow. Although the air was thick with loud talk and the stereo blasting, I had the feeling I could hear myself breathe. *This is my home and these are my people*, I thought. I poured myself another glass of wine.

Now Ian and Pedro talked about the Free Papua march they were organising. Pedro, a socialist from Sydney, had come to Darwin in solidarity for the movement. Pedro and his girlfriend Jasmine were staying with us and had set up their swag under the house. My concentration kept lapsing. I heard something about 'Australia's mining deals with Indonesia' and the 'torture of freedom fighters'.

I was drunk enough not to care if I appeared stupid. 'Are you saying Australia is involved in the torture?' I asked

Pedro stopped his rapid flow to stare at me. 'Australian Federal Police have been training the Indonesian forces that are torturing and killing the freedom fighters,' he said. 'You don't know about this? It's been in the news for the last month!'

Shelley filled my glass. 'Natasha wouldn't have had time to follow the news while she was looking after her mum,' she said.

'I've been in another world,' I said. 'Charismatics aren't interested in human rights or the environment. They're only interested in our souls.' The joint came around again.

'They're obsessed with sex, you mean,' said Pip's girlfriend, Ruby, standing up. 'My brethren, God made Adam and Eve. Not Adam and Steve!' she intoned in the style of an American evangelist.

'Natasha's family aren't like that,' said Pip, stroking Ruby's arm.

'I wouldn't be so sure,' I said. 'But don't worry – they don't hate you. They love you. They just hate your sin.' That got a laugh from the table.

'Someone should assassinate all the fundamentalist leaders. They're dangerous people,' said Pedro.

'Whoa, settle down, Pedro,' said Ian.

I had drunk too much. 'Yes, dangerous people,' I kept saying. Letting the talk flow around me, I filled my glass and drank some more. I couldn't stop giggling.

I heard myself say, 'Did you know that my mother is going to get up and walk?' I was gabbling on now, not knowing what I was talking about. Somewhere in my ramblings, I was conscious of telling them about Mum's dream of jumping the three-metre-high back fence, and the ramp to salvation, and the ridiculous healing party and the look in Mum's eyes when she opened them after the marathon of prayers and knew she wasn't healed.

The room was spinning, I was zoning in and out. Someone was laughing too loudly. I realised it was me. The faces around the table were alarmed. *Are you okay?* Shelley's and Pip's faces were right in front of mine, they were holding me under my arms and pulling me to my feet.

*

Waves of shame rolled over me, waking me in the dark before I was aware of the drilling in my head and my dry, filthy-tasting mouth. I put my hand up to wipe my brow and knocked something hard next to my pillow. Someone had put a bottle of water there. I gulped it down.

How vile I was, putting down my family in front of others. At least Dad knew how to inspire Mum, my sisters and his admirers; I knew nothing except how to judge and destroy. *Admit it*, I said to myself, *you couldn't help your mother. You weren't there digging things up for her, or for Bonnie, or for the sake of the truth. You were doing it for yourself. You wanted some bloodletting. You're nothing but a nasty piece of work.*

I was heavy, pinned to the bed, burning up. Every creak and clang of the fan spinning above me hurt my head. The light from the half-moon outside was too much. *Now Jason and your friends know what you're like, too. They are good, balanced people, and they know that you're not.*

*

I woke with the sun blazing into my room, head hammering and my body slicked in sweat. Panicking, I grabbed my watch. Thank God there was still time to call.

After a shower and Panadol, I rang Mum's ward number. It would be 9 a.m. over there and the best time to speak to her before the visitors arrived. The smell of the miso Shelley was cooking for breakfast wafted through the house, making me feel sick.

'Hi, Mum,' I said.

'Natasha,' Mum said. 'No need to ring again, la. You already rang last night.'

'That was just to let you know I arrived. Remember I told you I would ring you every morning after breakfast?'

'Are you sure? You are busy.'

'I'm not too busy to give you a call.'

'Don't worry. The Lord is looking after me.'

'I just want to say hello every day.' I hoped she didn't hear the catch in my voice.

'Okay,' she said. I heard other voices in the background. Mum spoke to someone.

A sharp pain drilled into my head. 'Do you see Doctor Richards today?' I said.

'Supposed to,' she said.

'He'll let you know when you can go home?'

'Yes, supposed to.' She sounded distracted.

'I'm going to work today.'

'Tell your boss to give you back the same job,' she said.

'I can't do that. I left that position.'

Mum was speaking to someone on the other side. Her voice came on again. 'What did you say?'

'I have to take whatever is available because I quit my old job.'

'Okay, I will pray for you. Bye-bye.'

'Bye, Mum. I'll ring again tomorrow morning.'

I went into the kitchen. Shelley was rushing around in her work clothes. 'There's coffee in the pot. I have to leave in two minutes,' she said, smiling at me. 'How are you feeling?'

'Pathetic. Did you put the bottle of water and the bucket next to my bed?'

'Pip and I did.'

'Thank you. I'm sorry I was so gross last night.'

She waved a hand across her face. 'Don't even think about it. We've all been there,' she said.

No, they haven't, I thought. They became even more suave and charming when they drank or smoked too much. I had never seen them be repulsive.

*

The receptionist at the Disability Advocacy Service was new. I told her I had an appointment with Katrina. She didn't seem to recognise my name even though I had worked there for two years and only been gone for three months.

'Take a seat,' she said. 'The director shouldn't be too long.' I sat down, feeling like an outsider. I looked at the posters on the wall: 'Domestic violence, break the silence', and another one, 'Kava, not Aboriginal way'. Two clients walked in, fidgeting and tense in their sweaty T-shirts.

Three of my old workmates spotted me at reception and came out of their offices to say hello. Their concerned looks made me aware that my eyes were probably still bloodshot and I looked terrible. *Welcome back, how's your mother, it's been full-on here, Sam left to work for the Aboriginal Health Service, let's do lunch* ... They had a busy air while we chatted, and quickly returned to their work. Despite their friendliness, I wondered if I sensed a wariness in them, as though Katrina had told them I wasn't a team player.

Katrina and I had worked on a project together before I left. We had found the ideal house to set up a group home for people with mental illnesses who were reintegrating into society after hospitalisation. Katrina instigated a doorknocking and consultation campaign to gain the support of neighbours for the home. Even though she had around eight years in the sector and I had only two, I was convinced that Katrina's approach was wrong. 'These people have the right to live in the community,' I said. 'Your consultation strategy will just give a voice to prejudice, and prejudice is not a valid reason for a proposal to be knocked back.' Half our management committee supported me, but in the end the chair decided in favour of Katrina's approach. We went ahead and the objections to having people with mental illness as neighbours were so vociferous and well publicised that the application for the house had to be withdrawn. I was furious, but she was adamant she had done the right thing. If we hadn't gone down that path, she said, things would have been worse in the long run.

Katrina called me into her office. Once we would have hugged, but now she just enquired politely after my mother before getting down to business.

'As you know, the first group house was abandoned,' she said. 'But we've found another house and are going to have a consultation campaign similar to last time. You wouldn't be a project manager this time, but we can give you a job doing the doorknocking and consultations. It's a lower level than you were on.'

She looked at me searchingly. 'Obviously you need to be onside with it. I'm not offering you this job to bring up old issues. That's water under the bridge. But if you are going to take this job' – her eyes became flinty and her voice flared – 'you need to be fully committed. You need to be a team player. I won't have you running your own show.'

I didn't say anything for a while.

'I will understand if you don't want to take it on,' she said.

'I'll do it,' I said.

*

In the next week, I doorknocked about forty households. The proposed group home was on a respectable middle-class street, with many households of young families with new four-wheel drives in their garages.

I wore my badge and gave them my spiel. Four men and women at a time will live in the house with a supervisor until they are ready to shift into their own homes. They need to live in a neighbourhood setting to help them regain family, work and social networks before they move out on their own again.

The neighbours were keen to have their say. The home shouldn't be located in a residential area, they said. It will pose a danger to families and children. Our children will not be able to play in the street. The sense of community will be destroyed. Our properties will be devalued. These were the usual responses. Only five households in the street supported or were neutral about the home. I found I couldn't pick who was going to be in favour. I would go into a house with people who seemed open, kind and intelligent, who had Aboriginal paintings on the wall and community-service jobs, and they would give the stock negative responses.

For the first couple of days, I corrected residents who used the words 'schizos' or 'psychos', and responded with an appalled silence to those who told me that people with mental illnesses were dangerous, or sex offenders. To the neighbours I felt could be reasoned with, I talked about de-institutionalisation, the right to housing and a community, and told them to put themselves in the shoes of that person or their family. The drive in me to scourge and to scold and be the truth-sayer was strong. But when I spoke like this, I could see faces harden and the walls go up further. One young mother said, 'Don't look down your nose at me,' and I felt ashamed at how self-righteous I was. *I'm like my father*, I thought, *only without the charm and the charisma.*

*

By now I'd seen Jason three times. The first time I had glimpsed him in the distance, cycling with a woman in an aerobics outfit. I expected the stomach-churning insecurity to start, but it didn't.

The second time was at the opening of his exhibition. It was a group show titled *Strange Fruit*. For years, Jason had made drawings of weird and macabre deep-sea creatures. Grabbing any blue biro close to hand, he would scratch vigorously onto paper until the marks became a powerful mass. The scribbles were an antidote, he said, to the constraints of his work as a graphic designer. Seeing them on the wall, I could see they were much more than that. His creatures exuded a deep aloneness and an alien quality.

I wanted to tell him that, but he was surrounded by people. He was fit, fair and clean-cut, dressed neatly, without any hint of the bohemian artist. His glazed eyes and deadpan look might have led others to assume he was bored, but I knew that was the mask he wore at social occasions he found terrifying, and that he probably would have been vomiting before the show. I had to smile to see him trapped there, hating being the focus of attention. Our eyes met across the room. I waved and started to leave. But when I got to the door, I felt a hand on my shoulder.

'Hi, thanks for coming,' he said.

My stomach flipped. 'Of course, I had to.'

'What do you think?'

'They're everything I imagined you would do and more. They're totally otherworldly.'

'I'm really glad you came,' he said. There was no mask now. His eyes were tender and troubled. 'How's your mum?'

'She seems okay. She's still in hospital, but should be out soon.'

He nodded, and looked as if he wanted to say something else.

I felt like hugging him. 'Are you okay?'

'I'd better get back,' he said.

The third time I saw him, all my housemates were at a party and I was at home by myself. Candles, stuck in old beer bottles, were the only light on the verandah. The mosquitoes were bad that night. I had lit half a dozen mozzie coils and retreated to the dark back corner, where there was a mattress and net. I must have dozed off. Then Jason was on the verandah. I got to my feet, startling him, and softly said his name.

'Shelley said you haven't been well,' he said. He was looking over to my corner, his face troubled. I realised he couldn't see me. I was happy to stay there in the shadows. Grabbing a candle from the table, he walked over and held it out. Now his face was hidden and all I could see was a dark, hulking figure before me. For a long time, it seemed, he looked me over. He stood so close that I could hear him breathe and feel an intensity coming off him. If I took one step forward, we would be touching. I yearned to do that.

We heard voices and footsteps coming up the verandah stairs. He put the candle down and walked away, passing Pip and Ruby on the steps.

*

I waited for the nurse to hand the phone to Mum. I had rung her every morning for a week, but she felt more distant than ever. When I asked when she was going home, she replied, 'Maybe soon.' To find out what was going on, I spoke to my sisters. Patsy said that Mum was on antibiotics as a precaution against infection, and that she would stay in hospital for two more weeks, until the course was completed.

In the time before Mum's cancer, I had rung her once a fortnight from Darwin. Our chats floated on the surface. We always talked about the same things: what we'd been eating, news about the Charismatic community, church, and so forth. I didn't go into detail about anything, not because I didn't want to, but because her mind would wander, and I'd realise after a while that she wasn't listening. It was different, though, if I said I was ill or tired. Then she would scold, 'Aiya! See, I told you – you work too hard, you need to rest more, don't worry about things so much, pray to Jesus. You eat too many heaty foods. What time did you go to sleep last night? What? Too late – no wonder you get sick, going to sleep so late. Tell your boss not to give you so much work. Don't be frightened to tell him. Go to church.' The tirade would go on and on. When she scolded, she was animated and present, and it made me feel cared for.

Now the nurse put Mum on. I didn't ask her how she was feeling about the antibiotics, as I knew she wouldn't want to talk about it. As usual, I asked who had stayed the night, how many people were at prayers, what she had eaten for dinner last night and breakfast this morning, how Dad's projects were going, and who was visiting today.

I felt like telling her, *I haven't been sleeping since I returned to*

Darwin. I feel so depressed all the time. I don't know what's happening anymore. I want to bring you cheer, but I can't.

'I haven't been feeling well,' I said.

I waited, but the scolding didn't come. 'Never mind,' she said in a faraway voice. 'Give it to Jesus.' She was interrupted by someone. 'What were you saying?' she said, when she came back to the phone.

'Never mind, Mum. I'll ring again tomorrow. I'd better leave for work,' I said.

*

Ten days after returning to Darwin, I received the phone call. It came in the small hours of the morning, when the bats cried like babies and the sun had not started its ascent, or the birds commenced their calls.

Maria's voice was low and stern when I picked up the phone. 'Natasha, say goodbye to Mum,' she said.

'What?' I said.

I heard voices in the background, then thuds and crackling as if the phone had been dropped. I started to sob.

'I'm putting the phone next to Mum's ear. She can't talk. You can say goodbye now.'

'Mum, I love you. I'm sorry, I'm so sorry,' I cried.

'Are you okay, Natasha?' It was Maria again.

'Yes,' was all I could say.

'I have to hang up now,' she said. 'You can pray with us from over there.'

'Yes.'

The phone clicked.

SPRING HAD COME TO MELBOURNE IN THE TWO weeks that I'd been gone. Outside, the wind blew warm and unsettling. Particles of dust, yellow pollen and dried-up blossoms swirled past my window.

There was much to be done before the funeral the following day. I sat on the bed in my old room. *Just two more minutes*, I told myself, *before I face the others again.*

The funeral program was shiny and gold like a Chinese New Year card. On the front was a photo of a young woman with sparkling eyes and alluring lips, posing in a silk cheongsam. Bust out and shoulders back, she held a long-stemmed rose in one graceful hand. Her rich black hair was gathered up in a bun, a few tendrils falling loose around her face.

Of all the photos we had of Mum, Dad's choice was this glamour shot taken when they were courting in Hong Kong almost forty years ago. My sisters agreed with Dad's choice. The photo I would have chosen for the program was taken at Mum's last outing to St Kilda beach. When they rejected this photo, I blurted out that choosing an image of her as a 23-year-old instead of the person she was before she died was like saying she was no longer beautiful. Dad looked away, hurt. Anita told me to shut my mouth, that I never had anything constructive to say.

I liked Mum's hair in the St Kilda photo. It was before she got the wig. Sea winds had tousled the thin tufts, giving her a messy, boyish charm. Her face was beautiful and determined, though age and illness had sucked the vigour away and left her skin worn and pale. Only her eyes remained bright. 'You should always make your eyes look big for photos,' she had said. Exaggerating, she had widened her eyes as Maria clicked the camera. I picked up the photo and held it to my face. I couldn't stop crying.

Dad was to give the eulogy. He would tell the congregation that when he married Mum, she had been the belle of Hong Kong. He would say that her life was a testament to faith, a faith as strong as rock, and she was truly a saint. He was going to have me read out a passage from 1 Corinthians 13 that he said embodied her saintliness: 'Love bears all things, believes all things, hopes all things, endures all things.' I scribbled notes in an exercise book. There was something I needed to say. But my notes were incoherent. I flung down the pen.

I placed side by side in front of me the program photo of Mum at twenty-three and the photo of her taken at St Kilda beach. Both photos captured her beautiful lopsided smile. But now I could see the essential difference. When she was young, the tilt in her smile was born of uncertainty. When she was older, it had deepened into a quality of eternal endurance and hope.

She smiled most at prayer meetings, but her eyes were glazed, her shoulders stiff and raised. There was an overwrought quality to it. That was her public smile. I never trusted it. When she caught my eye, I would demonstrate this to her with a withering, resentful expression. I regretted that now.

I tried to think of the times I had seen Mum happy. I could recall her joy when Dad gave his life to Jesus, and when Anita gave birth to Will. I remembered how in our early teens, when Dad was in his studio and we thought Mum was watching TV, Maria, Patsy and I would closet ourselves away in my bedroom. On went the radio, tuned into one of the stations Dad disapproved of. Maria would start thrashing around like a lunatic to the music. When Patsy and I weren't on the floor convulsed with laughter, we were trying to follow Maria's moves. On two or three of these occasions, I saw Mum standing outside in the dark night, peeping through my window at us, thinking she couldn't be seen. How happy and at ease she had looked, watching us!

I had dreamt of her last night. She was sitting shyly by the altar in our large rectangular church. Wearing a shawl over her patient's gown, she looked just as she had the last time I saw her in hospital. This time, however, her face and body were relaxed, without the stiffening that pain forced on her. The line to greet her travelled down the centre aisle, all the way back to the doors of the church.

I stood in the line as well, not too far back, my eyes always on her. I was content to wait and admire the poise and the sweetness with which she greeted each parishioner. When I reached her, she smiled and gently raised her hand to my face. With the back of her hand, she brushed my cheek. I could feel her touch. Immersed in my dream, I felt joy that she was still alive, that we had another chance to put things right. But then I saw the sadness in her face and I became aware that she was dead. I woke up, my face wet with tears.

Since Mum died, I'd had a stone in my stomach, weighing me down with the knowledge that I'd let her down.

I could hear Anita in the kitchen. I made myself go in there to speak to her. She was taking baking pans from the oven and counting them. I could tell from looking at her that she was angry. After tomorrow's funeral, the congregation would come back to the house for lunch. 'Twelve baking pans. That should be enough. We won't need as many as we did for the healing party,' she said.

Traces of the party from six weeks before were still all through the house. No one had taken down Dad's handmade posters. 'Don't remove them, they're so cute,' he had said. Stuck to the front gate a faded poster with an arrow said *This Way for a Miracle*. We hadn't even returned the crates of glasses borrowed from the parish hall. In the backyard, the ramp to salvation leant against the back fence.

Anita clanged the pans down on the table. 'Line these pans with alfoil, will you,' she said over her shoulder, her voice sharp. 'Then mop the floors and make Dad a hot drink and some banana loaf with butter.' I lined the first pan. 'You're using way too much foil!' she barked. She wouldn't look at me.

Realising there was no right time to talk, I forced myself to begin. 'I was wondering if something happened at the hospital while I was away that I don't know about,' I said.

Anita gave a dismissive snort.

My voice was shaky. 'I mean, it sounded from the phone calls that everything was pretty much the same as before I left. Did anything change – her diagnosis, her medication, anything?'

She opened the freezer and started rummaging through its contents. 'Probably not,' she finally said.

I picked up the pan I was lining and moved closer to her. 'What about her pain level?'

'Same, I guess.'

'She was up early as usual, greeting visitors all day, going to mass, was she?' I was nervous and speaking too fast. 'You still had the prayer meetings and someone always stayed the night with her?'

'Yep.' Anita's tone was mocking.

'Was she eating normally?'

'Yep.'

'And what was her mood like?'

Anita slammed the freezer door shut and swung around. 'Look, what's this about?' she said. The bitterness in her eyes stunned me.

I took a step back. 'I just wanted to know if Mum was going downhill,' I said. 'Because if she was, why didn't anyone say anything to me?'

Anita exhaled loudly. 'Don't think you can just come back and start interrogating us.' She paced back and forth, opening and slamming cupboards. 'You think we had the time to report back to you? Who do you think you are? If you're so concerned, you shouldn't have left, should you!' Picking up a stack of plates, she stalked out of the kitchen.

I brought Dad his afternoon tea in the family room. He was sitting in the easy chair with Maria behind him, massaging his head, her fingers weaving in and out of his hair. If we felt compelled to protect him like a child when he was happy and rejoicing, the drive to protect him when he was sad was even stronger. None of us could bear to see Dad lowered by grief, that urging voice quietened, the blaze in his eyes dulled. We offered him his favourite foods, said the things he liked to hear, and my sisters, particularly Maria, gave him the treats he craved. Now his hair was dishevelled, his thick lips softly open and his heavy-lidded eyes wet and sensual from the massage. At the sight of his pleasure, even though I knew it was unfair, a jolt of hatred shot through me.

Maria rubbed Dad's scalp with clinical detachment. Her lips were pursed, her jaw was tense and her eyes were on the alert for how she might be useful next. There was something particularly distant and dissociated about her, and I thought about the strength and control she had needed to be alone with Mum while she died, to be the one to tell the rest of the family and wait for them to arrive.

'Sing it again,' Dad said to Patsy, who was kneeling on the carpet next to the altar, playing her guitar. Patsy looked lost, her voice was thin and eerie. When Patsy wasn't singing, she was eating – bread, cakes, chocolate, all the things Mum had wanted her to enjoy.

The phone rang. Anita spoke to the funeral director. Mum's body had been delivered to the church. 'I want to see her,' I said. Maria volunteered to go along with me.

*

The coffin was in an annex on one side of the church foyer. We waited for the caretaker to arrive with the keys to the door of the annex. It was cold inside the high brick walls of the church. The light was bleak, but we were hidden from the gaze of passers-by. Outside, the wind blew and we could hear the pop of balls and an occasional exclamation from the tennis court next door.

I was grateful that Maria had come along to support me. She walked around the foyer, picking up pamphlets and hymn books that parishioners had scattered on tables and benches on their way out after mass.

'Can you sit down for a minute and talk, Maria?' I said. I sat on a vinyl padded bench next to the annex door. 'You were the only one with Mum when she died. Can you tell me what happened?'

'Why do you ask me? No one else has.' Maria said. Holding a pile of hymn books, she walked over. I slid across the bench so that she could sit down. She remained standing.

'I wish I had been with her. I need to know,' I said. 'I spoke to her that morning. It was just our usual conversation. She didn't say anything about feeling worse.'

Maria looked down at the books. We avoided each other's eyes, as we usually did in my family. 'The nurses that day were not nice. They kept wanting Mum to have more morphine,' she said.

'Why? Was she in pain?'

'No. Well, she might have been, but she wouldn't know because they kept giving her more drugs.'

'What? Do you mean topping up the dose? I was with Mum once when she complained to the nurse about that. The nurse said you had to do it to stop breakthrough pain.'

'But maybe her pain had gone and she didn't need any morphine,' Maria said.

'What makes you think her pain would have gone? Obviously the doctors didn't think that.'

Her eyes flickered. 'You know that's the way they euthanise people in hospital – morphine?'

Euthanasia. That was on the Charismatics' list of pet issues, along with abortion and homosexuality. 'What are you saying?

That they euthanised her?'

'Maybe . . .' Maria wiped her mouth with the back of her hand. 'Not really.'

I rubbed my face. I wanted to shake Maria out of her fog. 'Then why did you bring it up?'

'Hospitals do it all the time . . . Never mind.'

'If you seriously think that the nurses were giving Mum too much morphine, then we should talk to the hospital.'

'Don't worry about it,' Maria said, and walked to the other side of the foyer. She wandered around, arranging the books on the trolley and the pamphlets on the wall shelves.

When she was done, she walked over to me. 'What did you want to ask?' she said. Her eyes were more focused, her voice less dreamy.

'What happened when she died?'

Maria looked down at her hands. 'Mum woke up coughing blood. I called the nurse.'

'What time was it?'

'Around three.'

'How much blood was Mum coughing up?'

'I'm not sure. She was coughing into a towel. It was soaked red with her blood.'

I was too shocked to say anything. My heart raced.

Maria did a half-turn and gazed out at the foyer. I worried that she was going to walk away again. 'Did the nurse come?' I asked.

'Two of them came. They checked her airways, gave her something to stop the coughing, cleaned her up.'

'Was she suffering? Was she in pain?' I asked.

'I don't think so. She started to panic at the coughing and the blood. But I got her to hold my hand and told her that God loved her and everything was all right. She calmed down. She became unconscious.'

'How long was she awake before that?'

'I'm not sure. An hour? The nurse told me to ring the family. Dad and the others only arrived after she died. We sat around her. Her mouth was still wide open from trying to breathe. I held her face and forced her mouth closed.' She cupped her hands around an imaginary jaw and pushed it.

I was finding it difficult to breathe. Maria turned around, about to walk away.

'Wait,' I said. 'Did Mum say anything before she became unconscious?'

'We started to pray the rosary together, then she couldn't say anything more.'

'Do you think she knew she was dying? Was there anything she said that day, before she went to bed?'

Maria hung her head. 'After evening prayers she asked if Dad could stay the night as well as me. But I said no, Dad needed to be well rested so he could be in good health for her.'

Voices outside startled us – cheery voices. The caretaker was talking with a tennis player.

'Thank you, Maria. You gave Mum a lot of comfort. I'm so glad you were there when she died. Thank you,' I said.

Emotion filled Maria's eyes for a moment. She sat down. For a while we were silent, seated side by side. Then she coughed, stood up and started searching again for things to tidy.

We heard a quick step and whistling, and the caretaker, old

but sprightly, bounded up the entrance steps. He apologised for being late, commented on the warm, windy weather and unlocked the annex.

The room was small and dim. Chairs stacked high up against one wall tilted forward. It struck me how the casket gleamed. The wood of the box and the steel handles were so polished that they looked wet.

Maria and I lifted the lid. It was surprisingly light. We stepped back. Mum's body lay stiff and straight, dressed in the same gown she'd worn at the healing party. Her hands were clasped below her breast. A white sheet covered her lower half. The skin was hers, so were the brows, the hair and lips, the hands, the shape – but it was all wrong. I wanted to close my eyes so that this false image would not infiltrate my memories of her. At the same time, I could not look away. The funeral worker had somehow wrested away signs of her sickness and pain. Her twisted neck and torso had been smoothed out, the bloat in her stomach flattened and her legs stretched out, straight and firm. Loud, awful sobs erupted from me.

Calm and dry-eyed, Maria hugged me and I held onto her. 'Now I remember,' Maria said. '"What beautiful children I have!" That's what Mum said before she died.'

She poked through her handbag, pulled out a tube of Mum's pale-pink lipstick and told me to put it on her lips. First I touched Mum's cold cheek with my hand, then I drew the lipstick over lips that were as hard as cured clay. I apologised to Maria for being unable to stop crying.

*

Sitting next to Maria as she drove us home in her car, a realisation grew in me. I turned to Maria. 'Mum didn't really say what you said before she died, did she? I mean, she didn't say, "What beautiful children I have," did she?'

She kept her eyes on the road as if she had not heard.

'I know you mean well. But there was no need to say that.'

Maria put her window down all the way and then back halfway up. She started to cough and wipe her face. I had forgotten how much hayfever affected her.

'I'm not saying that she didn't think we were beautiful,' I continued. 'It's just that it's not the kind of thing Mum would say.'

'She did. Something like it,' Maria mumbled. She wouldn't say anything more after that.

Before we turned into the driveway, I asked her another question. 'Are you moving back into your place after the funeral?'

'Dad wants me to stay,' Maria said.

'You'd be mad to move in with Dad,' I said.

She didn't say anything.

*

As soon as we got home, Anita told me to mow the back lawn. Tomorrow would be a fine day, and we planned to set up tables in the backyard. I went outside. The neat, open spaces of the backyard surprised me. In my thoughts, it hadn't been cleared; it was still the backyard of my childhood, impenetrable and infested with weeds, cacti and junk. I dragged the mower out of the shed. On the open stretch of grass, it moved steadily, cutting the lawn into long, neat strips. Then I got to the back fence and had to struggle, pushing and pulling back and forth and sideways to skirt around the cacti and the ramp. The old mower was powerful in my hands, its clatter and roar loud enough to obliterate thoughts, but still they came – a towel soaked in her blood, her mouth open and gasping for air, a premonition that made her ask for Dad to stay.

The wind was dusty and irritating. I lunged too close to the cacti and fantasised about slamming into their evil thorns. Instead I rammed into the ramp. The impact cut the engine, dislodged a plank and threw me backwards. I ran to the shed and grabbed the first tool I saw, a pick. I liked the feel of the long wooden handle in my hands and the weight of the metal head at the end.

I returned to the ramp and raised the pick above my head. *Chop, chop, chop*, it hacked into the ramp. One plank started to cave in. Anita was out of the back door in a flash. She strode towards me.

'What do you think you are doing?' she shouted.

'It's hard to mow around the ramp,' I said.

'You can't just destroy it. It's Dad's ramp.'

'It was supposed to be Mum's salvation ramp, actually.'

Anita's eyes narrowed. 'Just shut up and put that pick down.'

Patsy came out and stood next to Anita. I dropped the pick. 'I don't know why Mum died,' I said. 'Why did Mum die?'

'Are you crazy?' Anita said. 'She had cancer.'

'Yes,' I said. 'But no one was expecting her to die. You all said she was getting better. I need to know how this happened.'

'Mum had a tumour as big as a fist above her stomach. The doctor said it was like a ticking time bomb, that it could burst any minute,' Anita said.

I gasped. 'I didn't know that. Why didn't anyone tell me? Who else knew this? Did you know, Patsy?'

Patsy shook her head. 'No,' she said. 'I didn't.' Her face was pale and tense.

'Did Mum know?' I asked.

'Look, what's the point in bringing all this up?' said Anita.

'Did Mum know?' I asked, louder.

'Yes, Mum knew!' Anita yelled. 'Listen! If it wasn't the tumour above her stomach, then it was the one in her spine that killed her. It doesn't matter. She had cancer!'

I heard my voice breaking. 'What about the miracle, the healing?'

Anita looked at me with a combination of pity and disgust. 'The miracle you never believed in?'

'You all said she was going to be healed,' I said, holding back tears.

Maria came out. 'Shhh. We can hear you from inside. You'll upset Dad.'

We looked up at his studio window. He was watching us, partially concealed by a curtain.

I turned to Maria. 'Did you know? About the tumour the doctor said was a ticking time bomb?'

Maria scratched her face with both hands. 'Yes.'

'Why didn't you tell Patsy and me?'

'I don't know. I didn't really think of it . . . Sorry. She was going to be healed.'

'Look, the main thing is to stay positive.' Anita was being placatory now. 'And as Dad said,' she continued, 'it wasn't the miracle we expected, but there were other miracles. God works in mysterious ways. Now we need to move forward.'

I hated her work voice. Her 'let's be nice and reasonable' voice. 'I don't know how you do that,' I said. 'When the miracle doesn't happen, you just change tack. You must be a lot more sophisticated than me. I can't do that doublethink. Or is it all just pretence for you?'

Anita's eyes hardened, and a mirthless smile creased her face. 'So selfish.' She shook her head slowly. 'So selfish.'

'You think we're all better off pretending, don't you? You think it's harmless,' I said.

Anita threw her hands up in the air. 'Just let her stew and feel sorry for herself,' she said to the others, walking back into the house.

Patsy stepped closer to me. 'The miracle has manifested!' She was breathless. 'Look at how many people Mum inspired to come to the Lord. And I'm not anorexic anymore. Haven't you seen? I've started eating.' She gave me a desperate smile.

'That's good you're eating, Patsy,' I said.

'It's okay to feel disappointed, Natasha. I was disappointed with Jesus too,' said Maria, her eyes compassionate and sickly sweet. 'But then I forgave Him. I know He is teaching us something.'

I looked up at the window again. Dad was still there. 'I need to ask Dad if I can take the ramp down. So I can mow the yard,' I said, and went inside.

*

I climbed the stairs two steps at a time before I lost courage. The door was ajar and I entered without knocking.

'Dad, I want to take down the ramp,' I said.

He was studying a large photomontage on an easel. His face, in profile, had a deep and intellectual cast. I wanted to apologise for interrupting him before I had even started. Without turning his attention from the piece, he addressed me.

'That's fine. Take the ramp down. It has served its purpose. You feel your mother wasn't healed and you are angry with Jesus. I saw you talking with your sisters. Do not hurt the memory of your mother, please, by quarrelling with them. I pray one day you will have the same spiritual maturity and wisdom that they do.'

Images covered the studio walls. He stood up, the man at the centre of his creative output, and turned to me. 'I believe with all my heart that the miracle did occur. The *outward* deliverance is not granted, but the *inward* deliverance is *glorious.* One day you will see it. She found peace. She found forgiveness.'

A million inexpressible thoughts and feelings screamed inside me. His voice continued, authoritative but lilting. 'Did you see how happy she was? She prayed every day that you would reject your New Age self-gods and find Jesus. I know that she is in heaven now, interceding for us. Your mother was a saint.'

'No, she wasn't!' I heard myself say, and it was like in dreams, when I was falling and falling and unable to scream, until finally I found my voice. 'Don't say she's a saint!' I sounded shrill and ugly, but couldn't stop. 'You make her meaningless when you do that. She suffered. You tried to silence her. We couldn't even talk to her when she was dying. You make us all pretend. You make us deny things that happen right in front of us.'

For a moment he was too shocked to speak. 'Ask for forgiveness, ask for forgiveness right now from the Lord for your abject thoughts. Your mother would be very disappointed. She and I have always been forgiving of you. Consider whether it was you who didn't want to talk with her. You wouldn't even go to church for her.'

'I'm not listening to you. You lie all the time. You lied to her and you lie to us.'

He was livid now, his face contorted. He jabbed a finger at me. 'You are the bad, destructive child. You hurt her, but most of all you offend Jesus.'

'No, *you* hurt and humiliated her. You cheated on her from the start. We knew about the affairs – everyone knew. Then you became born again. You did try to be good – I'll give you that. But then you became the great holy man and you still couldn't keep your hands off the girls. And Bonnie. We all knew it deep down. But you made us think we didn't know it. I don't know how you do that.'

His eyes widened, big and terrible. 'You are mad! The devil is using you to attack me.'

I saw the fear in his eyes, but kept going. 'You made Mum doubt what she saw with her own eyes. You told her the demon of suspicion and jealousy was in her. You —'

Suddenly Anita was there. She raised her arm and struck me hard across the face. I stumbled. Maria, appearing at my side, put out a hand to steady me. Dad collapsed into a chair. Maria went to him. Anita dragged me by the arm out of the studio and down the stairs. At their foot, Patsy stood with her back tense against the wall. At first I thought she was softly wailing, then I realised she was singing in tongues.

Anita, sweating and panting, yanked me across the lounge room. In her rage, she was far stronger than me. I couldn't stand the pain of her nails biting into my flesh. 'Let me go!' I cried. 'What are you, his bodyguard? Why, you're more angry with him than I will ever be.'

'You bitch!' she snarled. 'How could you do this when everyone is trying so hard? I'll never forgive you. Just get away from me. We don't want to see your face.' She let go and I walked out the front door.

*

The oval was too close to home. I had no money or bag, so I just walked, turning randomly, going deeper into the labyrinth of residential streets. I walked fast at first, striking the footpath. But soon it felt as though all my energy had drained away. My limbs became heavy and slow and I longed to stop. There was nothing in these streets but rows of houses shut tight. If I stopped to rest in front of one, it would arouse suspicion. When it was almost sunset, I turned around and headed back to the oval.

My cheek was still hot and throbbing where Anita had struck me. Although it was dusk, the oval in the half-light reminded me of the early-morning walks I would take before getting Mum out of bed. How different, though, the feel of those walks. With the beginning of each day, there had been new hope – maybe this would be the day I would talk to Mum, find common ground and get to know her better.

If only I could have told her I loved her. She was in a coma when I finally did. Why didn't I say it on the last day I saw her? I winced as the image surfaced that I had been trying to suppress. She was sitting at the hospital window with its glass so thick that no sound penetrated; the light that filtered through was weak and grey. 'I'll see you at Christmas,' I had said, and walked out. I saw her turn and stare out the window with haunted, grieving eyes. She knew it was our last time. I could have turned back then and told her I loved her.

Liar! Liar! I punched my cheek where it was sore. I was so good at lying to myself. I could have stayed. I should have stayed. I could only think I'd been punishing her. On the night I stayed with Mum in the hospital, after everyone left, taking their rejoicing and verve with them, I had reminded her that I was leaving the next day. In the deathly quiet, in the smallest of voices, she had said, 'Do you have to go?' I had pretended I didn't hear.

*

Maria opened the door. 'Good, you're back.' She ushered me in, locking first the security door and then the inner door. She double-checked the locks. Anita and Patsy had left. I told her I would cook dinner. She said Anita had already bought some noodles, but Dad wouldn't eat any. She was wary and distant, though not hostile.

I climbed the stairs to his studio. There was no light coming from under his door. I knocked. No one answered. I knocked again and pushed it open. The lamp on the landing cast a triangle of light on the studio floor. Beyond that, I saw darkness, shadows and menacing shapes. I could smell the chemicals and paints, and underneath that, sweat and something bitter. Now I saw him, a black, breathing form, skulking in the back corner.

'Dad? Dad? Are you all right?' I searched for the light switch on the wall.

'Leave the light off!' His voice came out strangled and animal-like.

I felt my way across the room to him. He was crouched on the ground. I knelt down near him. 'Dad, are you okay? What are you doing on the floor?'

'Leave me,' he growled. His breath was loud and ragged, his shoulders rose and fell heavily. An intense tang came from him, the smell of heat and shame. I felt we were back in Rowling Road.

My eyes, grown more accustomed to the dark, could now make out parts of his face – the gleam of tooth and eyeball, and his mouth gaping and panting.

'Dad? We know how hard you try. We all love you.' I took a deep breath and started to shiver uncontrollably. 'I love you.'

He was silent. Then he cleared his throat. 'Thank you. You're a good girl. Don't be angry.'

'I'm sorry, Dad, for hurting you with what I said before.'

'I forgive you,' he said. 'You didn't know what you were saying.' His voice was a hoarse whisper.

'I knew what I was saying.'

'You were angry with God for taking your mother. I understand.'

I shook my head. He probably couldn't see me in the dark. 'No, Dad.'

'Your mother loved all her children very much. I know I have been defective. Sometimes I feel like a monster. I will be in purgatory for a very long time.' He gasped sharply, then he was sobbing and heaving.

Tears started to fall down my face, too. I tried not to make a sound. I took his hand and he gripped mine back with a warmth that flooded through me. I was on the verge of telling him I had failed Mum and that I wished I had stayed. The memory that I couldn't trust him stopped me from doing so.

'At first I felt, oh no, now that Irene is dead, she will know all my thoughts and all my deeds past and present and all the sins I have hidden from her.' He shook his head from side to side. 'But God put on my heart that Jesus wipes the slate clean. He not only forgives, but forgets. So she will not see anything.'

He believed in God's mercy. I was struck by his innocence – the innocence that in spite of everything, in spite of his need to dominate and control, had stayed alive.

'You must look at the big picture. Within the big picture, your mother was a saint,' he said. We were silent again. 'Yes, your mother was a saint. Now go and get some sleep.'

He would not get up or let me turn on the light, despite my entreaties. I left him there on the floor, my insides twisted with love, pity and guilt.

An hour later he was still up there. Maria and I tried to take him some food and drink.

'Leave me alone,' he growled when he heard us on the staircase.

It took me a long while to get to sleep that night. I lay in bed listening for his footsteps. I thought of Dad alone and tormented in the blackness of his studio, and of Mum locked up in the cold church annex with its teetering chairs stacked to the ceiling. Pushing away thoughts of her coffined body, I fixed an image of Mum's essence as something diaphanous and softly sparkling, and wondered where it might be.

*

The family, Ed, the drama group and two funeral directors arrived at the church early to set up for the service. The church was not yet unlocked, so for some minutes we milled around, tensely exchanging commiserations on the concrete steps. Dad leant against the wall like an old man.

Dad had slept in his studio. When he came down in the morning, he walked stooped over, with slow shaky steps. At breakfast, he was quiet and aloof, passively chewing the noodles that we served to him and mumbling flat responses to the questions we asked. Before we left for the funeral, Maria tried to get him to pray with her but he waved her aside. She looked at me in consternation. I was sickened to think what my outburst yesterday had done to him. I wondered that Maria did not condemn me.

Now Anita, taking Dad's arm, guided him to the piece of lawn at the front of the church where there was a bench under a willow tree. Patsy followed a few steps behind, looking lost. Anita brushed the leaves off the bench and waited for Dad to sit down. Then she went up to Maria, who was on the stairs, talking to Ed. Anita had not looked at me once all morning.

'Tell everyone to gather round,' Anita told Maria.

'Can everyone come down here for a prayer before we go in?' Maria called out.

We clustered around Dad where he sat on the bench. I wore dark glasses to hide a purple bruise that had come up under my left eye from Anita's blow. Even through my glasses, everything was too bright. The tree swayed in slow motion, each blade of grass was too precise, the wind and voices too loud and artificial.

The group, even the funeral directors, formed a circle around Dad. His hands were trembling, his mouth panting. He appeared to be barely in control. The night before, in the darkness of the studio, when my eyes made out his shadowy form in the corner, I had had the impression of a crouching, injured animal. Images had come to me of Dad's caged brother, and of the chaotic narrow house on Rowling Road. I remembered the out-of-control fear I would feel back then that something terrible and disastrous was about to happen. Unable to breathe, my head prickling, I felt the same fear now as we stood in a circle waiting for Dad to start.

What would happen if he was stripped of his beliefs? It was terrifying to imagine. As much as I fought against the Charismatics, I had not questioned the family belief that our faith had kept the wolves at bay. It had stopped Dad from going off the rails, from leaving Mum, and the family from falling apart. We had been saved.

Dad did not look up from the ground. He started to mumble, 'What is heaven like? Irene knows. The Lord knew it was time for her reward in heaven.' We strained to hear him. 'Tell me, what is heaven like?' he said.

We were silent, not knowing if he was talking to himself or to us.

'Are you asking us a question, Dad?' said Anita.

'Describe heaven, someone, come on,' he said, his voice quavering.

'The bible says the walls are made of jewels and the road paved with gold,' said an older member of the drama group.

'Heaven is better than that,' Dad said louder. He looked up now. His face, usually so animated when he talked, was drawn and severe, his thick lips downturned. 'Someone else. What is heaven like?'

'There's manna from heaven. It's full of the love and the joy of Jesus?' said Maria.

'It's better than that,' Dad said. 'What is the most beautiful thing you can imagine?'

Troy stepped forward. 'Angels singing, every day is a sunrise and every single one of our loved ones is with us.'

Dad stood up. 'It's better than that! Whatever any of you might say, I say back – *heaven is better than that*. Our earthly minds cannot even begin to contemplate its magnificence.' His eyes were fierce. There was a desperation in them.

'Let us hold hands and pray. We thank you, Lord, for the miracle of Irene,' he began. As he prayed, he slowly came back. His voice growing stronger with each word, he exhorted us to rise, to mingle our tears of grief with tears of happiness, for the miracle had occurred. 'Each and every one of you,' he proclaimed, 'your life has been changed and you will now go out and inspire others. Today will be a victory for the Lord.'

Then he cried, tears rolling down his dignified face, and Bridie and another member of the drama group comforted him.

He was in fine form. With each triumphant word he uttered, I felt myself sinking. After the dread I had felt that he would be somehow changed, I was shocked that it was not relief I felt now, but devastation. I wondered what it would have been like if he had broken down, cried words of shame and regret, if he had even renounced the prophecy and the miracle.

A dangerous, powerful thought took hold of me. What if they had not been born again? What if the day Dad and Mum gave their lives to Jesus had not been our salvation? What if it had actually stopped us from growing, from seeing things, from finding courage? The thoughts were making my head spin. I leant against the tree to stop myself from falling.

The doors to the church opened. The group on the lawn gathered up guitars, flowers, costumes and their belongings and made their way inside. Maria called me in.

'Just a minute,' I told her. I sat on the bench under the tree. The funeral would start soon. Mum's body would lie in the coffin at the foot of the altar. Dad would give the remembrance speech next to the altar. From there, he would descend the red-carpeted steps, dragging the microphone, to sing 'I Believe', standing by the coffin. Anita would be mistress of ceremonies, Patsy would sing and lead the music ministry, and Maria would perform a short piece accompanied by four members of the drama group. They were going to run down the three aisles, writhe and roll on the carpet, and shout 'Jesus!' at the end, with arms held high.

I decided to sit a bit longer until the people arrived. I closed my eyes. I could see Mum's face. She was in the car, being rushed to Emergency. She was confused, asking for her lipstick over and over, but then she turned around to look at my sisters and me, sitting in the back. She looked at us with such love and heartache. I had never seen her eyes so clear.

Acknowledgements

Firstly I thank Helen Garner for spurring me on to write and be published, and for being the voice in my head as I wrote, calling for fearlessness, clarity and compassion.

Thanks also to Michael Gawenda for encouraging me to write at a time when I was at a crossroads.

It has been a privilege and pleasure working with editor Chris Feik. Chris showed me meanings in the story that I couldn't see myself and made it a better novel. And I am grateful to Jo Rosenberg for her fine skill and generosity as project manager and copy editor.

I acknowledge the warm support received from family and friends, including Joanne O'Mara, Lorena Wright and Paula Chatfield, who read the first draft.

Finally, my thanks to Stephen Gray, who gave me the guidance and love I needed to write.

Born in Malaysia, Micheline Lee migrated to Australia when she was eight. She is a former human rights lawyer and painter, and is currently completing a PhD. Her most recent publications are non-fiction works about how people respond to disability and difference. *The Healing Party* is her first novel, and was shortlisted for several awards, including the Victorian Premier's Literary Award.